Integrating the
Shattered Self

Integrating the Shattered Self:

Psychotherapy with Adult Incest Survivors

Nicki Roth

JASON ARONSON INC.
Northvale, New Jersey
London

Production Editor: Judith D. Cohen

Library of Congress Cataloging-in-Publication Data

Roth, Nicki.
    Integrating the shattered self : psychotherapy with adult incest
survivors / by Nicki Roth.
      p. cm.
    Includes bibliographical references and index.
    ISBN 0-87668-562-9
    1. Incest victims—Mental health. 2. Psychotherapy. I. Title.
    [DNLM: 1. Child Abuse, Sexual—rehabilitation.   2. Child of
Impaired Parents—psychology. 3. Incest—psychology.
4. Psychotherapy—methods.   WM 420 R84451]
RC560.I53R68   1992
616.85′83—dc20
DNLM/DLC
for Library of Congress   92-10687

Manufactured in the United States of America. Jason Aronson Inc. offers books and cassettes. For information and catalog write to Jason Aronson Inc., 230 Livingston Street, Northvale, New Jersey 07647.

To my father Morton Roth
who gave me unconditional love
and
to my daughter Erika
who allows me to carry on that family tradition

Contents

Preface

While traveling around the country during the past five years, training psychotherapists in the treatment of adult incest survivors, I have heard the following story repeatedly. An experienced therapist who has felt successful in her or his work for at least ten years feels completely confused and inadequate when treating an incest survivor. What has worked with other clients seeking long-term reparative work seems to go completely awry with these clients. All of the usual sound and respectable techniques of the trade don't seem to work. The therapist thinks, "Is this resistance? Is this a poor transference or negative countertransference? Am I dealing with a borderline? Is this some form of pathology I've never seen before?" In recounting this story the therapist then explains to me that even these questions seem to be the wrong ones. Then comes the question I am asked continuously: "Could it be that adults who experienced childhood incest need a unique treatment approach that is particular to this kind of trauma?" Relief fills the room as I respond with a resounding, "YES!"

Earlier in my career I experienced the same dilemmas as do these therapists. I was doing very solid family systems work with a distinctly Bowenian approach with my clients at the University of Michigan Student Counseling Services. I had a developmental and social psychology undergraduate background, with family systems and group work graduate training under my belt. I caught the first wave of dysfunctional family work before there were books and groups and labels for everyone. In short, I felt confident. Then I encountered my first incest client. She was a 20-year-old junior at the university who entered counseling to facilitate her newly found sobriety after five years of using drugs and alcohol. Several months into our work she suddenly recalled her grandfather sexually abusing her when she was about 3 years old. This flashback did not relate to any of our work. It seemed to come out of nowhere. The panic reaction was very severe for her. Accustomed to crisis intervention work at that Center, I sprang into action. We got through the crisis just fine, but we were then left to deal with her revelation. I asked all the usual therapeutic questions: "What do you remember feeling? How do you feel now when you think about your grandfather? Where was your mother?" I was met with blank stares and a lot of "I don't knows." Every road seemed to lead to a dead end.

Little did I know that this moment would open a whole new avenue in my work. For two years I continued to work with this woman, as well as with several other clients who were recalling incestuous experiences. At that time hardly anyone was actually entering treatment with incest as the presenting concern, but it usually surfaced during the course of therapy. I began combing every bookstore and professional book service for anything on the topic of incest treatment. What I found were some good sociological explanations for why incest occurs, a few books on treating abused children, and a few books describing the consequences in adulthood of the incest trauma. However, I could not find any books on therapy with adults. So I began to seek training and supervision and eventually had the great honor of attending training sessions with Eliana Gil and David Calof. By the time I heard them I was already formulating my own theories and interventions. I was as relieved as the clinicians I now train when I listened to Gil and Calof. They confirmed that I was on the right track, and they used some language that helped me to articulate what I was already learning in my work. I was beginning to develop a bit of confidence in my approach with incest survivors.

And then I met Mariah. . . .

She entered therapy to resolve her childhood incest experiences in order to be healthy enough to maintain her relationship with her lover. She knew her past was interfering with her present and she wanted to move ahead. From that first session I knew there was something unique about this woman and that treatment could not be conventional. What was different about Mariah was that she had never forgotten any of the abuse—she had not repressed it and therefore had full access to all the information we would need for her recovery. The other striking feature about her story was the severity and duration of the abuse. What I had encountered up to this point with other clients were isolated or short-term abusive experiences. Never before had I heard of nearly an entire childhood and adolescence filled with sexual, physical, and psychological abuse. And yet, sitting before me was a competent, independent, articulate, open woman who was desperately seeking relief from her nightmares. Never before had I met such an outwardly high-functioning adult with such internal damage and turmoil. And so we began our work together.

Over the course of five years, my work with Mariah has reminded me of Alice in Wonderland. At one moment we are sliding down the rabbit's hole, and in the next moment we are encountering strange characters along the road who speak in verse. The unexpected always seems to happen and we end up in some new adventure. Not all the adventures are pleasant or fruitful. We have tried potions and cookies in an attempt to get out of one spot or alter what is happening. Sometimes we are delighted with the results. For however mysterious our journey has been, there are two absolutes. One is that Mariah has healed from her childhood trauma and is very content in her long-term love relationship. The other is that I have learned an immeasurable amount about how to treat incest survivors. This book is my effort to share my understanding of what works.

What follows is a comprehensive description of long-term psychotherapy with adults who suffered from incest as children. I discuss and illustrate what happens behind the therapist's door, and I invite you to enter that room with me and these clients. Try to hear and perceive the world as these clients do and allow that to inform your treatment decisions. Try to develop an awareness of the duality of this work, of treating the functional adult and the damaged child, both embodied in the client before you. Try to interweave several perspectives all at once. Read what follows with an attempt to expand your current understanding and approach. Try to comprehend how incest recovery follows a unique form of treatment that draws on many different modalities. I hope that when you have finished reading this book, you will share my deepest respect for these most triumphant individuals.

The clinical information presented here represents what I have discovered in the course of treating countless incest survivors. Not only have I had the opportunity to learn which approaches are most effective, but (sadly) I have learned through my clients that which did not work in their previous therapies. It has been striking that rarely have I been the first therapist a survivor has encountered. In fact, I am more often the third, fourth, or fifth therapist. Earlier in my work I worried that I was getting swept into the drama of a chronically disturbed client until it became apparent that a pattern was emerging with these clients. Their unbelievable will to find what it was that they needed kept them plugging away until they found satisfaction. Through their recounting of their past therapeutic work, I was able to determine further what actually works in the treatment of incest recovery.

Additionally, I have had the opportunity to supervise other clinicians' work in this area. Through consulting and teaching I have had many of my hypotheses tested by others. The clinical results have been quite consistent: the treatment of incest survivors is unique, creative, intense, and highly rewarding work.

For reasons of simplicity and predominance I have used the pronoun *she* throughout the book in reference to the client. Although my clinical experience covers the treatment of male survivors as well, the overwhelming majority of incest clients are female. Where relevant, I have made separate comments about male survivors, but in general the treatment does not vary a great deal depending on client gender. I have also used the generic word *partner* to describe the significant primary person in the client's life. This is to be inclusive of both heterosexual and homosexual relationships, as well as legal and nonlegal commitments.

The treatment population I am writing about are highly functional adults who do not fit easily into any of the prescribed psychiatric categories. Although the symptomatology may have pathological elements, these are healthy individuals who are struggling to overcome the aftermath of severe trauma. I am not describing those individuals who develop distinctly borderline or narcissistic personality disorders or multiple personalities. There are many abuse survivors who clearly fall into those psychiatric classifications, and the treatment I will be describing is not appropriate for them. The best *DSM-III-R* category for the clients I am writing about is "Post-Traumatic Stress Disorder."

It has been my experience that labeling is not particularly useful for the client or the therapist in this work. For this reason there are very few references to schizoid traits, paranoid tendencies, codependency, enabling, and the like. It is not that these categories are not accurately descriptive of many clients; it is rather that I find the treatment more dynamic and energized when neither the client nor the therapist relies on these labels. Too many of my clients have felt more trapped than liberated when they have happened upon the notion of—for instance—codependency. For numerous reasons, that label seems to lead them to the conclusion that they are forever stuck with that cross to bear. My focus instead is on delineating the client's *coping strategies* as a child and as an adult and how to help her move toward experiencing herself as *a powerful* individual. My intent in this book is to move behind and beyond the labeling to offer information about how to conduct the treatment. As my long-term colleague and friend, Joan Zald, said to me every time I struggled with finding the right diagnosis for my clients, "Nicki, how will having just the right label inform or change what you'll do in the therapy? Will it ultimately cause you to intervene any differently?" This comment was inevitably followed by a rich and lengthy conversation about strategies in any particular case. Her wisdom constantly returns to me in the course of treating incest survivors.

I have included a great many case examples throughout the book. In some cases there are summaries of particular moments, and in others there are verbatim dialogues. Some of my clients have generously allowed me to use their own private journal entries. For the sake of confidentiality, all identifying information has been altered and all case illustrations have the client's full permission to appear here. As those of you who are already working with incest survivors know, their own words are more powerful and expressive than any objective observer could recreate. My clients' permission to share their experiences here has uniformly been granted so that, in a client's own words, "other clients can receive the help they deserve from therapists."

It is my hope that this volume will contribute to the burgeoning literature about incest treatment and stimulate further discussion and research. Incest is an area that has been ignored for too long within our culture and within our profession. We need to engage in active dialogue to understand better the phenomenon, the pain, and the healing from incest. We still know so little about the effects of childhood trauma on bodies, minds, and souls.

On behalf of all my clients and incest survivors everywhere, I welcome you into my office and the world of these remarkable people. It has truly been my privilege to be invited into their very private and hidden realities. Together we wove our way through the darkest forests of their pasts to emerge into their bright and hopeful futures.

Acknowledgments

This book would never have needed to be written if it were not for the countless incest survivors. It has been an immeasurable honor for me to have encountered so many courageous, spirited, clever, unique, and remarkable survivors over the past years. It has been their willingness to trust me with their secret inner beings that has made this book possible. When I was recently interviewed by a prospective new client, she inquired about my credentials to treat incest survivors. I found myself stopping mid-sentence as I was listing all my degrees and years of training to reply, "I have learned the most about treating incest survivors from my clients. Over the years they have shared so openly with me what they need, what works, and what doesn't work. They were willing to experiment with me until my own ideas became more formulated." This book is my testimony to their strength and hard work. In particular, I want to thank Mariah for her exceptional openness and endurance in this process of experimentation. All the clients who followed her benefited from her contribution to this work.

I never would have considered, let alone begun, this project were it not for the urging and support of Barbara Kessler, Susan Kelly, and Julie Zuckerman Brennglass. All three of these dear friends convinced me that I had a book hidden inside of me that needed to be written. Although I had my doubts along the way, their continuous encouragement from start to finish was a driving force for me. I am extremely grateful to all of them for their faith in me and for their friendship.

Throughout the writing I received excellent technical assistance from the staff at Jason Aronson. I offer special thanks to Anne Patota for her interest, enthusiasm, and editorial guidance. The production staff, headed by Judith Cohen, pulled things together so nicely to create a wonderful finished product. On the homefront, I want to thank Jean Lieverman for her computer assistance and for fine tuning the layout of the manuscript.

I will always be appreciative of the wisdom, skill, and guidance I have received over the years from Zona Scheiner. Her insights, understanding, and warmth have helped me through the roughest moments in my life. She resides in a special place in my heart and soul.

I am so fortunate to be surrounded by the love and support of wonderful friends. They have celebrated my ups and consoled me during my downs. Their patience about my sporadic presence in their lives during the writing of this book has been invaluable. I can't thank them enough for the playful "study breaks," encouraging phone calls, dinners, entertaining of my daughter, and constancy in my life. In particular I want to thank David Hiller, Mickey Price, Joan Zald, Penny Turner, Sara Schreiber, Lia Wiss, Marshall Lee, and Howard Meyerson.

I am convinced that I was able to do this work and write this book because of my extended family. My brothers, cousins, aunts, and uncles have provided me with love and acceptance throughout my life. They are a constant source of warmth and strength. In particular, I want to thank Barry Roth for always being there for me. I can't imagine what life would have been like without him.

There is no question in my mind that Veronica Massey and Gail Green spirited me through these many months. Both of them gave me their time, attention, editorial skills, and patience. They went far above and beyond the call of duty at many moments. I love them both dearly and I could not have completed this book without them.

Throughout this all-consuming project, my mother, Marcy Roth, has offered constant support, encouragement, patience, and pride to spur me onward. I want to thank her for all her love and help.

Most of all, I want to thank my daughter Erika. She has been so understanding about all the times she wasn't allowed to disturb me. She has actually been one of my best cheerleaders—always supportive without pressuring me. Being her mother has given me great insight into my work because she allows me to see so vividly what children really need. She lets me be the kind of parent I always hoped I would become. I love her with all my heart. I know that we are both ecstatic that this book is completed so that we can have more time to play together.

1

Through the Eyes of the Child

In order to understand fully the impact of incest after the fact, it is necessary to go back to the childhood experiences and attempt to comprehend the child's reality. Herein lies the first obstacle for the adult trying to unravel her past. How does an adult recapture memories from the point of view of a 4-year-old or an 8-year-old? How does an adult strip away the grown-up language, interpretations, and censoring to get back to the child's understanding? How does an adult retrieve memories that are buried under layers of protective defenses? How does an adult give credibility to a child even if that child is herself? Our culture holds two beliefs about children that even an incest survivor believes: that children exaggerate and embellish reality to the point of creating fantasy, and that children are remarkably resilient and can survive anything unscathed. So an adult incest survivor, with the agreement of many adults around her, will say, "What's the big deal? It happened. It's over. I probably exaggerated the extent of the abuse. And I'm okay now."

Although currently there is horror and shock over the tremendous frequency of incest in this country, there is still a serious lack of understanding about the long-lasting impact incest has on its victims. Adult survivors regularly appear on national talk shows tearfully describing their childhoods and their course of recovery. Audience members and hosts offer sympathy and applause for these individuals' courage. What is missing in these presentations is the child's point of view—not the child who is currently being molested but the child who is now an adult. A child doesn't have the ability or emotional preparedness to talk about

1

incest. An adult who survived has a unique perspective that needs to be part of any incest discussion. The most powerful depictions of the severity of the incest trauma can be offered by an adult survivor who can speak the words she could not have known, formulated, or expressed as a child. These accounts can inform adults, especially therapists, of the truest nature of the devastation of incest.

MARIAH'S STORY

I grew up in a conservative upper-middle-class neighborhood where everyone went to church every Sunday. Our family seemed like all the others. There was my dad, the upwardly mobile engineering executive, and my mom, the housewife. I had a bunch of brothers and sisters and we played with all the other kids on the block. We all were good students, obeyed our parents and the church and did all the things kids generally do. We were just a normal family and I was sure that whatever I was experiencing inside my family was what all my friends experienced too.

I don't have a lot of memories about my mother, and a few years ago I figured out why. I suddenly realized then that my mother has always been a pretty severe alcoholic. The reason I don't have many childhood images that include her is because she had usually passed out. I remember seeing her asleep in her bedroom, but I don't remember her being at the dinner table too often, or going grocery shopping or making meals, or taking care of my brothers and sisters. I remember that I did a lot of those things from about the time I started school. The only times I thought all this was a bit unusual were those occasions when I'd be at a friend's house and her mother would be up and dressed and making dinner and offering us freshly baked cookies. I loved those moments but never let myself feel bad that my mom didn't do those things. I just figured it was a special deal every now and then at my friend's home.

When I was really little, I remember feeling a bit confused about my father. There were times when he'd hug me and kiss me and tell me how special I was to him, and then there'd be other times when he'd call me "Dummy" or "Stupid Head" and yell at me to do certain household chores. I definitely remember feeling humiliated because he often said these things in front of other family members. I was also convinced that I deserved those names. I usually felt pretty lousy about myself and spent a lot of energy trying to be good enough or smart enough.

When I was 6 years old my dad starting touching me differently. It wasn't the hugging and kissing that reassured me that he really did love me. Instead it was uncomfortable and embarrassing. He'd pull me onto his lap and thrust his pelvis against my butt while he held me tightly around the waist. I would panic and freeze up trying to figure out what this was all about. Although my back was turned to him, I could hear his breathing getting heavy and quick. I was too afraid to turn my head to look at his face. He didn't speak to me while this happened. After he stopped moving he would gently say, "You're my special girl." So I figured that even though I was scared and uncomfortable, this was just something daddies do with their special daughters. Even so, I became very wary around my father.

By the time I was 8 my father began the "Saturday Ritual," as I call it now. Since my mother was passed-out, my dad did the grocery shopping on Saturday mornings. I was instructed to watch the younger kids while he was away and to send them outside when he arrived home with the groceries. Then he and I would put the food away. We were in the house alone (except for my sleeping mother upstairs). He would corner me in the pantry and rub against me and stroke my chest and my butt. He would kiss my neck and breathe heavily and get red in the face. I was paralyzed. I couldn't speak. I couldn't move. I couldn't think. I couldn't cry. I remember looking out the kitchen window at my siblings playing in the yard while my father rubbed against me. I began to hate being "special." It was overwhelmingly confusing. My father was actually being gentle with me and saying loving things to me. But all I felt was frightened and sickened. I knew *something* was wrong but couldn't figure out what. The best I could surmise was that there was something wrong with me. But I had no idea what it was.

My 10th birthday provided more answers to the riddle. Every year on my birthday I went through the whole day hoping that my parents would give me a present or make me a cake or just wish me a happy birthday. But nothing like that ever happened. The day of my 10th birthday was no different. I went to bed that night with a familiar sense of disappointment. I remember hearing the stillness of the house as I lay awake feeling very sad. Then I heard the click of the light switch at the bottom of the stairs. It was one of those old-fashioned switches that echoes throughout the house. Then I heard my father's shoes slowly clump up the wooden stairs. I remember thinking, "Oh goody. He didn't forget! He's coming to give me my birthday present." There he was standing over my bed and I looked up in anticipation. He didn't say anything. He just began unbuttoning his shirt and pulling his pants down. I couldn't believe my eyes. Then he pulled up my nightgown and lay down on top of me. I remember the weight of his body making it difficult for me to breathe. I remember the scratchiness of his stubbly cheek against my cheek and I remember what he smelled like. It's a distinct odor that is not pleasant but one I can't describe. I was so scared that I actually did whimper, "Don't Daddy. Don't. Please don't do that." His only reply was to tell me that he was going to show me how a daddy loves his daughter.

I don't have much memory about what happened next. All I can say is that the pain I felt was unbearable. I can only tell you now as an adult that my father put his penis inside my vagina. What I could have told you then was that my father was splitting me in two and then I went away. I wasn't underneath my father anymore. I was floating near the ceiling drifting over a beautiful sunny meadow. I remember the meadow very well because I've been there so many times. But that night was the first time I visited the meadow. I have no idea how much time passed but when I became aware that I was curled up in the corner of my bed holding myself, I was alone in my bedroom. Then I felt the burning, piercing pain between my legs and in my stomach. Then I felt something wet. I reached down to touch my thigh and it was then that I realized I was bleeding and that my sheets were soaked. The next thing I remember is being in the bathroom with the sheets, being terrified that my mother would discover the blood. I became obsessed with washing all the blood out so my mother wouldn't punish me. Once I was satisfied that the sheets were okay I got a wash cloth and cleaned the blood off my vagina and thighs. I never looked down at myself. I was disgusted. I felt dirty. I kept washing and washing, hoping to rid myself of this filthy feeling. All the while the pain I felt was tremendous.

Eventually I changed my sheets, went to bed, and managed to sleep a short while. That marked the beginning of what I would call becoming a zombie. I was in a daze most hours of any given day. I went through the motions of attending school and doing my chores, but I wasn't really there. My mind was consumed with what I could do to prevent or avoid my father's nocturnal visits. I had already become convinced that this was my punishment for being such a bad girl. I was obsessed with being good. I mopped and waxed the hardwood floors at one o'clock in the morning in hopes this would save me. I cleaned the house every day after school and kept my brothers and sisters in line. I never bothered my mother if she was sleeping and never crossed my father. I bravely withstood the rapes, beatings, burns, and berating. I became good at not feeling anything physically or emotionally. I never cried or yelped out in pain. I was a walking zombie. A disgusting piece of shit that deserved what I got.

But there was another part of me. A very private part that I never told anyone about. I was sure that if I ever spoke of it that it, too, would be taken away from me. It was a place inside of me that was connected to that meadow. It was like a small, good, peaceful, and strong version of myself. It was the total opposite of that zombie. Inside of me I was brave and powerful. I was free of pain and punishment. I could do and be anything I wanted to be. It was that *inside me* that planned my escape from this nightmare. That inner self eventually got me involved in music and playing the violin. I made a plan to become so accomplished that I would be offered a music scholarship to attend summer camps and college. My violin became my ticket out. Not only was music going to set me free by getting me out of the house, but the music itself transported me when I most needed to *go away.* And, in fact, I was offered a college scholarship at a music school and that's how I left home.

While other children were enjoying the smells of mother's home cooking, a gentle paternal caress, the sounds of laughter in their homes, verbal praise for their accomplishments, and goodnight kisses, Mariah's senses were being assaulted with inappropriate touching, sexual smells and sounds, angry and hushed tones, verbal belittlement, and nighttime rapes. This was her world, and from this world she developed a particular understanding and point of view about herself and her life. This was the context for her ego formation and cognitive development. She was forced into adult roles and behaviors with the knowledge of a child. From that primitive place of magical thinking, crude logic, egocentric causality, and dependent relationships, Mariah formulated a rather elaborate mental labyrinth to explain and cope with her circumstances. If Mommy is always sleeping, she must be sick. If Daddy says I'm stupid, it must be true. If Mommy pushes me down the stairs I must have deserved it, so I will figure out what bad thing I did so this doesn't happen again. If Daddy climbs on top of me and hurts me between my legs, I must be being punished for not cleaning up the kitchen well enough. If Daddy tells me he is doing this to me because I am his special daughter, then I must have been chosen among my sisters to have this honor. If Daddy hurts me and I show my pain, then he'll hurt me more.

The list of reasoning is endless, and it is this very thinking that serves to protect the child. To Mariah as a child, these conclusions made perfect sense and provided her with something to hold onto—some illusion of comprehension. It is like a 7-year-old child trying to put together a jigsaw puzzle with 1000 pieces. Since she doesn't have the developmental skills to perform the task with accuracy, she will take all the existing pieces and force the connections by jamming the pieces together. By luck she will occasionally fit two interlocking pieces together easily. In the end she will have all the relevant pieces mashed together without forming a coherent picture. These faulty linkages do not fade in adulthood without major effort.

Some would say that by the time this child reaches adulthood she will have been exposed to many experiences and people who will contradict her earlier learning and, thus, she will arrive at a more optimistic and healthy outlook on life. Whatever damage she suffered will have been remedied, so what's the big fuss? Besides, so many of these incest survivors go on to lead very successful lives. The incest is in the past, it was survived, the person is all the stronger and more determined as a result of it, so why dredge up old business? But the reality of childhood incest is that it is *not* over when it's over. The aftershocks are omnipresent in a survivor's psyche and existence. A developmental description of Mariah's experiences tells many survivors' stories.

DEVELOPMENTAL HISTORY

Early in her life Mariah's attachment to her mother was severed due to her mother's alcoholism and the birth of several new siblings. She did not have a permanent love object in her mother and struggled to find ways of coping with the resultant anxiety and insecurity. Before she was 6, Mariah's father provided the most consistent adult bond. For the most part, his behavior was appropriate—nurturing, loving, and caring. He was Mariah's most secure attachment, and she developed a modicum of trust, dependence, security, and a sense of separate self. From this base the molestations occurred. This trustworthy adult upon whom Mariah was totally dependent, and with whom she experienced a mutual love, began behaving in ways that disturbed her. A small and egocentric child has no way to evaluate the parent's behavior as inappropriate, so she easily draws the conclusion that she has done something bad to create these situations. All possibilities for normal development are interrupted, as this child can no longer depend on feeling safe or good in her father's presence. But because she *used* to feel fine with her father, Mariah will become obsessed with discovering the magic formula to retrieve those lost feelings. This becomes the organizing focus for Mariah's continued ego development.

As the incest continues Mariah's experiences become more bizarre and overwhelming. The only way she can cope is by shutting off her physical and emotional responses to the abuse, and so ordinary development in these areas is also disrupted. This spills over into her whole life. Another child will tease her at school or a boy will lift up her dress to peek at her panties and Mariah will not register any emotion about the incident. This is just business as usual for her.

Trust has become a thing of the past that Mariah can no longer even remember, let alone experience. By the age of 10 she trusts no one except herself. She becomes obsessed with self-control, assuming that absolute mastery over her entire being will protect her from further abuse. Even though this plan is not successful, it is all she has left to depend on. She makes sense of her world through unsophisticated mental processes and holds on tight to her conclusions. Her outlook boils down to this: "My father doesn't love me anymore because I'm a very bad person. If only I can figure out how to be the kind of good person he wants me to be, then he will be kind and gentle again. His anger and actions toward me are correct, and I deserve them because I am so awful. I've got to work really hard to notice everything and take care of everything and be really, really good so that my father will be happy with me again." This becomes the basis for Mariah's self-image and self-esteem.

So the years pass; the incest continues and Mariah still has not found the secret formula. She never develops positive feelings about herself, continues to be obsessed with attempting to be good, keeps to herself, and outwardly accomplishes endless chores more adeptly than most adults. She finally leaves home at the age of 18 and enters the greater world. What does she bring with her? Mariah has grown into a perfectionistic overachiever who tries to accommodate herself to the needs and whims of others. Behind this flurry of generous and successful behavior is a frightened, empty, lonely shell of a person who believes she is completely unworthy of any praise or affection. To those around her, Mariah is a marvelously accomplished, giving, and cheerful woman. No one would ever suspect that she had endured years of sexual and physical abuse in her childhood or that she thinks so little of herself. Her performance is believable. She spent years honing it. But Mariah knows the truth and her truth is that there is no person behind her mask. Her opportunity to develop a sense of herself as powerful, good, efficacious, loved, and worthy was taken away from her so long ago. She goes through the motions without feelings, reactions, or substance. She still lives in constant fear that she will be hurt or invaded by others or, worse, that she will be discovered to be the disgusting, terrible, wretched person that she really is.

HOW THEY SURVIVE

A child who survives incest grows into an adult who may look fine on the outside but is a fragmented mess on the inside. Whatever developing sense of self and security was established before the incest occurred is shattered. Without a protective adult present, this child has no chance to proceed through ordinary developmental stages. She is prematurely forced into adult behaviors with a child's mind. What does develop is a complicated and idiosyncratic coping structure, which is not at all the same as an autonomous identity. Many are fooled because this grown survivor appears to be just fine.

Incest is a crime of the most devastating proportion. Not only are the child's physical boundaries, innocence, and security ripped away, but her very self is obliterated. It is appalling to consider that: (1) a child would exaggerate or fantasize such horrors or (2) she will bounce back from them without much difficulty. Before this child has had the opportunity to feel any secure sense of competency or coherence in her world she is thrust into a bizarre and destructive reality that becomes the context for her perceptions. Without intervention, the impact of childhood incest will be felt throughout a person's entire life.

The current psychiatric diagnostic category for dysfunctional adult incest survivors is "Post-Traumatic Stress Syndrome" (*DSM-III-R*, 1987). Other survivors included in this grouping are disaster victims, Vietnam War veterans, hostages, and Nazi Holocaust survivors. Holocaust survivors provide an interesting and apropos comparison with incest survivors in terms of the severity of the victimization and the necessary elements for survival. Bruno Bettelheim (1980), in his essay "The Ultimate Limit," writes: "It can become completely shattering to a person's integration when the system of beliefs on which he relied for his integration, and for offering protection against death anxiety, not only lets him down, but worse, is about to destroy him psychologically and physically. Then nothing seems left that can offer protection. Furthermore, we now no longer can feel confident that we will be able ever again to know reliably what to trust, and what to defend against" (p. 10). Bettelheim was speaking here of adult prisoners who had to transform themselves psychologically in order to survive extreme circumstances. His statement is equally true for incest survivors, with the additional difficulty that they never completely formed a "system of beliefs" upon which to base an integration outside of the context of their imprisoned childhoods. With incest, the child's belief system has abuse at the center of it. Much has been exposed and written about the horrors of the concentration camps, the evils of Hitler and his S.S., the devastating loss of human lives, and the tenacity of those who survived. Incest warrants the same exposure.

Like the Nazis, adults who sexually abuse children in their families terrorize, threaten, and assault innocent victims. They wield total control over the child's very existence by stripping away any sense of self-pride, dignity, privacy, or power. If the child resists the mistreatment, the threats escalate to include greater physical harm or potential harm to the people the child loves. The random nature of the assaults leaves the victim constantly wary and anticipating the next attack. Over time the only hope that still burns within the child is that someday she will be set free and all will be well. Once she finally does leave home, her liberation is not all that she had hoped it would be. This terrorization, the deterioration of self, the will to survive, and the recurrent traumas after liberation are the very issues that plague Holocaust survivors and freed hostages. Many survivors of these acts of terrorism have written eloquently detailed accounts of their captivity and the psychological aftereffects. Incest must be viewed as a similar crime against human life. The only difference is that incest must be evaluated as the most severe of all, because it is perpetrated against children who do not have the physical and psychological skills to cope with their "extreme situations," as Bettelheim refers to the concentration camps.

As has been mentioned earlier, there is a lack of understanding about the child's reality within an incestuous family. Not only is this evident in the minimization of the long-term impact incest has on human development and the reluctance to label this a heinous crime, subject to serious legal punishment and public outrage, but it is also apparent in the current educational-prevention programs aimed at children. Across the country school children are being instructed to tell someone or "just say no" to unwanted adult intrusions. This approach shows a remarkably naïve understanding of the total power an adult can have over a child's psyche. When incest occurs, the child becomes numb with confusion and terror. Almost without exception, the physical acts are accompanied by verbal threats of greater harm if silence is not maintained. Although it is useful to identify "safe adults" within the school setting that a traumatized child may turn to, it is unlikely that such a young person could overcome the control of the abuser by "telling someone." For these programs to be more effective, the approach must be through the eyes of the terrorized child.

When a child who is sexually molested considers telling her mother or teacher or grandmother about the abuse, she cannot think her way out of the maze. Her thoughts sound something like this: "Daddy said that if I tell anyone about our little games together, that he will kill Mommy. I have to protect Mommy." "Grandpa said that if I tell anyone about this that no one will believe me. They'll think I just made it up. I'm sure he's right. Who would believe a kid over a grown-up?" "Mommy says she doesn't know what we'd do without Daddy. We'd go to the poorhouse, for sure. If I tell Mommy what Daddy does to me they'll have a big fight and Daddy will leave and we will go to the poorhouse and it will be all my fault." "My mom always says how lucky we are that she met my stepfather. Now we have someone to take care of us. If I tell Mom what he does to me, she'll get mad at me and maybe she'll send me away. I don't want to leave my mom." Unless the child still experiences some trusting reliance on a significant adult, it is unlikely that she will reveal the incest. She has been convinced that telling will only make matters worse. However awful the abuse is, destroying the rest of the family is more awful. Only under rare circumstances would a child think: "I don't like what Daddy does to me. I think it's wrong and

I'm going to tell Mommy all about it. I don't believe Daddy when he says that no one will believe me. I am sure that Mommy will believe me and that she will tell Daddy to stop. Then we can all live happily ever after." It would be erroneous to assume that children will come forward when something is wrong. Incest and other forms of child abuse create an enormous amount of emotional and cognitive isolation and panic that renders the victim speechless. When adults finally do speak of their incest experiences they are invariably asked, "Why didn't you ever tell me/anyone?" The answer to that can only be understood through a child's mind.

In lieu of ordinary development, the sexually abused child organizes her sense of self around surviving and coping with the abuse. She addresses the developmental tasks of autonomy, competence, self-control, and mastery (Erikson 1950, Piaget 1963) through her attempts to end the incest. Unless the incest ceases, she deems herself a miserable failure. Even if it does end before she leaves home, she never quite trusts that it won't happen again. The molested child creates layers of protective defenses to guard her innermost fragile sense of self. It is similar to Bettelheim's (1980) point of view in the concentration camps: "If the author should be asked to sum up in one sentence what, during all the time he spent in the camp, was his main problem, he would say: to safeguard his ego in such a way that, if by any good luck he should regain liberty, he would be approximately the same person he was when deprived of liberty" (p. 62). Victims of senseless, continuous, and assaultive persecution focus their energy on self-protection and eventual escape.

What, then, is required of the child in order to survive the incest? How can she protect herself? How does she achieve the developmental goals of autonomy, competence, self-control, and mastery? How can she look as *normal* as possible? How can she gain control of her destiny? With remarkable cleverness, the abused child creates an elaborate system of repression, fantasy, idiosyncratic logic, physical numbness, hypersensitivity, defiance, and responsibility (Fine 1990, Sgroi and Bunk 1988). All of these help to protect her from completely evaporating into the ether. What little ego she has, she protects for dear life.

This is accomplished through an egocentric perspective. The sexually abused child believes she is the cause for this mistreatment. If she is the cause, then she can be the cure. The list of "if only's" is infinite. If only she were . . . then the abuse would stop. This creates the "illusion of control" (Calof 1987) for the child. Feeling a sense of control over her actions, her body functions, her emotions, and her duties offers the child the illusion that she might—through proper actions—be able to control the situation. To acknowledge that she is completely at the mercy of this adult would be too devastating, so she denies the extent of her captivity and pours her attention into figuring out the exact formula that will finally end the abuse. Her response to her failure at this task is to say, "I'm just not smart enough yet to figure this out. If I keep at it, I'm sure I'll eventually get it right." Mastery for the abused child only comes when she is able to prevent, avoid, or end the incest.

Fantasy serves an especially important function for the abused child. Not only does it provide moments of relief, creativity, and playfulness, but it also keeps the hope of escape alive. As was true for hostages or Holocaust survivors, dreaming about a better future keeps the spirit from being broken. It is a private form of resistance to the victimization. As long as the child can envision a carefree life, she can continue to cope with her conditions. The moment she can no longer dream, she becomes dangerously susceptible to vanishing altogether.

On a more profound level, the child coping with incest will develop a defiant posture towards her abuser. Inwardly she says, "I dare you to try and destroy me! Nothing you do can get to me anymore." Outwardly she stops shedding tears, displaying any affect or registering any pain (Goodwin 1990). Unfortunately, this can often provoke her abuser even more. His intent *is* to break her will and gain power over her. The more she exhibits resistance, the more likely it is the abuse will escalate. Most adult survivors will describe that this defiance was the most solid part of themselves. Even though they observed that it intensified their pain, they were not willing to relinquish this last ounce of dignity. It is striking that this furious drive to resist develops at such a young age. This is the very same force that survivors such as Viktor Frankel (1959), Natan Sharansky (1988), and Bruno Bettelheim (1980) describe. "Somehow I will get through this. My basic decent self will remain intact. Some meaning will emerge from all of this and I will be triumphant." Even the small child will create whatever mental illusions or coping strategies (no matter how bizarre they may be) she needs in order to preserve some sense of self.

It is these same thoughts and mechanisms that the grown child brings into adulthood. Once released from her "prison," these very beliefs that contributed to her survival may not be so effective outside the prison walls. This can be exceptionally confusing and often leads to a degree of dysfunction. It is somewhere in this state that an incest survivor may present herself for therapy. It would be a therapeutic blunder to identify these defenses as pathological. Rather it is incumbent upon the therapist to view these strategies as the safety deposit box for the client's ego. By serving as the "enlightened witness" (Miller 1990b), the therapist provides the opportunity for this client to move through developmental stages that had previously been interrupted and to reorganize the pieces of the shattered self.

2

Beginning the Therapy

As an incest survivor I feel that I am starting a new life. I have to learn the proper way to feel, think, trust and live. I need proper guidance. As an incest survivor I feel that I need and ask for a lot of help in seeing how wrong my old world was. It makes me want to get all the proper knowledge and guidance I can get.

—Client just beginning therapy

As I look back (over our therapy together) I will always cherish the fact that you are always available for me and that you have always given me *genuine* human responses. These are things I never experienced as a child or as an adult in therapy. By giving me your time and thoughtful gestures I've come to know that you really want to help me and see me through all this. I don't feel like just another name in your appointment book. I know my pain and suffering are important enough to you that you go out of your way to help me. The therapists I've had in the past were rigid and mechanical in their treatments and with their time. I wasn't an individual to them; I was just another incest victim who had lots of problems. Maybe, then, successful and meaningful therapy for the incest survivor is in a way a direct result of the therapist's ability to be genuine, creative, compassionate, and available in her therapeutic relationships.

—Client near the end of treatment

TREATMENT GOALS

Incest clients make it perfectly clear that their goals for therapy are to receive what they deserved but never got in their childhoods in order to recover from

11

their traumatic pasts. This is exactly what therapists ought to be offering. Clients are straightforward about their desire for a safe, protective, and healthy relationship with a therapist so they may learn what they need to know to live productive *and* happy lives. This hope and goal is the primary focus of incest treatment.

In order to achieve this goal, long-term psychotherapy for incest survivors must accomplish these specific goals: (1) telling, feeling, and releasing the incest experiences, (2) gaining new insights about the family dynamics surrounding incest and the impact on the child's coping and surviving, (3) developing positive self-esteem leading to a sense of empowerment, efficacy, and health, (4) integrating the traumatized child with the functional adult, allowing the child to blossom and heal, and (5) experiencing a reparative relationship with a significant adult that reflects, models, and teaches about well-boundaried and caring relationships. These goals must be approached by the therapist with an extensive understanding of incestuous family dynamics and the psychology of incest survivors. Incest is not like any other family dysfunction. (For more extensive background information about incestuous family dynamics, see Courtois 1988, Finkelhor 1979, Forward and Buck 1978, Gelinas 1988, Groth 1982, and Kluft 1990.)

Telling, Feeling, and Releasing the Incest Experience

Incest occurs in silence and secrecy, leading to feelings of shame, isolation, worthlessness, and anger. The first step toward recovery from these wounds is to begin to talk about the incest. The forbidden territory needs to be revealed to end the oppressive consequences. For many, therapy will be their first opportunity to speak. Beyond the telling is reexperiencing the feelings that were not safe to express at the moment of trauma. Although coping mechanisms may have intervened at the time to protect the child psychologically and physically, causing her to block out the trauma, the memories have been stored within. The client will need to release all the thoughts, perceptions, sensations, and emotions that have been stowed away inside her. There has been a flood dammed for years within the client that needs to flow outward. By sharing her past and permitting the resultant emotions, the client can drop the burdens of her secretive past (Courtois 1988, Gelinas 1988, Gil 1988).

Gaining New Insights About Incestuous Family Dynamics

All incest survivors assume full responsibility for the provocation and occurrence of the incest. They were developmentally egocentric when the incest happened and drew the (faulty) conclusions that they brought this on themselves because of their behavior or inherent badness. They never developed the concept that the adults were responsible for the sexual abuse and that they lacked protection from it. They have grown up continuing to believe these childhood thoughts. Therapy will unravel the past through very different points of view, teaching the client about the entire family and their role in the incest. The client will move away from the notion of being the instigator and come to understand her victimization and how she managed to survive such horrors. This forms the basis for a new self-concept (Bowen 1978, Kerr and Bowen 1988, Kramer 1985).

Developing Positive Self-Esteem

As new insights emerge, the client has the opportunity to assemble a very different picture of herself. As she perceives her cleverness and courage in coping with the abuse, she begins to sense that she is not so evil or weak or damaged as she had thought. Through a variety of treatment modalities, the client will develop a new and empowered sense of self-worth.

Integrating the "Child Within" with the Adult

Incest treatment gives attention to both the adult-client and the child-client that resides within the functional, though troubled, adult. Sexual abuse creates devastating developmental arrest and damage that must be repaired within the therapy. The child's emerging sense of self is shattered by the incest, creating an individual who is called upon to participate in adult behaviors with a child's confusion. The end result is a child with overdeveloped adult traits and under-developed ego integration. This calls for very painstaking reparative work for the therapist and the client. As the child-client feels safe enough to appear, she receives guidance, care, and information that she never got when she was small. Simultaneously, the adult-client is called upon to offer her resources to embrace that child within herself, thus forming an integration of self that was not per-mitted before (Bradshaw 1988, 1990, Courtois 1988, Erikson 1950).

Experiencing a Reparative Relationship

The therapeutic relationship becomes the vehicle, the laboratory, and the metaphor for teaching the client about healthy, appropriate, well-boundaried, and caring relationships. This encompasses experiencing trust, consistency, safety, guidance, nurturance, and worthiness. A good therapeutic connection provides the opportunity for the client to reveal her entire reality (Kirschner and Kirschner 1986).

To attain these treatment goals, the most comprehensive theoretical under-standing comes from a mixture of family systems theory (including the most recent Women's Project work), developmental psychology, post-traumatic stress phenomenon, and psychodynamic theory (Bowen 1978, Calof 1987, Courtois 1988, Erikson 1950, 1968, Kramer 1985, McGoldrick and Carter 1980, Piaget 1955, 1963, 1965). It is essential to think about incest within the context of individual and family dynamics and human development. To see incest from only one of these perspectives is a mistake. Incest is an extremely complex occurrence in the life of a family or individual. Its impact is traumatic, multilayered, and long lasting. It would be damaging to a client to approach treatment from a more individualistically dynamic point of view as the client is the victim of someone else's illness. Incest involves people outside of the client's own psyche and they must be part of the therapist's understanding of the client's past. Conversely, it would be shortsighted and potentially harmful to the client to understand incest only from a family treatment perspective. The client will require far greater privacy than family treatment allows. In concert, however, family systems, developmental, post-traumatic stress, and psychodynamic theories offer a thorough understanding of the phenomenon of incest.

These are clients whose learning about reality in childhood was disturbingly interrupted and distorted. They became adults before they had a chance to be children. The specifics of incest and its aftermath suggest a multidimensional therapeutic approach. For the therapist to be wedded to primarily one theoretical perspective and one stylistic stance is to offer a very limited healing opportunity for the incest client. There is no one treatment modality that can meet all these goals. Instead, a very eclectic and broad range of methods will be employed. These techniques generally fall within six categories: intrapsychic exploration, reparenting, cognitive and behavioral adjustments, life skills learning, expansive and creative experiences, and adjunctive resources. Table 2–1 lists a potpourri of treatment strategies from each of these areas. It is to be seen as a sampling of the most frequently used methodologies rather than a finite list.

Every incest client wants to know how long it will take to undo the incestuous damage. Although there is no definitive answer to this question, there is a reasonable range. One to five years of individual psychotherapy is a general estimate. The severity and duration of the incest often determine the course of treatment. Meeting once a week for one or one-and-a-half hours is acceptable, although many clients choose to meet twice a week. There is no proof that meeting more than once a week brings termination about any faster, but it does seem to regulate the anxiety better for some clients. There are some moments during the treatment when the material is particularly painful, and more frequent sessions on a short-term basis are a good idea. The duration of the treatment is dependent on so many variables that it is hard to be more accurately predictive and it is prudent not to set up false hope for a speedy recovery. This work is slow and intense and need not be constrained by time pressure.

These goals, orientation, and methodologies seem to be most effective in the

Table 2-1. Treatment Modalities for Incest Therapy

Intrapsychic Exploration	Reparenting	Cognitive and Behavioral Adjustments	Life Skills Learning	Expansive and Creative Experiences	Adjunctive Resources
Talk therapy	Child	Behavior	Problem-	Guided	Group therapy
Introspection	psychotherapy	modification	solving skills	visualizations	Family or
Insight-oriented	Play therapy	techniques	Decision-	Imagery and	couples
Journal writing	Therapeutic	Stress	making skills	metaphors	therapy
Expressive-	reparenting	management	Communication	Art, music, and	12-Step
emotive	Developmental	Relaxation	skills	movement	programs and
catharsis	learning with	training	Understanding	therapies	support
Exploration	therapeutic	Assertiveness	relationships	Psychodrama	groups
of family	guidance	training	Sexual	and role-	Medical or legal
dynamics	Unleashing the	Nutritional	education	playing	resources
Genograms	developmentally	management	and discovery	Gestalt	Bibliotherapy
Memory work	arrested child	Addiction	Physical health	techniques	Spirituality
	within	recovery	attention and	Rituals	
		Recreational	maintenance		
		therapy	Money		
		Neurolinguistic	management		
		programming	skills		
		Rational	Employment		
		emotive	issues		
		therapy	Parenting skills		
		Cognitive			
		restructuring			
		Reality testing			
		Family systems			
		coaching			

treatment of incest because they optimize the client's potential to become empowered and in control of her destiny. More traditionally analytic approaches are founded on the notion of therapist omnipotence. For incest survivors this would feel all too familiar: the all-knowing, all-seeing adult who has total control over the small, helpless child. Although traditional therapies are not intended to create abusive dynamics, the incest survivor cannot experience this kind of relationship in any other way than harmful and disempowering. As Alice Miller states in *Banished Knowledge* (1990):

Both basic rules—the psychoanalytic setting as well as the method of free association—assume that on the one side there is a superior, informed interpreter, the analyst, and on the other the uninformed patient to whom the analyst explains his situation, his unconscious desires, thoughts, and impulses. For the analyst to be able to do this, the patient must as it were uncover, betray, and expose his unconscious with the aid of free association. Thus the authoritarian structure of childrearing is preserved unthinkingly in both basic rules. Parents, too, told the child from their perspective how he felt, or how he was supposed to feel, and the child believed that they knew better than he did. [p. 183]

The overall goal of incest recovery therapy is to guide the client through a developmental progression that will leave her with a whole and integrated sense of herself. The treatment is an interactive process that gathers together broken pieces, fragmented bits, dropped stitches, and missing connections and then produces the glue that creates a complete and healthy sense of self. To accomplish this, the therapist needs to be eclectic, creative, flexible, and willing to establish a meaningful human connection to the client.

CLIENT PRESENTATION: ELIZABETH

Elizabeth entered therapy at the age of 29; she wanted to confront the traumas of her childhood because they were intruding into her marriage of three years. She loved her husband very much and felt safe and secure with him, but she was aware that she had become noncommunicative and no longer interested in being sexual. She was very concerned that although her husband was understanding and patient with her, he would decide to leave the marriage unless she became more functional as a partner. She had revealed to her husband that her father had sexually abused her throughout most of her childhood and adolescence and that she needed help to "get over it." She had tried therapy twice before her marriage but was unable to feel comfortable enough with the therapist to delve into her childhood memories. These experiences had soured her toward psychotherapy but she now felt desperate. She felt her marriage to be in jeopardy if she did not move past her nightmares and so sought out a third therapist.

Elizabeth had been teaching fourth grade for seven years. She was continuing her education during the evenings and summer months, and was one class away from completing her master's degree in guidance and counseling. She had met her husband, David, through mutual friends five years earlier. Initially they had become close friends sharing many similar interests. After one year their romance began to ignite, and Elizabeth was overjoyed that she had met such a gentle, kind, and caring man. They were married the following year and shared a solid relationship until last year when they began discussing having children. They had previously acknowledged their mutual desire to have children, but as their conversations became more serious Elizabeth began dramatically to withdraw from David. She became robotic in her verbal responses offering no signs of affect. Her facial expression seemed permanently blank and her body posture became rigid. Even the smallest sounds or movements in a room would make her jump and cause her to flee toward some safer spot. She became hypersensitive to people's responses to her, fearing that she was being watched or ridiculed. Although she could not tolerate David being physically close to her, she could not bear to be alone in their home. She would be overcome with severe panic attacks that left her fetally crouched in a corner. Only after gentle verbal coaxing would she unfold and rest in the comfort of David's arms. Although her parents lived in another state she developed a chronic fear that they would arrive at her doorstep unannounced at any moment. If she received a telephone call from her mother or father, Elizabeth clicked into her best "good daughter" voice and carried on an ordinary conversation. Immediately upon hanging up the phone she would reach for a glass of wine.

At school, her teaching began to falter. Although she continued to enter the classroom each morning well prepared for the day's lessons, discipline became a severe problem for her. She began to experience the children as unruly, yet she felt torn about seizing control of the situation. If she heard her voice rise to firmly request the children to behave, she would instantly panic that she had been too harsh. If she allowed the disruptive behavior to continue, she would feel enraged and helpless at the same time. Her principal was aware of the changes and spoke with Elizabeth on several occasions. Because she had been such an exemplary teacher up to this point, the principal simply expressed concern and wondered if she was getting "burned out." Elizabeth reassured her boss that she was just feeling a bit stressed but that she was getting it under control.

Meanwhile Elizabeth and David awkwardly tried to discuss the situation. David expressed concern for his wife and worried that he had done something to create this. They traced back to the beginning of Elizabeth's anxieties and recalled their discussions about having a baby. Elizabeth burst into tears proclaiming that she would make a terrible mother. It was this moment when they both made the connection to Elizabeth's childhood and they agreed that therapy would be helpful.

Elizabeth's presenting symptoms were depressed affect, anxiety, panic attacks, loss of appetite, disrupted sleep, loss of sexual drive, paranoid tendencies, lack of self-esteem, irrational fears of impending doom, retreat from social interactions, mistrust of adults around her, and confused perceptions. These are several of the most common traits in adulthood for people who survived the childhood traumas of incest (Courtois 1988, Gelinas 1988, Gil 1988, Sgroi and Bunk 1988). In spite of these troubles, many of these people continue to function adequately in their jobs and home lives, although they are not performing as flawlessly as they might be.

How does a therapist begin to conceptualize this configuration of symptoms? Is this an organically based depression? Is it the onset of a schizoid personality? Is this a completely irrational, potentially psychotic episode? What about a borderline personality? Although the *symptoms* may have some pathology, it would be a mistake to immediately diagnose from a medical stance. Upon closer assessment there *is* the possibility of severe pathology involved for this kind of client, especially in the borderline and multiple personality categories (Braun 1990, Masterson 1976, Stone 1990). But in the majority of cases these symptoms are an indication of trauma aftermath. A more open-ended diagnostic approach that depathologizes an incest client is to view her presentation as an *adult version of childhood coping mechanisms that have become dysfunctional.* There is very little therapeutic value in labeling the incest client as sick. In fact, this can lay the groundwork for therapy recreating the earlier abusive dynamic where the victim is identified as the "bad, ill, crazy" one, and the adult is "good, right, and justified" in his or her behavior. This will perpetuate the client's sense of helplessness and negative self-worth. It is essential, then, that the therapist begin with a perspective that deems the client to be healthy but in trouble, rather than sick and chronic. After a period of time, if the treatment is not progressing as expected, then it is appropriate to begin considering other psychiatric evaluations and recommending new courses of treatment.

It is extremely useful to look more closely at the coping strategies an abused child develops and how those skills translate into adult behaviors. Most adults entering therapy to recover from incest will exhibit some combination of the traits listed in Table 2–2. Many of these traits appear in the current *DSM-III-R* to describe Post-Traumatic Stress Disorder (1987, pp. 247–251).

Table 2–2. Presenting Symptoms

Coping Strategy	Childhood presentation	Adult presentation
Dissociation	Flat affect, withdrawn, "spaced out," not crying, high-pain threshold	Withdrawn, depressed, false or flat affect, does not experience bodily sensations
"Leaving" Mind or Body	Mentally cuts off from physical experience	Mentally "goes away" while operating on "automatic pilot"
Splitting/ Compartmentalization	Good child–bad child	Successful public self = false self; horrible, disgusting, private self = true self
Rigid and Obsessional Thinking	Idiosyncratic cause and effect logic that creates a rigid code of behavior	Individualized code of morality, extremely rigid rules for behavior
Denial	Dreamlike disbelief about the abuse	Repression of childhood memories
Overly Responsible	Taking on adult responsibilities for household and child care	Persistent overattention to the well-being of others
Overly Nurturant	Extremely gentle with children and animals	Choosing nurturing professions, the caretaker in relationships
Self-reliant	Wary of adults, not asking for help, figuring out tasks for self	Difficulty trusting others, does everything for self, does not want help
Self-nurturant	Rocking, hiding in closets, fantasy play, excessive reading, outdoor play, overeating, prolonged thumbsucking	Eating problems, excessive spending, excessive reading, "spacing out," safety in the outdoors, fantasizing
Hypervigilant	Heightened startle response, acute attention to minutae	Overly attentive to inconsequential behaviors, misinterpretation of subtle nuances
Self-abuse	Head banging, hitting self, creating physical pain to block emotions	Cutting, head banging, nail digging, distracting self from emotions, addictions

COPING STRATEGIES

Dissociation

Childhood presentation. An abused child appears withdrawn and depressed. She almost never cries and grows to have an exceedingly high threshold for physical pain. It is as if the child's thoughts and sensations leave her, especially as the abuse is taking place. There is carryover into daily life as this child seems affectly flat and "spaced out." She appears cut off from fully experiencing certain events.

Adult presentation. Dissociation continues into adulthood for the incest survivor. When events get too intense she will withdraw physically and emotionally. She is very detached from her physical being and often does not experience feelings of hunger, satiation, exhaustion, sexual desire, or pain.

Leaving in Mind or Body

Childhood presentation. During sexual abuse many children will "leave their bodies" while they mentally float somewhere above and away from it all. This is a unique form of dissociation that enables the small child to withstand extraordinary pain or humiliation.

Adult presentation. In adulthood, the survivor is able to "go away," "space out," "go on automatic pilot," or "drift into the ozone." The outer shell of the person remains, but mentally she is not present.

Splitting/Compartmentalization

Childhood presentation. An abused child often develops two or more selves. There is the good child who works hard every day to do well, and there is the bad child who "deserves" to be punished. This is the child's explanation for the pain and humiliation suffered. The different parts of the child perform different tasks. The good part cleans the house, the naughty part experiences the sexual abuse; the frightened part hides in the closet, and the grown-up part takes care of her siblings. (This is not a description of Multiple Personality Disorder.)

Adult presentation. The adult survivor maintains these different personae in a slightly more sophisticated version. Often the adult is very successful and accomplished in her outer life but is certain that it will all fall apart as soon as the world finds out the "truth"—that her real self is horrible and disgusting. It will take only the tiniest mistake for people to discover that she really deserves to be at the bottom of the heap. She is cut off from any awareness that she is competent, worthwhile, or valued. Her true self is bad while her achievements are the false self.

Rigid and Obsessional Thinking

Childhood presentation. Because sexual abuse makes no sense, a child will create her own explanations for why and when the abuse will occur. It is the child's attempt to create order out of chaos—her own logic for cause and effect. What develops is a primitive and restrictive code to live by that the child hopes will bring protection and control. For instance, the child may become aware that the abuse happens in the evenings when it is dark. She concludes then that if she leaves several lights on in her room she will be free from harm. Even though her hypothesis is not supported in reality, she will persist in these magical, ritualistic thoughts and behaviors.

Adult presentation. Highly developed, detailed, and rigid causal thoughts are characteristic in adult incest survivors. "*If* I always get out of bed on the left side and *if* I always drive exactly at the posted speed limit and *if* my clothes are pressed just perfectly . . . *then* nothing bad will happen." When something occurs to upset this unique set of rules, the adult becomes very upset, angry, or confused. If another person challenges the survivor's thinking, she is apt to defend herself angrily to the point of rejecting the other person.

Denial

Childhood presentation. A dreamlike quality sometimes develops in an abused child. She will wonder if she only imagined these bizarre and painful episodes. Denial of the incest helps her to distance from the devastating reality.

Adult presentation. Denial in adulthood can be so profound that all memories of the incest or other childhood events can be repressed for many years. As vague recollections begin to surface, the adult survivor will think, "I must have dreamed all of this. . . . I'm sure it didn't really happen. . . . I'm probably just going crazy." Denial continues to allow the adult to distance from the painful reality and leaves her feeling confused about what really happened.

Overly Responsible Behavior

Childhood presentation. The abused child perceives that she is the one who is responsible for causing the event that led to the abuse. It stands to reason, then, that she can prevent the abuse by being a better child. This usually comes in the form of taking on adult responsibilities, such as household maintenance, cooking, and taking care of the other children. She thinks, "If I do a really good job of cleaning this floor then everyone will be free from harm." Even though this strategy does not work most of the time, she will persist in her frenzied adult habits. This behavior is usually reinforced by her parents.

Adult presentation. Many incest survivors as adults feel perpetually responsible for the bodies and souls of those around them. They can fill all twenty-four hours every day with cleaning, cooking, shopping, caring, working, and volunteering in a desperate hope to keep everything in order so that nothing disastrous will befall anyone. If something bad happens in someone's life, these survivors often worry about what they forgot to do to have avoided such an awful moment.

Overly Nurturant Behavior

Childhood presentation. There is a huge deficit of nurturing in the life of an abused child, yet somewhere she develops the awareness that all creatures require love, affection, and tenderness. The molested child often experiences deep compassion for younger siblings, neighborhood children, animals, or the "less fortunate." She demonstrates high levels of nurturant behavior with others, secretly hoping that someone will do the same for her.

Adult presentation. Countless incest survivors go on to choose such professions as teaching, nursing, and mental health as avenues for their abiding urge to offer nurturance. What qualifies the behavior as *overly* caring is the contrast to how little nurturing this adult has come to expect for herself. Even if she still harbors a secret desire to be taken care of, she is often extremely resistant to allowing others to do so.

Total Self-reliance

Childhood presentation. Because her trust in important adults has been betrayed, the sexually abused child will become completely self-reliant. She stops asking for help with school work or chores. She stops asking questions to clarify her confusion. She tries to figure everything out for herself because she cannot trust an adult response. Surprisingly, she will often develop a fairly high level of competence around tasks that are far beyond her developmental capabilities.

Adult presentation. This independent perseverance is a dominant trait in an adult incest survivor. She has learned that she *can* accomplish most tasks all on her own and is often frustrated in team or group situations. She has a great deal of difficulty trusting others and is frightened of more intimate exchanges. She likes to do things her way and is not comfortable negotiating for shared control.

Self-Nurturance

Childhood presentation. Abused children are exceedingly clever at discovering methods to soothe themselves from their constant fears. Hiding in closets, rocking themselves, finding solace in the outdoors, developing rich fantasy lives, reading incessantly, and eating too much are common behaviors in children who are coping with incest.

Adult presentation. Some of these childhood behaviors continue into adulthood. There are often two or three habits that still bring comfort to the adult survivor. Feeling safe only outdoors, hanging on to a special stuffed animal, superhero fantasies, or "going off into my own little world" are just a few.

Hypervigilance

Childhood presentation. An abused child is constantly on the alert trying to protect herself from further assaults. She attends to the tiniest of details in her environment: sounds, smells, tones of voice, rearrangement of objects, subtle nuances, and any other changes. She believes that if she notices every possible factor, she can then figure out ways to avoid the abuse.

Adult presentation. Most adults will outgrow their hyperawareness of subtle changes. Incest survivors do not. They continue to notice the slightest body language in the people around them: the tip of a head, a glint in an eye, a more nasal tone of voice, a sideways glance. They will often give great meaning to these movements and can become defensive when their interpretations are rejected. This attentiveness prevents the survivor from trusting others.

Self-Abuse

Childhood presentation. Although self-abuse is clearly maladaptive, it is important to understand its function in the life of an abused child. This child is used to feeling physical pain. She has also become adept at "going away" when there is such pain. When the emotional confusion and humiliation become overwhelming for this child, she will often resort to hurting herself to deal with the more manageable of the two pains. She understands physical pain better than emotional pain and can make herself disappear in the process. Such a child is likely to cut or hit herself, bang her head against something hard, scald herself with hot water, or create pain in her genitals. There are times when the child will hurt herself before her abuser has the chance to so that she can be tough enough in that inevitable moment. This is also a child who is used to being punished for being "bad" or molested for being "good." Either way she goes she will suffer great harm. She assumes this is her lot in life and continues the abuse herself at times to fulfill her purpose on this planet.

Adult presentation. The most common reasons for an adult to continue self-abusing behavior are (1) she still feels she deserves to be punished for just about everything and (2) she still feels overwhelmed by emotional matters and uses the physical pain to distract herself. At particularly overwhelming moments, a survivor will hurt herself to be reassured that she is alive or real. Most adult survivors are very secretive about these behaviors.

It is beneficial to the therapeutic process for the therapist to see these symptoms as part of an elaborate coping system that the child was forced to develop in order to survive. Part of what brings an adult into therapy is the desire to curtail or to end some of these ways of thinking and behaving. There is comfort for the client if the therapist can congratulate the child-client for being so clever about taking care of herself and to reassure the adult-client that, in time, she will no longer need to be so vigilant, rigid, spaced out, or destructive. The therapist must understand that these strategies are all this child has had to rely on. This is a good part of how she has organized her ego up to this point. To move too quickly to dismantle these strategies will leave the client without anything to hold on to (Sgroi and Bunk 1988). It is important for the therapist to approach these traits as strengths rather than flaws. After all, it is likely this client would not have survived the abuse in some intact fashion without the aid of these defenses.

THE THERAPEUTIC RELATIONSHIP

In the treatment of adult survivors of childhood incest, the client–therapist relationship becomes the context and metaphor for growth and healing (Calof 1987, Courtois 1988). These clients enter therapy deeply wounded from past relationships with important adults who should have been supportive, protective, and nurturing. The therapist is initially viewed by the client in that same category of potentially helpful yet highly mistrusted authority figures. In order to establish an appropriate relationship to the client that will ultimately lead to recovery from the childhood traumas, the therapist must infuse the treatment with a clear sense of boundaries, a reparenting dynamic, and an opportunity for empowering the client. Without these three elements treatment cannot be successful.

Boundaries within a relationship refers to a clear distinction between two individuals, defining where one person ends and another begins (Bowen 1978). Two separate individuals exist who interact, but do not overlap and become entwined in each other's concerns. They are influenced by each other's presence but do not invade each other's psychological or physical space. Within a well-boundaried relationship there is clarity of role assignments. For example, a parent is the caretaker of a child who is in a dependent position. The therapeutic connection must define the roles of the therapist and of the client, and it is the responsibility of the therapist to maintain this appropriate posture throughout treatment.

Psychotherapy recreates some elements of the parent–child relationship. A client seeks an authority figure who will offer insight and encouragement to foster growth through some developmental phase. In the treatment of incest recovery the therapist must be especially astute about the *reparenting dynamics* (Kirschner and Kirschner 1986). The therapist has the potential to offer the client a reparative parenting experience or to recreate an abusive situation. These parent–child dynamics must be viewed simultaneously through the eyes of the client and the therapist so that the therapist can make informed interventions that allow the client to experience a safe and appropriate relationship to a significant adult.

The client must be given a sense of self-determination and control within the therapeutic relationship in order to feel *empowered* (Bass and Davis 1988). The client must feel effective, heard, and respected. This means that her opinions and feelings can influence the course of treatment or modify the therapist's outlook.

These three factors play an essential role in the establishment of an appropriate and pivotal relationship for the client. The childhood damage occurred within the context of an important relationship and the therapeutic bond must repair this. As the therapist brings these elements into the relationship, the client will have the best opportunity to recover. What is recovery for these clients? Healing occurs when the client has achieved a reasonable level of resolution around the abusive events, has unraveled the resultant distortions of self and reality and replaced them with healthier views, has learned new skills that were not taught in childhood, has the ability to establish and maintain positive relationships, and has an experience of herself as efficacious in her world.

Defining the Therapeutic Relationship to the Client

From the first contact, the therapist is demonstrating and defining the terms of the therapeutic relationship with the client. Certain assumptions that may be implicit with other clients must be verbalized with incest survivors. It is important for the therapist to describe what it means to enter a therapeutic agreement because the client will enter with many preconceived notions (or even past negative experiences) that will form the basis for her own behavior. The therapist should offer something to this effect: "Therapy is a unique arrangement. It is a one-sided relationship where I will get to know you very well and you won't get to know much about me at all. I know this is unusual and not like anything else you've probably experienced. But our task here is for me to listen to you and help you untangle the pain you are experiencing. You won't have to take care of me. It's my job to take care of you. We will work together to help you heal."

This clarifies immediately for the client who will play what role and that her needs will be the focus of the interactions. She will react internally with very mixed feelings. There will be relief that she will not need to be a caretaker coupled with her fear or anger about being displaced from what she does so well. She will feel intrigued yet cautious about this one-sided arrangement. Her heart will leap at hearing the words "it's my job to take care of you," and simultaneously squelch that thrill. She will like the notion of joining forces to help her but will be very puzzled about how that would feel. This will all be whirling around inside, yet her overt response to the therapist will either be to accept what has been laid out or to challenge the guidelines. The therapist must address each question in a straightforward and honest manner. In so doing the therapist is reflecting that the client is being taken seriously and that the relationship will be conducted above board.

It is imperative for the therapist to continue defining the relationship by saying: "A client–therapist relationship is *not* a friendship and it is *not* reciprocal. What each of us brings into the relationship will be different and what each of us does will be different. Our relationship will *never* be a sexual one. You must know that I offer a 100 percent guarantee that I will never enter into any sexual interaction with you. In the course of therapy you may experience sexual feelings toward me. You need to know that is not unusual nor will it end the therapy. We can talk about it and you have my assurance that talking about it will not lead to any sexual behavior on my part."

These clients have experienced sexual activities occurring in the context of powerful relationships; they often assume it will occur. If the client enters therapy concerned that this relationship will evolve like many others, she will help recreate the dynamics that led previously to her victimization. To begin treatment with emphatic statements about what will and will not occur helps the client to know what the parameters are and optimizes the possibility that she will risk new behaviors.

It is also important to emphasize the importance of the therapeutic relationship and how it can provide a unique opportunity to experience a secure, consistent, nurturing, and safe adult. The therapist can reassure the client that she will not be exploited and that she will be an equal participant in the process. An acknowledgment needs to be made of the great difficulty it will be for the client to trust the therapist. This aspect is a key element within the therapeutic process and it will certainly take time to develop. It can make a huge impact on the client to know that the therapist anticipates being tested and does not demand her confidence right away. The client will have the luxury of time and scrutiny before she decides whether or not the therapist can be trusted.

If a client does not seem relieved and receptive to the boundaries established by the therapist and attempts to defy or forcibly modify the definition, there is a good possibility of presenting pathology. The most common diagnosis for this type of symptomatology is borderline personality disorder. If the therapist assesses the client to exhibit borderline traits this form of treatment will not be effective. An approach set forth by Masterson (1976, 1981) will be more successful for those clients. If, however, the client heaves a sigh of relief after these explanations about the therapeutic relationship, then treatment has already begun.

Treating All Five Senses

Psychotherapy with adults focuses a great deal on verbal communication with some attention to nonverbal clues. Incest survivors have coped with trauma or new experiences by using all five of their senses. They are highly sensitive to the subtlest of details: a tone of voice, a scent, a color, a facial expression. Verbalizations within their families were often confusing, so they learned to rely on many other perceptions to form a sense of reality. Their conclusions may not always have been accurate, but they have become convinced of the need to survey the entire environment. They will enter the therapist's office with all their senses sharpened and ready to calculate. This will influence their decision to work with a particular therapist and provide a sense of being able to trust the therapist they selected.

The therapist must be aware in the early stages of treatment that she or he is under a microscope. The client is determining if there is enough evidence to feel safe with this new adult. The therapist's furniture, pictures on the walls, clothing style, sound of voice, gesturing, language selection, cologne, facial expressions, music in the waiting room, nervous habits, hair style, and age will be closely examined. Although there is a range of positive responses to therapists' style, most incest survivors will find a more relaxed person more approachable. This means that a therapist who generally wears a suit will feel too threatening and distant compared with a therapist who wears slacks or skirts and sweaters. A clear and soothing tone of voice will be better received than a mumbled and gruff tone. An office that is not too sterile, calming waiting room music, soft lighting, and comfortable furnishings will put the client at ease. The client will be looking for signs of warmth, comfort, safety, and humanity in the therapist and surroundings. This does not mean that every therapist needs to adjust personal taste to suit these clients. It means that the client may inquire or comment on any of these items.

Therapeutic Style

This treatment occurs within a family systems approach. By definition, a transference–countertransference relationship will be minimized in preference to a more dynamic and interactive style. The therapist has the latitude to enter the relationship as a more multidimensional human being rather than as a "blank screen." In fact, the human qualities of the therapist often determine the development of positive rapport between the incest client and the therapist. The client will not experience a distant and analytic therapist as a potentially safe person. Instead, the client will perceive this therapist as potentially dangerous, which will necessitate the reinforcement of all her defense mechanisms. At best, she will experience a more traditional therapist as a constant object in her life. At worst, she will become more entrenched in protective coping mechanisms.

Because of the cleverness of the client's defenses, the therapist must adopt a therapeutic style that is open, approachable, and human while maintaining consistent boundaries. It needs to resemble an ordinary relationship while maintaining its own unique features. In the course of normal human interactions an appropriate response to a question such as "Are you tired today?" would be "Yes, as a matter of fact, I am." It would be highly unusual to respond by saying "What makes you think I am tired? Could it be that you are feeling drowsy yourself?" The more inclined toward interpretation or deflection a therapist is, the greater possibility exists to recreate crazy-making dilemmas within the client. This is a place for the client to learn about relationships in general. If there is a fair amount of distance and very little interaction, the client's learning will be skewed and not empowering. The more *human* a therapist can be with the client, the greater the opportunities are for the client to understand ordinary reality (Courtois 1988).

The Parenting Function of the Therapist

Although an adult walks through the therapist's front door, a small, damaged, and lost child enters the room with her. The client presents a blend of high functioning adult traits mixed with many coping mechanisms and the periodic emergence of a small child. At some moments the therapist is treating that grown person and at other moments she or he is dealing with a small child. This has implications for the therapist who will function to reparent the wounded child and who will need to synthesize treatment modalities for children and adults.

A developmental background will inform the clinician of the tasks of childhood and the role of constant adults in human growth (Bowlby 1988, Erikson 1950, Piaget 1955). These clients did not have "good-enough" parents who could provide the secure basis for healthy development. There are many moments in the course of therapy where basic issues of trust and dependency, for instance, are awesome and frightening for the client. Treating it from the viewpoint that the client never received adequate bonding in childhood to achieve these developmental goals frees the therapist to step into the parental position. In short, the therapist will "raise" this child into a healthy and independent individual.

Because of the mixture of childlike and adult traits within the client's presentation, the therapist will need to draw on techniques that span both treatment groups. While adult psychotherapy is most primarily a verbal interchange, therapy with children is creative, flexible, and incorporates play. Both styles of treatment are useful and important in incest recovery. The therapist will need to be proficient in both schools in order to move freely between the two.

The issue of separation anxiety provides an excellent illustration of these points. When a therapist announces to an adult client that he or she is taking a two-week vacation, there is anticipation that this will create a degree of anxiety for the client. The announcement is made far enough in advance to give the client an opportunity to express any concerns or irrational fears she may be having. An adult client would say, "I know this is all in my head but I worry about you never coming back. What will I do if I need you while you are away?" The therapist will respond reassuringly to each concern, drawing out earlier themes of abandonment within the client, giving the date of return and leaving the name of another therapist who will be on call. This will usually quell the client's anxieties. If a child in treatment is told of the therapist's vacation, she will exhibit a fairly high level of anxiety or mask it in a severe withdrawal. The psychotherapist will deal with this by helping the child to express her feelings in many creative ways (using dolls, drawing, play, and so forth), and give a calendar to the child to mark off the days while the therapist is gone or offer the child a transitional object to keep until the therapist's return. The therapist might allow the child to select a toy from the office that she can take home and bring back at the first appointment after the break.

When a therapist announces an upcoming vacation to an incest survivor, the client will usually exhibit a combination of adult and childlike responses. She might say, "I know you will be coming back and that nothing bad will happen to you but I'm so anxious! I feel like I'll never see you again. I worry about what will happen to me if I need you, and I worry something bad will happen to you." Her anxiety will escalate and the name of the therapist who will be on call will be of no comfort. She may appear inconsolable. Blending methodologies from adult and child therapy is a useful way to respond. Some degree of talking and reassurance will be taken in by the adult, while offering a transitional object will calm the child. Appropriate items to lend to the client are an object from the waiting room or office, a handwritten note with reassurance of the therapist's return, a picture of the therapist, a calendar page, or a stuffed animal (used with young clients). Although it is usually frowned upon within the mental health field to give things to clients, it is sometimes very curative for incest clients to receive something tangible from the parent/therapist. Insofar as the therapist is treating an adult and a child simultaneously, some creative interventions will be appropriate and important.

Recurring Themes in the Development of the Therapeutic Relationship

Trust building will be an ongoing issue during incest recovery. For the incest survivor, trust is a foreign concept (Courtois 1988, Sgroi and Bunk 1988). If she ever had an experience earlier in her life of trusting a significant adult, it is long forgotten. Because of the severity of betrayal created by incest, these women have learned to trust only themselves. Trust is not something that lends itself to dictionary or clinical description; it is something that must be experienced. It will take a long time in this treatment for the client to have a small understanding of the meaning of trusting the therapist. Constancy and consistency will be the first steps toward this goal. As it is in infancy, trust begins with the repeated appearance and predictable behaviors of the caretaker (Erikson 1950, Fraiberg 1959). Week after week, the therapist is there and offers a standard greeting. The surroundings become familiar and the client begins to relax.

"Even though you say you care and that you will be here to help me, I don't believe you. Why should I?" Challenges to the therapist about her or his credibility, trustworthiness, and motives are constant. The therapist must exhibit a great deal of patience and compassion. These clients have made it into adulthood without feeling safe in the world around them. They made it by their own wits and self-reliance. Letting anyone into their private world will be very threatening, and it is the therapist's role to respect this and to be steadfast in the midst of this testing. There are myriad subtle clues the client uses such as gestures, verbal expressions, changes in the surroundings, and tone of voice of the therapist. The more consistent, real, open, comfortable and well boundaried the therapist can be, the more easily trust will progress.

A unique form of testing exhibited by incest clients is the manner in which they tell their story. It is not uncommon for a client to reveal a great many gruesome details about the incestuous experiences. Her affect will often be flat with a touch of defiance. It may be punctuated with "I bet you've heard worse than this" or "Do you think you can handle this?" She is throwing down the gauntlet trying to discover if the therapist is (1) repulsed, (2) overwhelmed, or (3) unbelieving. She does not expect the therapist to respond by saying, "How awful that this has happened to you! You must have been a very brave and resourceful little girl to have survived all that. I'm glad that you found your way to me for I would welcome the chance to help you heal from this." Although the client has heard the unexpected-yet-longed-for response, she cannot allow herself to trust this. She will reservedly agree to give it a try. There is a big difference between being offered a great deal of information from an incest client and establishing a trusting rapport.

The arbitrary nature of cause and effect within her family contributes to the degree of mistrust within the client. If Dad came home from work at 7:00 every night, and some Wednesday nights and some Friday nights he visited his daughter's room when the house was silent, the child begins to conclude that Wednesday and Friday are dangerous days. But then Dad visits her room on Monday and not on Wednesday. The child is confused and looks for a pattern for anticipating her horror—only there isn't one. Her next thought is an egocentric one—"I am doing something to bring this on." She becomes hypervigilant about her own behavior and checks that against her father's reactions. For instance, she may notice that if the TV is on when he arrives home from work on the nights the abuse occurs, she will rush to turn off the set before his arrival. If the abuse still occurs, she will lie awake during the night retracing her every move to determine what little behavior triggered her father's actions.

There is an element of this dynamic of searching for patterns in the therapy. The client notices a particular facial expression on the therapist when she reveals certain information. If she has a negative interpretation of that expression she will modify her own behavior to see if that affects the therapist's face. Often this deduction will occur out loud. "Whenever I talk about my father you have this bored look on your face. I'm obviously not very interesting to you." It is important to draw out the client's behavioral observations as well as her interpretation.

Therapist: What did you see on my face?

Marge: You yawned after I said ... about my father. And you look really uninterested in general. Like tired or something.

Therapist: I guess I did yawn. I wasn't aware that I look so tired. It seems my yawn and expression are bothering you.

Marge: Well, yeah. I don't feel like you're interested in what I have to say.

Therapist: I'm terribly sorry that you feel that way. I guess I am a bit sleepy today, but I have been very immersed in what you are saying. I am taking it all in. Maybe the expression you see on my face is one of pondering. Do you think maybe that's what I look like? Like I am thinking really hard?

Marge: Yeah. I guess so. Maybe.

This type of interchange will occur frequently and it is important to *validate* the client's perceptions while offering a *new interpretation*. An open and honest response from the therapist provides building blocks for trust within the relationship. The client is not harangued for asking simple questions nor is she deemed crazy for having her perceptions. This will present her with such a new experience of human relationships that she will begin to understand what it feels like to trust.

Closely related to trust is the issue of *privacy* and *confidentiality*. Although confidentiality can be taken for granted by most adult clients seeking therapy, incest survivors need to hear the words. The therapist must explain what the guidelines are around confidentiality and privacy. This includes whether or not the therapist will be speaking to partners or family members about the client. A very private one-to-one relationship is very important to establish. This implies that couples or family treatment is contraindicated early in therapy. As healing progresses and the client is able to invite other relevant people into the treatment, new agreements can be made (see Chapter 6, Intimate Relationships). Initially, however, it is wisest to work only individually with these clients. They may never have experienced an exclusive relationship where nobody else had access to their privacy. For example, if the notion of couples treatment surfaces in the assessment phases, an incest client will often readily agree to whatever method the therapist recommends. She will not offer her desire for privacy because she is used to intrusion. It is imperative to offer only individual treatment at the outset. This invitation for an exclusive relationship with the therapist will be a great relief.

Note taking is standard practice for therapists. It is important to understand the meaning it will have for the incest client. If the therapist chooses to take notes during the session, the client will continue to feel mistrustful and to see the therapist as constantly distracted. Whereas this discomfort would be therapeutic to work through with other clients, an incest survivor will not get past this obstacle. If the client inquires about notes being made after the session, the therapist needs to reply honestly about this practice. If notes are jotted down and kept for reference, the client will want to know what is in them and who will see them. If it is explained that they are simply for the therapist's benefit and no one will see them the client may relax, although the issue may resurface many times. There may come a time either during or after treatment that the client might request the therapist's case notes. Legally, she is entitled to them. Psychologically, she may need them as a piece of herself she wants to retrieve. As this retrieval of lost pieces of herself is the entire theme of the therapy, it would be curative for the therapist to turn over the notes if requested.

It is important to be rigid within ordinary ethical guidelines around confidentiality with these clients. This would apply to consultations as well. If the therapist is receiving ongoing supervision, she or he must divulge this to the client right away. She must be made aware of any queries or conversations regarding her treatment. Again, this furthers the client's ability to trust the therapist.

Without exception the incest client will announce to the therapist, very early in treatment, that she does not intend to become attached to or dependent upon the therapist. The very thought of such an attachment can make her balk from entering therapy. It is useful for the therapist to describe that treatment will foster moments of dependency or temporary dependency, and that the ultimate goal is for the client to no longer need to depend on the therapist. Again, the words need to be spoken. "In order for healing to occur, you will need to experience me as a dependable, caring, and trustworthy adult. But I will only permit you to lean on me for short periods of time—like during a crisis or a particularly hard piece of work. I will always be reminding you of your ability to stand on your own two feet. It would not be helpful for you to become overly dependent on me. You will, however, come to feel attached to me. This means our relationship will become important to you and you will develop strong feelings towards me. Sometimes they will be positive feelings and other times they will be negative. This is normal in the course of therapy."

The client needs to be reassured that temporary dependency and attachment will not lead to weakness and helplessness. As a child she was dependent and attached to her parents and that led to pain and betrayal, not protection. She has learned well not to need anyone other than herself. The therapist must understand how terribly vulnerable this will make the client feel and how hard she will resist this attachment. Reinforcing the client's other important relationships to partners, friends, and family members diffuses that anxiety. It also gives the message that the client can have other important relationships, that she can move outside the therapeutic relationship. This is a very different dynamic than the abusive relationship. The child often received threats of greater pain (physical or emotional) if she ever spoke about the nature of the incestuous relationship or developed important attachments to other people.

The history of negative self-esteem and conditional positive feedback makes it impossible for the incest survivor to welcome praise from the therapist. Most incest clients will evoke a great deal of positive regard from the therapist and it would be customary to express it. However, if verbal praise is given too soon or too intensely, the client will react in anger. The context is essential here. In childhood a little girl was told by her abuser "You are so special," or "You're not like the others," or "You're so pretty/smart/stubborn," and then the abuse occurred. Compliments seem to carry price tags. Praise is often linked to abuse. A child's logic takes over: "If I am so special and this is what happens, I don't want to be special!" If the therapist praises the client for some special trait, the client will assume that abuse is soon to follow. Even if she is convinced the therapist will do no harm, she will reject the compliment because it does not match her self-image, and she will conclude the therapist is not very perceptive at seeing her true nature. This is very complicated because while all of this is occurring on the surface, the client is also hoping for the therapist's acceptance. It is also important in the treatment that, in fact, the therapist offer positive feedback to the client. A less loaded way to express a compliment to an incest survivor is: "I know that must have been very scary for you to have shared that with me. I want you to know that I appreciate the courage it took, because this information will help me to know you better. That way I can be more helpful in this process with you." The message combines the client's and the therapist's points of view—the client's internal experience of fear and the therapist's experience of awe over this person's unusual strength. It is more likely to be well-received by the client.

One way the therapist can offer protection to the client is by pacing the treatment. Most incest clients will burst through the therapist's front door full steam ahead to "get over this stuff already." They envision the work will go faster if they reveal more. It does not take long for the client to become overwhelmed at her breakneck speed. The therapist needs to hold the reins and slow the process down early in the treatment. This work is actually very slow and plodding, with many intense spurts. The client will not be able to remain functional if she tries to race ahead. If the therapist maintains close watch on the pacing of the therapy, the client will experience this as protective of her well-being. This is not necessarily what she received from her parents and she will come to appreciate the therapist's effort.

It is interesting to note how the client attempts to control the pacing of the treatment. It is common for the client to pull away after revealing particularly painful memories, which she may do in a number of ways. She might call to cancel next week's appointment, or she might be unusually chatty the following session, or she may become hostile, or she might avoid direct eye contact. This is her way of protecting herself while she observes how this new information will affect the relationship. Will the therapist reject her or overwhelm her? Was she believed? Will the therapist *now* pronounce her crazy? Was the therapist disgusted by these details? The client is struggling with her own shame and embarrassment and pulls inward, regretting that she revealed so much. The therapist needs to remain steady during these moments, trusting that the client will reemerge fairly soon. This is healthy self-regulation on the client's part and need not be interpreted beyond that.

Potential to Re-create an Abusive Dynamic

Many traditional therapeutic models have the hidden potential to re-create an abusive relationship for the incest client. What are the elements to a more orthodox therapeutic approach? The therapist is positioned to become the projections of the client so that transference can occur. With these projections, the client will react to this neutral adult and reveal longstanding anxieties and will, in time, move through past unresolved feelings. This is accomplished by the therapist remaining distant and offering periodic observations to the client. The therapist becomes omnipotent and powerful in the client's view (Freud 1940). This is certainly a sound and worthwhile treatment approach for other clients but will set in motion all too familiar dynamics for the incest client. If the client is in therapy truly to recover from the incest trauma she must have a more empowering relationship with a therapist. An incest client will become immobilized in her defensive functioning within the confines of more traditional treatment models. A simple example can illustrate this.

After revealing a particularly upsetting memory, the client awaits the therapist's response. It may be absolutely appropriate for the therapist to sit quietly. In the silence the client's mounting anxiety may be apparent and the therapist may allow it to linger. Many clients will yelp at the therapist, "Why don't you say something?" Then the therapist will reply, "Why does the silence upset you so?" With an incest client therapeutic silences are quite a different experience. For most of these women, silence means disapproval, rejection, and hostility. The silence means that she has not been believed. This is terribly debilitating for the client; she is rendered helpless and the therapist becomes all-powerful. That analytic dynamic is counterproductive for this treatment. After a client reveals painful details, the therapist needs to respond rather quickly. A simple "How awful that you had to experience that" will do. She requires the therapist's validation in order to know that she is not crazy. Ordinary therapeutic silence will increase the feeling of insanity that accompanies incest; these feelings are not the same as normal therapeutic anxiety.

For these reasons it is imperative for the therapist to understand the meaning the client assigns to some very ordinary behavior. With completely benign intentions, the therapist can often set off "land mines" within the client. While making an observation, the therapist may point a finger at the client only to watch a sudden wave of panic wash over the client as she prepares to bolt from the office. Asking what just happened can reveal that the client's abuser always pointed his finger at her and that it was a precursor to the abuse—an ordinary behavior that creates an extraordinary response. Responding to a client's negative self-harangue, a therapist might offer, "but you are a very special person," only to have the client scream, "*Never* call me special again!" Ensuing discussion uncovers the loaded meaning of being referred to as *special*.

Does this mean the therapist must constantly monitor or modify her or his behavior in response to these "land mines"? Yes and no. It is empowering for the client to witness the therapist avoiding certain behaviors or comments temporarily in order to make the client more comfortable in treatment. She will feel respected and heard and realize that her feelings count no matter how irrational they may seem. An excessive response from the therapist will undoubtedly backfire. It would be like giving a small child too much control over the environment. Some amount of control contributes to feelings of competence, efficacy, and autonomy. Too much control leads to anxiety, mistrust of the adults, and boundary confusion. A balance needs to be struck in which the therapist allows the client to determine some modifications in the therapist's behavior without feeling too much in charge of the situation. In time, as the client develops trust towards the therapist, some of the same loaded behaviors will take on new meanings, and thus healing occurs.

When conducting this treatment the therapist must simultaneously view things from three different perspectives: the therapist, the adult-client, and the child-client. In essence the therapist is maintaining two separate relationships with the client that must be interwoven and synthesized. The following case example highlights these different points of view by uncovering the thoughts of each person.

Trisha: I don't know if I should be telling you this, but I had a strange experience the other day.
(The child *and* adult-client are testing the waters.)

Therapist: If you'd like to tell me about it, I'm willing to listen.
(The therapist wants to invite without pushing.)

Trisha: Well, I was walking down the street and this woman passed by who had on the same perfume that you wear and it startled me. I felt kind of shook up at first and then I felt suddenly calm. I think it's really weird for me to feel like that, but it was like you were there all of a sudden in the middle of my regular day.
(The child is worried that she will be rejected by the therapist for having revealed this. She doesn't know if the feeling or the expression of the feeling is appropriate. The adult feels embarrassed by the whole experience and thinks it is inappropriate to have reactions to the way the therapist smells. The therapist is a bit taken aback as she was unaware that her perfume was that noticeable across the therapy room. She never imagined her scent to have a calming effect on anyone and considers the primitive nature of this revelation.)

Therapist: Why do you think your feelings are strange?

Trisha: I just don't think I'm supposed to have such strong associations.
(The adult wants to know if this is appropriate or crazy.)

Therapist: Ours is a very important relationship. I would expect you to be especially observant and to have strong feelings. I must say I was unaware that my perfume is so pungent.
(The therapist is letting the child and adult-client know that she is not crazy. At the same time the therapist is showing a genuine response.)

Trisha: It's not that you wear too much or anything; it's just that the office sort of smells like your perfume. Actually I've noticed other women with the same perfume and I've had the same kind of reaction—sort of calming.

Therapist: Well, then it seems this is a positive experience for you. I guess the smell of my perfume is rather comforting for you.
(The therapist is beginning to understand that her scent is helping the client to feel comfortable and familiar with the therapist. The client doesn't seem to be raising this in a way that blurs any boundaries. In

> fact, the primitive nature of this association leads the therapist to
> understand that the child is responding to the perfume. If this is
> creating a sense of comfort or trust within the client, all the better.
> The adult-client is a bit surprised that the therapist isn't making a
> bigger deal out of this or interpreting her behavior. This is a relief.
> Maybe it wasn't so weird after all. The child-client is delighted that this
> response is acceptable and wonders where she can get this perfume
> so that she can recreate that feeling of safety and calm.)
>
> Trisha: By the way, what is the name of that perfume anyway? I'm just
>   curious. . . .

The therapeutic relationship in incest recovery is the most critical element of
the treatment (Calof 1987, Gil 1988). A well-defined, deliberate, and multiper-
spective connection must be maintained by the therapist. There are subtle nuances at every turn of the corner and these take a great deal of insight and
patience on the part of the therapist. Understanding that the therapy is treating
the damaged child as well as the vulnerable adult adds to the intervention options.
Blending adult and child psychotherapy methodologies is a challenge to the
therapist; yet it will optimize the potential for growth and healing in the client.

THE TREATMENT CONTRACT

When a client and a therapist agree to begin treatment together, there is usually
a short conversation about fees, appointment scheduling, cancellations, and
expected duration of the therapy. This is a fairly inconsequential conversation
dealing primarily with business matters. For incest treatment, initial contracting
between the client and therapist must be an extensive, explicit process that
becomes the first therapeutic intervention. These first sessions lay the groundwork for the unfolding of the therapeutic relationship and process. Establishing
a clearly articulated verbal (and/or written) agreement defines the treatment
parameters, the expectations for the client's and the therapist's behavior, and
offers control to the client. The following eight items should be discussed within
the first two or three sessions with a new client who is seeking help recovering
from childhood incest.

Anticipating the Consequences of the Therapy

The therapist needs to help the client anticipate the results of being in treatment
both in terms of present-day functioning and uncovering of the past. The client
needs to have a realistic picture of the process so that she can make an informed
decision about proceeding. She should be told how emotionally intense the work
will be, how painful the remembering and telling will be, how anxious she will

sometimes become, how intrusive into her everyday life the therapy can become, and how difficult it sometimes is to contain all of this. She also needs to anticipate that she will probably experience some dramatic changes in how she currently functions in her world. Of course, all this hard work is to allow her to arrive at a healthy and whole new place with herself, her past, her present, and her future. Additionally, the therapist should offer a general idea of the phases and course of this treatment—the ebbs and flows, the highs and lows, the breadth and depth. A rough estimate about how long it will take for the client to complete therapy needs to be suggested. The therapist should provide as much information as the client needs to anticipate this major undertaking. Not only does this help the client arrive at an informed consent for treatment, but if she is educated about the process it also short-circuits some of her anxieties.

Appointments and Fees

Together the therapist and the client must make agreements about the number of appointments per week, fees, cancellation procedures, and the time limit of each session. This needs to be explicit with incest clients, as it helps to define the structure and establish a sense of safety.

Phone Calls

Each therapist must be very clear about how willing he or she is to be reached by phone between appointments and after hours. It is crucial not to be vague about this point, because incest clients *will* sometime need to call between appointments and, if guidelines are not made clear, there can be serious disruptions in the therapeutic relationship. Assuming that the therapist has already clarified this for herself or himself, preferences about *how, when, where,* and *how often* the therapist can be reached by phone should be spelled out.

Confidentiality

Incest survivors will not make any assumptions about client–therapist confidentiality. They will have many questions about who will know she's in treatment, who the therapist will be speaking with about her, and whether any written records will be kept. They will have these questions but not necessarily ask them. It is a huge relief for the client if the therapist makes all issues around confidentiality explicit and open for discussion. The therapist might say, "I want to reassure you that I consider what happens in this office to be strictly confidential. If your husband calls me to inquire about your progress, I will need to ask your permission before I speak with him. If you don't want me to talk with him, then I won't. Unless you tell me otherwise, I will not be revealing any information about you to anyone." The client may have some additional concerns and these can be considered at this time.

Emergency Plans

The client needs to understand the therapist's methods for dealing with extreme circumstances or emergencies such as suicidal feelings or attempts, anxiety or panic attacks, or other life crises. This is described to protect both the client and the therapist. The client is reassured that the therapist will move into action if the need ever arises, and the therapist makes it clear that she or he will not necessarily act alone in cases of emergency (Gelinas 1988).

Unavailable Times

Periods in an ordinary week's schedule (such as staff meetings or evenings) when the therapist is unavailable, should be specified at the beginning of treatment.

Relationship Definition

To establish clear boundaries from the beginning, the therapist needs to initiate a conversation about the definition of the client–therapist relationship in order to explain that this is neither a reciprocal relationship, nor a friendship, nor a potential sexual liaison. It is important to be honest about the unusual nature of the therapeutic relationship while stressing that the therapist is there to help the client and not vice versa. All of the client's questions on this subject should be entertained at this time (for further discussion, see the Therapeutic Relationship section earlier in this chapter).

Termination

All clients worry about becoming attached to the therapy and the possibility that the "almighty therapist" will make a unilateral decision about when the client is finished with therapy or, worse yet, kick the client out of therapy. With incest survivors the therapist needs to describe how the decision to leave will be in the client's hands and that when the time to terminate seems evident, there will be a mutual feeling and input about it. Furthermore, the client must be reassured that once the therapist agrees to begin treatment there is a mutual commitment to staying together until the end. If the therapist is uncomfortable promising that the client will not be referred to some other therapist midstream, then the promise should not be made.

By setting forth these guidelines the therapist begins to shape the therapeutic relationship and begins the task of trust building. The clearer the expectations, the more predictable the situation feels for the client. This contract conveys the message to the client that the therapist is being realistic, is anticipating the general flow of things, is already aware of some of the client's concerns, and is taking this commitment very seriously. Accomplishing this within the first few sessions plants the seeds for establishing a trusting rapport.

3

The Four Phases
of Incest Therapy

The journal entries included in this chapter and Chapter 4 have been written by one client, Client X, who has been willing to share her experiences here. This is her introduction.

What I Would Like to Tell Therapists about Incest

I am an incest survivor. I am a woman, 37 years old. My father began molesting me when I was 6 years old. He continued until I was 19 years old. I worked with counselors for one year in high school and for seven years in college. Since that time I have entered therapy with five different therapists for a total, thus far, of twelve years. Some of my therapy experiences have been helpful, and some have not. I welcome this opportunity to discuss many of those experiences.

> *—I can't write my name here.*
> *I have a family, a job, friends, neighbors.*
> *Incest survivors are still in the closet.*

It is useful to conceptualize long-term incest treatment in segments that address separate goals, as this identifies groupings of tasks as well as a progressive development of the therapy. Relating to the treatment goals listed in Chapter 2, there are four basic phases in this therapy: validation, development of a new world view, emotional flooding, and new hope. The *validation* phase focuses on telling and remembering the incest. The *new world view* works

41

toward new insights about the family, the impact of the abuse, and the development of positive self-esteem. The third phase occurs when there is a release of the feelings surrounding the incest and the emergence of the arrested child. And the final stage of treatment deals with the client's sense of hope, empowerment, health, and freedom and indicates the end of treatment. These are general categories and are not intended as a rigid codification of this therapy. There is no singular, linear, upward progression in incest treatment. Rather, it is multifocused, multidirectional, and fluid (Courtois 1988, Gil 1988). A client may begin therapy at the point of emotional flooding only to slide into an affectively void state similar to Phase 1 and then suddenly face issues more pertinent to later stages. Each client will have a unique treatment journey. No two therapies will look alike. In order to understand this work, however, it becomes necessary to create some linear model. This allows both the therapist and the client to anticipate the major themes, the general direction, and the expected outcome of the therapy. It is important for the therapist to convey the idea that work can begin at point A, jump to point F, hop over to W, and circle back to A, in order to ward off the client's concerns about backsliding during treatment. Incest issues are so loaded that they *must* be dealt with repeatedly until there is greater resolution. It would be a mistake to think of incest treatment as mechanically linear. The metaphor of creating a tapestry is more appropriate. The therapy will weave various fibers together, changing colors, tying off threads, while leaving others hanging, doubling back to reinforce certain sections, working furiously on some patterns while feeling unexcited by others, never being quite sure exactly what the final product will look like until it is completed. It is a dynamic process that takes shape only as the client works the loom.

PHASE I: VALIDATION

Incest is an embarrassing, humiliating, experience. The pain of remembering and reliving those incidents, and all of the accompanying circumstances is incredibly painful. When I walk into a therapist's office I am already experiencing guilt, shame, and feeling unaccepted or unacceptable. I know that it was wrong for that to have happened to me, and I still struggle with the idea that there is something wrong with me. I continue to struggle with this idea through many levels of this recovery process. Whenever I share something sensitive with my therapist I carefully monitor her facial expressions and her body language. I am watching her, because I want to see whether or not she is okay with what I'm telling her. If she shudders, cringes, squints her eyes, shakes her head, bites her lower lip, or if she makes statements such as, "Oh, how awful!" "That's terrible!" or generally reacts with shock, discomfort, or apparent disbelief, then I immediately realize that what I'm telling her is something really, really bad. In my mind I also realize that what I'm presently telling her is only a tiny fraction of the painful feelings and memories stored inside of me. Indeed, it may even have seemed like a normal, everyday part of my life at that time, and if she is displaying this negative reaction to this small amount of my experience, then the rest of the story must be intolerably bad, and I'd better not tell her any more of the very sensitive stuff. Sometimes I continue developing that thought to the point where I believe that if whatever I told her is, *that bad,* then I must also be *bad,* for having had that experience, and for having told anybody about it. In other words, if my therapist reacts negatively to my sensitive sharing, I interpret that reaction as nonacceptance of my feelings and experiences, which I translate into nonacceptance of me. In all probability, I will not be willing to reveal to her further details of my abuse. Furthermore, not only do I feel that my experiences are unacceptable, but I will avoid discussing sensitive issues with my therapist in order to rescue her from feeling further shock or discomfort.

I feel most comfortable talking to a therapist who is sitting fairly still and looking directly at me while I'm talking. It's okay for her to become involved in my story by asking me questions such as, "How did you feel?" or "Where was your mother when this was happening to you?" I appreciate it when my therapist empathizes with me by making such statements as, "I'm sorry you went through this," or "That must have been very painful for you." A therapist's calm, gentle, empathetic reaction to my sensitive issues clearly communicates to me her acceptance and validation of my experiences and feelings.

It is vitally important to me that my therapist validates my feelings. When my thoughts and feelings are validated, I am free to feel more deeply, and I can find words to express those deeper thoughts and feelings. Only then do I feel safe enough to be able to completely let go emotionally, experiencing sadness, grief, anger, and rage by crying, yelling, punching pillows, and so on.

It is only after I feel total emotional safety with my therapist that I am able to trust her with those experiences and memories that are the most painful for me. In order for this to happen, I must feel not only my therapist's acceptance and validation, but also her empathy, compassion, sensitivity, gentleness, and patience. I must feel that she is *right here* with me. Then I am able to talk to her *regardless* of my feelings of shame and humiliation. I believe that it is essential for me to feel safe talking and crying through those experiences in my memory that are the most painful and humiliating. I am convinced that it has been this most intense level of trusting and sharing with my current therapist that has been the primary reason that I am now healing from my incest experiences.

—Client X

The child suffering from incest existed within a sense of unreality. Although her pain and humiliation were very real, they were shrouded in secrecy, darkness, and intimidation. She was left to wonder whether she had just dreamed up these horrible nightmares, because there was no overt confirmation that anything had actually occurred. These sensations are still with the adult who enters treatment. She is not convinced the incest happened, but she is fairly certain something was wrong. The initial stage in treatment deals with this uncertainty. The tasks of the validation phase are remembering and telling the story, sharing the secret, suppressing affect, facing the reality of the past, learning to trust the therapist while anticipating rejection, and coping with self-blame and self-destructive thoughts and actions.

Telling and Remembering

Words are very potent for the incest survivor. Almost without exception, sexual abuse carried with it a verbal threat from the perpetrator. "No one will believe you if you tell," or "Your mother would die if she knew," or "I'll kill you if you say anything," or "This is for your own good" are common lines delivered to the small child. Because children believe what adults tell them, the incest victim unquestioningly accepted these threats. Even though she is walking into therapy as an adult, she still believes much of what she was told as a child. Simply telling someone about the incest is an enormous act of courage and moves the client into forbidden territory. The therapist must appreciate this bravery and gently coax the client to continue telling what she remembers. Saying the words is the client's first step toward freedom.

It is important that the client and the therapist use explicit language when discussing the incest. The client needs to describe exactly what happened in all its horrifying detail and the therapist needs to exhibit the ability to handle the information. If either shies away from the specifics, the telling will be incomplete and will set the stage for euphemistic language throughout the therapy. Conversation must be direct. If the client says "My father touched me down there," the therapist needs to inquire "What is down there?" The client needs to speak the words herself. If the therapist says "Do you mean your vagina?" then the client will simply nod rather than saying the unspeakable. The spell must be broken and accurate language must replace the inappropriate and veiled language of the abuse. If a client is vague, the therapist must ask specific questions.

Pam: My grandfather would, you know, be in my bed.
Therapist: What exactly do you mean?
Pam: You know, like touch me.
Therapist: Where did he touch you?
Pam: All over.
Therapist: Can you be more specific?
Pam: Is this necessary? Don't you get the picture?
Therapist: Yes, I get the picture, but it is important for you to be able to tell me exactly what happened. You don't have to do that all right now if you are not comfortable. But eventually, as you are able to, it will be very powerful for you to tell your story in as much detail as you can remember. You were threatened not to tell anyone—that something horrible would happen to you. You will need to see that nothing tragic

will occur if you speak about the abuse. In fact, quite the opposite will happen.

Pam: You mean something good will happen? I don't believe that!

Therapist: You will be released from the evil spell your grandfather cast. For now, the words only need to be spoken right here in this office. Do you think you can tell me any more right now?

Pam: Maybe just a little bit. He would touch me under my pajama tops.

Therapist: Where exactly?

Pam: On my stomach and my chest. I didn't have breasts then. I was only 5. . . .

Upon hearing the words, the therapist's first intervention is to convey to the client that she is believed. The second intervention is to offer a small dose (because the client cannot handle a large dose) of empathy, and the third intervention is to congratulate her on her courage to survive the abuse and to tell about it. In doing so the therapist provides what the client never believed could ever happen; she has been believed and been responded to in a caring way. Although this will feel remarkable to the client, she will not be able to trust it or integrate it instantly. This is understandable. For most of her life the client has felt uncertain about the reality of the abuse as well as her credibility. It is not reasonable to believe that one statement from one adult will undo all those years of doubt. Therefore it is essential that the therapist frequently reiterate her or his belief in the client until such a time as the client has accepted her reality.

Most incest survivors do not arrive into adulthood with all their memories intact. Repression, denial, dissociation, detachment, and splitting occurred at the time of the abuse causing perceptions to be buried, skewed, and protected. Over the course of treatment many of these memories will surface, but initially the client may remember only a portion of the incest. What is more important than remembering absolutely everything is telling what has remained conscious. Sharing the secrets of her past starts the process of bringing the client literally into the light of day. As more images return to the client's consciousness, those can be verbalized.

The question is often asked if it is necessary to remember all the incest details. What about vague feelings that there was incest without specific memories? Can someone mend from incest if she cannot retrieve whole segments of her past? It is important to remember the context of the initial incest to answer these questions. For many, the abuse occurred so early in life that cognitions, perceptions, and language had not yet developed. Even without trauma, this is difficult information to uncover in therapy. It is likely that clients who were victimized as infants will never fully remember the abuse. Age-regressive hypnosis may reveal some important images but the pictures will not be as complete as those of an older child. What is more crucial than focusing on specific memory work is focusing on sensing work. If a client describes "feeling a presence in my room when I was 6 years old," the therapist can inquire what the presence felt like. It could be a generic sensation of darkness and threat that evokes great fear. Whether or not it is definitely determined that incest occurred, it could be concluded that this client experienced something highly intrusive. If she continues to feel this "presence" in her adult life, it could be conjectured that some kind of abuse may have occurred if there are other presenting symptoms that resemble childhood trauma. It is likely that during the course of treatment these images will take more form and offer more concrete information. In any event, it is not necessary to push at the client's defensive structure to force the memories out into the open. As she is prepared to cope with her past, the remembrances will surface quite on their own.

Lack of Affect

A unique trait among incest survivors is the near total absence of affect as they tell their stories. It is not uncommon for a client to recount gruesome details of the incest experiences without any revelation of feelings. Emotions are a mysterious realm for the incest survivor. She learned very quickly as a child that the more pain, anger, or fear she expressed, the greater her suffering. She may even have been taunted about her outcries. The only way to survive is to stop having feelings. Don't let the abuser see that he has affected her. What occurs is a flat or false affect to cover up any true feelings. This will still be evident in the adult survivor. Therapeutically it is not useful to ask the client how she feels about the story she has just revealed. She will not be able to answer this question with any degree of satisfaction at this point in treatment. She will need to experience a great deal of trust in the therapeutic relationship before she can express and unravel her feelings. This lack of affect should be viewed as a protective form of coping that will eventually melt away over the course of the treatment.

Acceptance of Reality

As the client proceeds to share her story, denial is slipping away. As the therapist validates the client's perceptions, reality is sinking in. This is revolutionary for the client. For years she has protected herself from the terrible truth by persuading herself that she was exaggerating or fabricating her past. Peeling this away can be very frightening, so it must be done slowly. The emphasis needs to be on making the past real rather than on racing toward interpretation or resolution. One way to accomplish this is through reframing. A client is likely to describe an incident by punctuating it with "I was such a rotten kid. I probably deserved it." Ordinarily a therapist might respond by saying "What makes you think you were so rotten? It sounds like it's your abuser who was rotten." If this statement is offered early in treatment, the incest client may bolt. Her entire belief system has been built on believing that she was to blame for the abuse and that her abuser was just doing what he had to do. If she is just beginning to reveal the actual details of the abuse, breaking through the years of secrecy, and then is asked to change her perceptions about who was in the wrong, she will be overwhelmed. A gentle reframing would be more effective. "It is important to remember that you were just a small child when this occurred and your stepfather was a very large man. Yes, kids are sometimes bad, but adults are not supposed to hurt children." The therapist does not want to confirm the notion that the client was a rotten child but can't point the finger yet. By speaking broadly about all children and all adults and their respective roles, the therapist creates the distance necessary for the client to develop some new ideas.

Trusting the Therapist: Part 1

Although trust and rapport building are important in the early stages of treatment with any client, there are unique variations on this theme with incest survivors. The concept of being able to trust a powerful adult is approached with extreme trepidation, so great is the fear that another violation will occur (Calof 1987, Courtois 1988). The incest survivor has existed on the basic premise that no one other than herself can be trusted. Her survival instincts have propelled her into therapy, but it will take quite a bit of assessment to determine if this therapist is trustworthy. Rather than seeing this as resistance, the therapist must perceive this testing as necessary and essential to the healing process. An atmosphere and tone of safety and nurturance must be present at the very beginning of treatment and the therapist should anticipate being challenged, questioned, and provoked. (For further discussion of setting a trusting tone, see the section on the Therapeutic Relationship in Chapter 2.)

In order to encourage the development of trusting feelings within the client, the therapist must convey a sense of warmth, consistency, confidentiality, openness, and clear boundaries. With each session in the early stages of treatment, the client will be looking for clues about whether it is safe to proceed. She uses all her senses to case out the situation. If the therapist smiles after the client's remark, the client will wonder if this was a smirk, a laugh, a jeer, or genuine warmth. If the therapist is five minutes late beginning the session, the client will try to ascertain the reason. If there was a particular picture on the therapist's desk one week but not the following week, she will have noticed this and wondered why. In many cases, the client will offer her observations. "I felt that you were making fun of me when I made that remark." "You were late this week because you weren't looking forward to our session." "You must have had a fight with your husband. I see his picture is gone." With each comment or question, the therapist needs to validate the client's observation while offering a more accurate interpretation. "I guess I did laugh a bit. I find your sense of humor delightful." "I'm sorry about being late. Some days I just get a bit behind. We will have our full amount of time." "You're so observant. Actually, we didn't have a fight. The frame broke and I haven't had a chance to replace it yet." This accomplishes three things. For one, it lets the client know that she is accurately observing reality. She is used to hearing that she is nuts or wrong or imagining very real occurrences. Secondly, the therapist is offering a different under-standing of the real event. This dynamic is central to the entire therapy. And lastly, the client has an experience of the therapist as open to a two-way communication. The client can share her perceptions without being cut off or feeling crazy. She feels the therapist taking responsibility for her or his behavior. This is a radical concept for the client.

As was mentioned in the treatment contract, defining the therapeutic relation-ship establishes an explicit understanding of the parameters. The more distinct and consistent the boundaries are, the safer the client will feel. If this clear-cut relationship can be offered in a warm and human spirit, rather than a distant and sterile one, it will help the client develop a sense of trust.

Early in treatment the client expects to be rejected by the therapist. She is certain that her revelations will create feelings of disgust toward her. The feelings of shame and humiliation are overwhelming in the client as she tells her story. She has no reason to think the therapist will want to help her after she shares her experiences. Even if the therapist responds with steadfast caring and concern, the client will not be convinced. She is thinking, "I'm just pulling a fast one on this therapist. Wait till she sees what a horrible person I really am." Frequent and consistent validating responses over time will reassure the client that no matter what she talks about, the therapist will still be available.

Self-Destructive Tendencies

Suicidal and self-destructive ideation will surface in these early sessions with incest clients. This is a recurring theme for survivors. When the feelings begin to surface or the pain is too awful or the confusion too great, a client will return to physical pain or annihilation as a familiar refuge. It is important to discover the meaning and purpose of these thoughts and actions for the client. Does the pain make her feel real? Does the pain distract her from what she is thinking or feeling? Does she feel the need to punish herself for her "complicity" in the incest? Is she letting the therapist know just how meaningless and worthless she is? Is she crying out for help? Most survivors know a great deal about why, when, and how these self-destructive acts occur. Once the therapist understands the client's intent, he or she is in a better position to be helpful. The majority of self-destructive acts are meant to recreate the familiarity of pain (Courtois 1988, Gil 1988). They are not intended as lethal attempts to end life. It is the therapist's job to comprehend fully the client's need to continue to feel the pain.

If it is clear that the self-destructive behaviors are not for suicidal purposes, the actions should be understood as part of the client's coping structure. These are ways she can punish herself or control the onset of feelings or validate her existence. By the time she enters treatment, the client has spent years mistreating herself. The therapist should not expect to bring an immediate end to these habits. It is more reasonable to begin a weaning process. The therapist must communicate concern about these behaviors and hopefulness about the day when the client will no longer need to perpetuate the abuse. In the meantime, a series of understandings can be made. Emergency plans for more harmful actions can be described. Suggestions can be made about other behaviors that will not inflict pain but offer some release. Short-term "no danger" pacts can be made to give more time to the therapy to deal with the feelings in safe ways. Above all else, the therapist must reassure the client that she or he does not want to control the client's behavior. During this early phase of treatment the client must feel in control of herself and the process. Although the therapist will be worried about these abusive behaviors, the less control she or he tries to exert, the less likely the client will be to revert to such acts. These self-destructive moments are about control and distraction from pain. Giving the client a great deal of control and suggesting other, safe diversions from agony will lay important groundwork in the therapy as these feelings and actions will appear frequently during the course of treatment. (See section on Self-Destructive and Suicidal Behaviors in Chapter 4.)

The initial phase of treatment focuses on the client's recollections of the incest, building the foundations of the client–therapist relationship, and the emergence of self-abusive tendencies. It cannot be stressed enough that the manner in which these sessions are conducted sets the tone for the entire therapy. At the very basis is the development of the curative, reparental relationship. How the therapist hears and responds to the client's story and confronts the self-destructive behaviors is pivotal. If the client feels cared for, honestly responded to, believed, respected, and in control, she is prepared to take greater risks in the therapy. If, however, she experiences judgmental distance, panicky crisis reactions, and horror from the therapist the treatment will not be effective even if the client chooses to remain with the therapist.

PHASE II: DEVELOPING A NEW WORLD VIEW

A therapist must be a teacher. She must have the ability to break down a concept into many components at a level to which I can relate. I do not have the training or background to understand those concepts that she takes for granted. What may seem a simple connection for her may be very difficult for me to grasp. Her mere mention of an idea is not enough. I believe that it's her responsibility to get on my level and gently explain ideas, concepts, and connections as often as necessary. She should be prepared to repeat and/or rephrase her ideas as often as necessary.

—Client X

Once the client has started the process of speaking of the long-forbidden topics and sensing that she has found a sympathetic and wise confidante in the therapist, she will be filled with questions. What is a normal parent–child relationship like? How do other families function? Can there be complete recovery from the trauma of incest? What are all these feelings whirling around inside? Why did this happen? What is a healthy adult relationship like? Are there other incest survivors? The client will begin to challenge the way she has come to view herself and her world. The second phase of treatment addresses these issues within the context of the continuing development of the client–therapist relationship. The therapist performs reparental and educational functions to help fill the gaps in the client's development. Through cognitive restructuring, skill-building, and the introduction of new resources, the therapist encourages the emergence of positive self-esteem.

Insights about the Family

Most incest survivors are stuck in an egocentric view of family events. Children believe the world revolves around them and that things happen because of something they have done. An adult survivor still holds the belief that the incest occurred because she did something to deserve it. There is little insight into family dynamics or individual personalities.

Tamar was removed from her parents' home when she was 4 years old because of negligence. Until she turned 17, she was bounced from one foster home to another. The reason she was always given by the adults (foster parents and social workers) about her frequent relocations was that she was "incorrigible." Although she perceived herself to be fairly cooperative, Tamar accepted this label. There was no doubt that she was unhappy and longed to return to her mother and sometimes behaved aggressively. By the time she was 8 she was molested by a foster father. Three more placements and three more molesters later, Tamar was quite convinced that this was what "incorrigible" children deserved. During a five-year-stay with one family, Tamar was repeatedly raped by her foster father. Although she somehow survived many trials and tribulations (including intravenous drug addiction, sexual promiscuity, and losing custody of her own child), when Tamar entered therapy at the age of 28 she still maintained that she was a terrible child who had deserved every single bit of abuse she received. It was not until the therapist began to explain family dynamics, the impact of foster care, the prevalence of alcoholism in many of the families, and what kind of care all children are entitled to did Tamar start to see things differently. Never before had she entertained the notion that the adults had mistreated her because of personal and family problems. She had many questions and much to learn.

The use of genograms and a multigenerational Bowen approach is instructive for the client (Bowen 1978, Kramer 1985, McGoldrick and Gerson 1983). The diagrams make the family patterns and transmission of abuse very clear. The therapist can illustrate how the client found herself in the victim role, where the other dysfunctional relationships are, who else was abused, and where her potential allies are. The paper-and-pencil concreteness of genograms is very compelling for the incest client. It immediately offers a completely different angle on the same story. As the client is able to see the inevitability of her victimization, she begins to take herself out of the position of being responsible for the abuse. She learns about the existence of the specific family dynamics within which she was trapped. However, she is still left with a recurring nagging question: Why me?

The incest survivor begs for a rational explanation for why she, in particular, suffered such abuse. She still wonders what it is about her personality, presence, or behavior that provoked the incest. Although the therapist can repeat over and over that she was the innocent bystander to some adult's illness, the client will continue to search for a more self-centered explanation. If she can only figure out what she did to bring about these horrors, then she can prevent them from ever occurring again. It is likely the client will complete treatment without a truly satisfactory answer to this query. It is difficult to accept that incest is simply an irrational act that defies any reasonable explanation.

Somewhere in the course of these discussions, the client arrives at an understanding of the psychology of both her abuser and nonprotectors. She can identify the cycles of abusive and inappropriate parenting within her extended family system. Although this does not bring her comfort, it does offer the client a new way of viewing her history. It is important for the therapist to keep a close watch on what the client does with this information. There is a danger that she will become disempowered by feeling too much compassion for her abuser. Once she understands that her abuser was also abused and suffered from myriad other problems, she may prematurely let him off the hook. If that were to occur at this stage in treatment, she would be precariously poised for revictimization at the hands of someone else. Compassion without experiencing rage and sadness leaves her vulnerable to tolerating mistreatment (Courtois 1988). The therapist needs to focus the client on understanding her position within the family system rather than on understanding her abuser's problems.

Feelings

Attaining answers to some confusing questions clears the client's mind enough to make room for the emergence of some emotions. She will begin to notice that she has flashes of anger or moments of sadness or glimpses of fear. These are usually small doses of volatile and suppressed feelings that leave the client confused. Her early learning about emotions was convoluted and this needs to be untangled. As her father molested her, he proclaimed that he was doing this because "this is how a father truly loves his daughter." Sexual abuse, violation, intrusion, shame, humiliation, and secrecy have all come to mean love to this client (Calof 1987). The therapist will need to retrain the client by instructing her in what individual feelings appropriately look and feel like. This is straightforward cognitive work that is coupled with self-awareness. For instance, the client may describe to the therapist that she notices a queasy sensation in her stomach after her parents phone her but she doesn't understand why. Having the client give a more detailed explanation of "queasy sensation" will quite naturally reveal anxiety or fear. It is useful to teach the client to tune into these bodily sensations and then attach them to a specific emotion. This reawakens her from the long-standing numbness and helps her to trust her feelings. The emotional exploration at this point in treatment has an educational and developmental function.

Trusting the Therapist: Part 2

By this time the client is beginning to have some notion that the therapist is dependable, consistent, safe, and caring. She may accompany that awareness with a rationalization such as: "It's your job to do all that, and besides, I pay you for that service." There is continued testing of the therapeutic relationship as the client is highly reluctant to allow herself to form an attachment. For possibly the first time in her life, she is having a good experience with an adult. This is too good to be true so she pushes and prods and challenges to see if the therapist will go the way of all other important people in her life, but secretly hoping that this will not happen. She finds the therapist has become a presence in her life that is comforting, sane, and predictable. Although she wants more and more of this, she also cannot tolerate that desire. The incest survivor has learned beyond doubt that having a little bit of what she wants hurts more than having nothing at all. She'd rather be alone than have *some* positive interactions with someone. This theme surfaces intensely and ambivalently at this stage of treatment.

> After several emotionally revealing sessions, Joanne announced to her therapist that she just wasn't sure it was worth staying in treatment. The therapist inquired why she was having these thoughts.
>
> Joanne: I just get so riled up after these sessions that I can't concentrate at work or home. I don't feel like being around anybody.
> Therapist: What is so difficult? Having strong feelings? Remembering the past?

Joanne:	All of it. The feelings, the memories, and just being here.
Therapist:	Can you explain that some more?
Joanne:	Everything gets all stirred up and I can't get it all back in its place before I get home.
Therapist:	Do you need to have it all put away at home? Can't you talk to your husband about some of this?
Joanne:	It's not that I can't talk to him about it. It's just that he doesn't listen so well. Not like you do.
Therapist:	What's the difference?
Joanne:	When I'm here I don't feel like I have to censor myself. I can say whatever I need to. You just listen and don't get all bent out of shape. I don't have to worry about what you're thinking or feeling. My husband listens pretty well, but he gets so upset when I talk about the abuse. He just can't handle it.
Therapist:	Yes, it's very hard for partners to hear about the awful things that happened to their loved ones. Your husband's response is very common. That's the luxury of having a therapist, though. You don't have to deal with my reactions.
Joanne:	Yeah, but it makes me want to talk to you every time I'm thinking about this crap. No one else feels as comfortable right now.
Therapist:	So why are you doubting the value of continuing in treatment?
Joanne:	Therapy is making me need and want you too much. That's not good. I can't handle that. I took care of this stuff all on my own before, I can do it now too.
Therapist:	Yes, you were quite capable of handling all this before. But I think you began therapy because you were tired of doing it all alone.
Joanne:	Yeah, I know. But I just didn't figure this would happen.
Therapist:	Figure what would happen?
Joanne:	That I'd get hooked. That I would actually want to come here and talk to you.
Therapist:	It can be rather surprising. Clearly, you are appreciating some of the benefits of getting hooked.
Joanne:	True. But it makes life too complicated. It was easier when I just didn't need anyone . . .

The client needs to be given the room to play out this ambivalence without the therapist using strong-arm tactics. The client must feel that she is fully in control of the decision to remain in therapy or not. She must know that she is choosing therapy for her own good and not because she feels coerced. These can be very frustrating moments in the treatment but they need to be weathered. It is not coincidental that this ambivalence surfaces at this time. What is about to occur is the unleashing of an emotional flood that has been building for years. Although the client does not know this consciously, she is testing the waters to make sure she can swim. The therapist's patience during this process is very reassuring for the client.

Another interesting way incest survivors test the waters of this developing relationship with the therapist is to keep an eye on evening the score. This means that if the client feels the therapist has "been nice," then the client must be nice in return. "Being nice" on the therapist's part entails ordinary positive therapeutic responses such as returning phone calls or arranging an extra session or changing the appointment time to suit an unusual need of the client's or not reacting negatively to something the client has shared. The client then feels compelled to express her gratitude and make it clear she does not take any of the therapist's behavior for granted. Her thanks may be expressed by bringing a cup of coffee or soda for the therapist, or baking bread or sweets, offering to clean the office, adding something to the waiting room, or bringing flowers. Within reason, the therapist needs to allow this to happen without interpretations. Favors for this child often carried big price tags. Until such a time as the client feels more secure in the therapeutic relationship, she will need to keep things balanced. If the therapist cuts this off prematurely, the client will feel hurt and mistrustful; therefore, it must be permitted for a while. It is important, however, for the therapist to be certain this does not get out of hand. "It was very thoughtful of you to bring me a cup of coffee. Thank you very much. I hope you understand that it is not necessary to do this regularly."

Educating the Client

Around this time the client wants to know if she is the only human being to have suffered from incest. She is curious about books to read or groups and lectures to attend. There can be a zealous quality to her inquiries. It is not uncommon for an incest client to show up at her appointment with an armload of books for survivors. She will voraciously dive into one after another, only to find herself utterly overwhelmed. It is important for the therapist to monitor this reading because it can set back the treatment. Most of the books available for survivors these days are quite informative and encouraging, yet also intense. If a client reads too much she will begin to minimize her own experiences or prematurely have her own buried feelings provoked. This can shut down or impede the therapy. The therapist should offer to screen the books and urge the client to read only selected sections. This will allow the client to know she is not the only incest survivor but provides a more protected pace. (See References for suggested readings for clients.)

Support groups or adjunctive group psychotherapy may become useful resources at this point. Again, caution must be exerted when making these recommendations. The therapist should be well informed about the various groups in the community to be certain that a referral to a group would offer support, education, and affiliation for the client. For a thorough discussion of these matters see the section on Group Treatment in Chapter 4.

In anticipation of the approaching volatile work, and to teach skills never before learned, the therapist can instruct the client in recreational activities. The abused child did not play very much or feel relaxed. This was too dangerous. She needed to stay tense and guarded, ready to protect herself. The adult-client needs to know that it is now safe and desirable to relax and play. Sports, exercise, or outdoor activities need to be introduced into the client's life. Not only are these healthy habits but they also help in the regulation of strong feelings. Time to read, write, watch TV, or just do nothing are unusual events for many survivors. They are apt to have every moment scheduled so they can minimize the potential for emotional or physical intrusions. The therapist should urge new routines to allow for "downtime" but should not expect immediate results. At this stage of treatment, too much downtime would create too much anxiety for the client, so she will avoid it. It is still important, however, to plant the seeds.

This is a good time for the therapist to teach progressive relaxation techniques. As described in more detail in Chapter 4, self-regulatory skills help to control the intensity and flow of strong feelings. The client is about to enter an emotionally intense period and she must have some mechanisms intact and ready to be used. Exercises in deep breathing, yoga meditation, and guided visualizations can increase her arsenal of coping techniques. Many survivors are concerned that once they begin to experience their feelings about the incest they will become totally dysfunctional. The therapist needs to reassure the client that it will be important to achieve a balance between difficult therapeutic work and ordinary daily functioning. These relaxation and coping techniques will allow the client to maintain a decent level of stability.

Sometimes it can be appropriate and effective for the therapist to engage the client in a playful activity during the therapy session. This could include playing with yoyos, blowing soap bubbles, using coloring books, playing *Candyland,* or reading a children's book. The child-client will delight in these moments while the adult-client is reserving judgment. It is a creative way of jump starting the client's move toward more leisurely and playful times.

Phase II, then, focuses on the emergence of positive self-esteem in the client, new insights about incestuous family dynamics, learning to identify specific emotions, struggling to trust and depend on the therapist, and developing new skills to live a more balanced life. This is fundamental work that creates the internal and external resources to proceed in the healing process. Once the client has broader and deeper understandings about her past and some new coping skills, she is ready to begin the tumultuous unearthing of her buried emotions.

PHASE III: THE EMOTIONAL FLOOD

Sometimes I'll discuss a painful incident, feel its accompanying emotions, then later in the healing process, experience the same incident on an even deeper level of feeling. Often the limitations of language prevent me from describing the incident on a more painful verbal level, but I am definitely feeling it on a deeper emotional level, and I need to tell my therapist about it, even if my verbal description is exactly as it was before. The only place I ever feel safe enough to experience these feelings is in her office, in her presence. At these times I need my therapist's empathy, compassion, gentleness, sensitivity, and patience. I need her validation and acceptance.

I believe that my therapist must try to understand how deeply the pain and humiliation are harbored within me. I believe that my therapist has the responsibility to gently bring it out of me, while she is letting me know that I am okay, because, oftentimes I do not feel that I am okay. Sometimes I feel that I am different from other people. Sometimes the shame and the pain are so intense that I just want to crawl deeper inside myself, and hide from everyone, including my therapist. Sometimes, in this process, I especially want to hide from my therapist, because I have shared so much with her already, I've reached a deeper level of pain, and I am ashamed about what I've already told her.

—Client X

As new understandings resonate within the client, Pandora's box flies open. This is the moment the client has been avoiding for so long by distracting herself in abusive behaviors or abusive relationships. She has not wanted to explore the rage, sadness, and feelings of betrayal that accompany incest, although she has known these storms were brewing inside of her. This is a very difficult phase of incest treatment because of the intensity of the emotional flooding and the demands it places on the therapeutic relationship. This explosion unleashes more memories and nightmares and this time the client will experience the concomitant feelings. She will spill over with things she wants to tell her therapist—all the events and reactions that were not safe to talk about as a child—but there is also a simultaneous desire to suppress and to purge all this material. How the therapist handles this stage determines whether or not the treatment can be truly cathartic for the client. The goal of this phase, then, is to offer the client the opportunity to unload the emotional burden that is the incest legacy. There are several themes that surface at this time: intensified flashbacks and memories, emergence of rage, sadness, and abandonment, awareness of inadequate parenting, development of individual needs, decision-making about present family relationships, and exploration of sexual feelings and sexual identity.

If great attention has been given to the tasks presented in the earlier phases of treatment, invaluable coping resources will already be in place for the client. If she has developed new insights about her family, gained new respect for her indomitable strength, and joined in an appropriate and dependable relationship with the therapist, the client will have some of the necessary tools for managing the intensity of her feelings. In fact, many incest clients will urge the therapist to move faster in the beginning phases of therapy in hopes of dashing through the pain as quickly as possible. The therapist can explain that taking things more slowly will not only protect the client from becoming unnecessarily overwhelmed, but will also create the proper environment for the expression of long-hidden events and emotions. The stage has been set to optimize safety.

Intensified Memories

When the mind becomes cleared of interference, repressed information surfaces. No matter how much a client has consciously remembered about her abuse there will inevitably be new memories. These may take the form of sudden flashbacks, associations triggered by present-day events, new unexplainable fears or nightmares. These are very disturbing and intrusive occurrences in the client's life. Sleep is disrupted, concentration is impaired, and anxiety increases. There is a sensation of being overwhelmed with horrible images that psychologically re-create the initial abusive dilemma. How can the client have control over these violations? Not only did she suffer as a child but now it is happening all over again. She will become angry at the therapist and the treatment process for stripping away her defenses. She used to be able to "go away" or "shut down" whenever she was being assaulted, and now she can't even turn off her own thoughts. She feels out of control and that returns her to a helpless position. It is not unusual for a client to threaten to end treatment during this tumult. But she feels caught in a catch-22 situation. Through the course of therapy she has learned to trust the therapist and to need her or his help. She knows this is a healthy direction. Now she faces all her worst nightmares and recalls the best way to cope with them is by *not* needing anyone—by turning off and inward. But she has come out of her isolated world enough so that some of those defenses do not work as well anymore. She is torn. Should she give into the process and fully trust that the therapist will be there or just split and pray that her old defensive structure kicks into high gear again?

Beth had been in treatment for just over one year when her rage at her father began to appear. She had developed a much broader picture of her abusive family and past and had established a good rapport with her therapist. She walked into her appointment one week, plopped herself down on the couch, and glared at her therapist.

Therapist:	I take it you're feeling angry today.
Beth:	No shit, Sherlock!
Therapist:	Can we talk about it?
Beth:	I don't even know why I came here today. I don't want to be here and I don't want to talk to you about anything.
Therapist:	But you did come here, so why don't we make the best of it?
Beth:	You would say that! Talk, talk, talk. That's all you therapists ever want to do. Can't I just sit here brooding for once?
Therapist:	Is that what you'd like to do?
Beth:	Yeah.
Therapist:	Okay. If that's what you want . . .
Beth:	(after a few moments) Well, since I'm paying for this session I might as well get my money's worth. I just have one question for you. Why did you make me do this?
Therapist:	Do what?
Beth:	Talk about this shit. My dad, my childhood, the incest.
Therapist:	Do you honestly feel I *made* you talk about anything?
Beth:	No, not really. It's just that now I'm really in a fix. I keep having all these bad dreams and shakes and scary moments and now I can't control them like I used to. I never should have started this whole thing. I was just fine the way I was. I could take care of myself and not feel scared. Now I feel scared and a million other things. I hate it!
Therapist:	Yes, this is one of those difficult realities of therapy. You start to see more things, remember more things, and feel more things. Everything doesn't get stuffed away like it used to. I know it feels awful for you.
Beth:	It's all your fault, too! You made me like you and trust you. You took away my old ways of coping.
Therapist:	I'm glad that you like me and trust me, Beth. We worked hard at that. One of the reasons we struggled so much with that trust issue is so that when you got to this point, you'd feel confident that I would still be here to hang in there with you. I know this will be bumpy but I am still here to help you. But you'll also have to help yourself. We haven't taken away all of your defenses. That would have been foolish. You can still shut down if you need to and you can use some of the new skills you've acquired to manage what's happening.
Beth:	I just don't know if I can do this. It feels like too much.
Therapist:	It *is* a lot. But here's the thing of it. You don't have to cope with this all alone. This time around you have the help of a reliable and trustworthy adult. Can you think of how you would like my help in the midst of all this intensity?
Beth:	Not really. I don't know. I can't even think about it.
Therapist:	There must be something you hoped I could help you with.
Beth:	Just one thing, really. But it's stupid. It makes me feel like such a baby.
Therapist:	Can you share it with me?

Beth: It's just . . . just . . . I need to know you're really here for me. Like when I'm feeling really scared I sometimes think that if I could just hear your voice I'd be okay. See, I told you it was stupid.

Therapist: It doesn't sound stupid at all to me. I think it's a very understandable need. We all need to feel like there's someone safe to grab hold of during awful times. It would be just fine with me if you called me when you felt you needed to.

Focusing on old and new coping skills and the availability of the therapist gives the client permission to proceed in her emotional upheaval. Knowing that she has internal and external resources reassures her that she can move through these disturbing memories. This is the time to try out all those new self-regulatory skills the client learned earlier in therapy. It can be useful to offer more frequent sessions during this period so the client has more opportunities to verbally share her flashbacks and dreams. The more she can get the material to surface, the more manageable this process can be. The memories along with the growing emotions create a pressure cooker effect within the client. The more opportunities she has to let out the steam, the less likely it is that her lid will be blown off. The therapist needs to be instrumental in regulating this flow.

Rage

It is at this point the client starts to feel her anger at her abuser and nonprotectors. She now understands in her gut that she was an innocent victim. She looks at the children in her own life and cannot imagine what evil force would prompt her to harm them in any way. She knows she has troubles as a result of the abuse she suffered, but she would not violate a small, defenseless child. She does not feel compassion for her abuser and his problems. Feelings of rage, abandonment, and sadness set in and she has no idea how to deal with them. This is new territory for the client, and the therapist must become guide, instructor, and comforter.

Hopefully the client has come to feel safe in the therapy setting since she will need to release her feelings in some rather dramatic ways. She needs the freedom to scream, yell, sob, pace, stomp, and beat. She needs to learn there are productive and safe means to release the build-up of emotions inside. The therapist can encourage these outbursts while offering support and protection.

Angie had reached this threshold in her therapy. She was plagued with flashbacks that were evoking a great deal of anger. She needed to know how her therapist was going to handle this.

Angie:	What do you do when your other clients are angry?
Therapist:	I'm not sure I understand your question. Are you asking if it's all right for clients to get angry in my office?
Angie:	Well, sort of. See, my last therapist told me I had to control myself because she didn't want to be held responsible for anything getting broken.
Therapist:	Well, I guess I have some different ideas. Because of the nature of my work, I expect my clients to eventually feel quite angry. I think my office would be one of the safer places to express that anger.
Angie:	Well, but what if I want to smash something?
Therapist:	It's likely that you will have that urge. My only restrictions are that I won't permit you to hurt yourself and that you will have to pay to replace anything that is broken. As you can see, my office is not furnished with the most expensive or delicate objects. But there are other ways to express that same urge and I will help you learn some of those ways.
Angie:	Like what?
Therapist:	Like pounding your fists on these cushions or screaming at that empty chair. That rage can feel really destructive, but it can be expressed just as powerfully without actually becoming destructive.
Angie:	Oh. I didn't know that. Well, what about if I feel like banging my fist on something harder than a cushion. Like the wall, for instance. Sometimes when we're talking about the incest I picture myself smashing my fist real hard through the wall.
Therapist:	As I said, I won't allow you to hurt yourself. If I see or you tell me that you're dangerously close to hurting yourself, I will grab one of these cushions and place it on the floor near you so you can punch it. I will be very aggressive about protecting you while encouraging you to release that anger.
Angie:	I'll need to think about all this. Nobody ever said anything like this to me before. Thanks for the information.

Two weeks later in the middle of a session, Angie asked her therapist to put the cushion on the floor. She spent the rest of the hour sitting on the floor with her fist resting on top of the pillow while ranting about her father.

Incest clients require more time, room, and creativity to express these forbidden feelings. This is a period in the treatment when the therapist needs to be more available. This implies new contracting with the client about phone calls and appointments. Again, the therapist must be explicit about how and when she or he can be reached to define the parameters for the client and to prevent any feelings of intrusion into the therapist's life. These arrangements are temporary, lasting only as long as it takes for the client to move through the most intense moments of this cathartic process.

One of the most critical reasons to encourage the overt expression of rageful and sad feelings is the potential for implosion. Incest survivors are accustomed to controlling their emotions by turning them inward (Calof 1987, Courtois 1988). When she was angry at her abuser, the child transformed that anger into self-loathing. When she experienced loss or sadness, she created physical pain to make the emotions subside. There is still the danger that the adult-client will be swallowed up by all these intense emotions and end up in a suicidal or depressed state. One client expressed this phenomenon quite eloquently.

It's so tedious, everpresent, and unrelenting . . . this thing in me. I wax and wane but it's always there. This solemn darkness surrounds me, permeates me, moves silently, deftly with me. It possesses me. I can't make friends with it. I want to be rid of it some way, somehow. It just will not go away by itself. It lives within every cell and fiber of my body, my being. It is encroaching upon my spirit, my soul, and taking up residence there, the nucleus of it . . . sending out its tentacles, invading my every part. It must go one way or another. I need to find a way to get it out of me. The confrontation is growing nearer and nearer. I feel it. I have little control over this thing anymore. It is stronger than I and keeps getting stronger. I am a bystander no longer in control. I am being used as a host. This parasite is taking me over and it will be me. I will be gone. This must be what death is like, a constant fading, fading until there is only darkness and silence. The thing having fully prevailed will then be satiated, having changed all lightness to darkness. It will settle in . . . having overcome and be still, satisfied in its accomplishment and hibernate, slowly pulsating its darkness through. Only darkness pulsing . . . pulsing. It feels good. The struggle is over.

(For more ideas about treatment strategies for guiding the client through these intense moments, see Chapter 4.)

Trusting the Therapist: Part 3

As the client is purging these volatile feelings, she is experiencing the comfort, safety, and appropriateness of the therapist. Reliving her childhood experiences so vividly in the presence of this trusted adult brings the client out of her isolation. To have a witness to her suffering and to be cared for during her painful remembering is very powerful. It lets the client know three things: she has needs, she *can* get them met, and her parents did not permit or provide for those needs. This revelation is a very painful one. Because the therapist has been patiently and respectfully responsive to her needs in the therapeutic process (even during the worst times), the client understands it is possible to be worthy of care and comfort. She has held the belief that since her own parents could not adequately love her, then obviously she is undeserving of anyone's positive attention. She has trained herself to deny the existence of basic human needs such as affection, positive regard, comfort, and security. The therapeutic relationship has challenged her life-long belief system. Her awareness that her parents can *never* give her the love and protection she deserves puts an end to her fairy tale ending. They will never live happily ever after as the ideal family. Sadness wells up and fantasies grind to a halt.

The reparental function of the therapeutic relationship has played a fundamental role in this development. The client has slowly come to trust that the therapist will not behave like her abuser or nonprotector. She has felt the honesty, warmth, respect, responsibility, dependability, self-control, and appropriateness in the therapist's behavior. This reflects what infants and children require from their parents but most incest survivors never received. Enough cannot be said about the curative nature of this experience for the client. It is not enough to just talk about what an adequate parent does. The incest client must experience that within the therapeutic context. This is central to her ability to move all the way through the childhood trauma and into healthy adult functioning.

In essence this flooding releases that small, frightened abused child. It is that arrested child who is revealing all these details and feelings to the therapist. The adult-client recedes and the child-client appears. The therapist must pay attention to the changes in the client's voice, language, posture, and facial expressions to fully appreciate the child's presence. It will be necessary for the therapist to adjust her or his style to adapt to the child's needs. If the client looks petrified, the therapist must be gentle and reassuring. If the client is weeping and rocking herself, the therapist can offer to hold her. If the client feels shameful, the therapist can let her know she has done nothing wrong. Treatment strategies more appropriate to child psychotherapy may be especially useful at this time. Children in treatment are coaxed very differently than adults to reveal their traumatic experiences and feelings. None of these new methods should be employed without the full permission of the adult-client.

These are dramatic treatment opportunities. The child-client can finally have a trusting experience with an adult authority figure. It is healing salve for her wounds and developmentally propels her forward. When trusting and secure attachments are not available in childhood, there is a great interruption in emotional growth and cognition. Survival is the only focus—must be the only focus. By adulthood, the survivor is painfully aware of the deficits in her learning. Relationships are confusing, people are a mystery, society doesn't make any sense. What she learned about these things as a child was distorted, perverted, and incomplete. Being able to trust a therapist enough to regress to her childlike state is a phenomenal accomplishment and serves to repair the damage and teach new outlooks.

Dealing with the Family of Origin in the Present

Having achieved all this, the client is left with the troubling dilemma about what to do about her present contact with her abuser and family. She has faced the truest reality of her past, unloaded many of her stored-up feelings, acknowledged that her parents were and are inadequate, and started to feel more complete as an individual. Now what? Does she confront her abuser? Does she reveal the incest secret to the entire family? Does she address her nonprotector? Does she cut off all contact? Does she behave as she always has with her family? There is no one universal solution to this problem. The therapist needs to stay on the periphery of this decision-making process, for each client will need to discover her own best strategy without undue influence. The theme of her solution must be empowerment. How can she maintain her newly found sense of strength without setting up the potential for another form of victimization? Most clients will experiment with a variety of approaches (either hypothetically in sessions or in reality) before they settle on their own conclusion. It is essential for the therapist to set aside any preconceived notions about what would be ideal. During this process the therapist should primarily provide guidance and forethought. For a more detailed discussion of these matters, see Chapter 5.

Sexuality

Inevitably, the incest survivor will have many questions about what is normal and healthy sexuality. She will wonder if she has ever experienced such a thing. Sex and touch to her have meant power, force, and control. She has very little concept of sex as a pleasurable and desirable aspect of life. At this point in treatment she will not necessarily be ready to experiment with new sexual habits but instead she will just want a lot of information. In fact, during this emotionally intense phase of treatment, sexual activity is overtly avoided. It is important for the therapist to validate the client's need to be temporarily celibate. She needs to know that it is permissible for her to exert control within her sexual relationship. Her partner's cooperation and patience can make this much easier.

As the therapist addresses the client's questions about normal sexuality, it is important to separate behaviors from values. Clinical textbooks clearly describe the range of appropriate consensual sexual behaviors on a spectrum spanning from exclusively heterosexual to exclusively homosexual preferences (Kinsey et al. 1953). The therapist can inform the client about these matters. When it comes to inquiries about sexual orientation, the therapist's own value system must not enter the discussion. The client needs to hear that normal preferences fall anywhere along the continuum between heterosexual and homosexual. Because of the inappropriately early introduction into the world of adult sexuality, the client may feel confused about her own natural tendencies. This is the point in therapy when she can express her various thoughts. Given the prevalence of homophobia in this culture, it is important for the therapist to remain completely neutral. In time, the client will uncover her own sexual preferences, values, and needs. (For further discussion on sexual recovery, see Chapter 6.)

This third phase in incest treatment is intense, demanding, and fast-paced. It is also the pivotal moment that creates the springboard for full recovery. Fortunately, for both the client and the therapist, it does not last too long. It seems to have a regulatory system all its own. For some, a piece of this work will occur, then other foci will be taken, and then there is a return to this type of cleansing. Many clients are struck by the repetition of their stories or the recurrence of the tidal waves. It is helpful for clients to understand that they may have to review these images, feelings, and questions many times before they are put to rest. It is much like a film. When the client was small, the event was filmed in silence and black and white. With each stage of treatment a new element is added to the film. Color, sound, and texture are the feelings and new perceptions. The film is rewound and replayed many times over, each time revealing something else that was missed before. At first the sound seems so loud and the colors too vibrant, but with many viewings it becomes more manageable. Of course, the client will want to know when the film will stop replaying. During the last stages of treatment, the client will find a shelf for the film and be able to choose when she wishes to view it.

PHASE IV: NEW HOPE AND TERMINATION

The following excerpt is taken from a tape that my current therapist made for me. The general subject being discussed was what I could expect in the future and in the therapy process: "It's very possible to feel (free from the pain of your past). . . . Will you be able to manage whatever pain . . . (comes) up in your memories?" "Yes! Most of the time." "Will you feel much lighter from your burden than you feel right now? Yes! Because this [therapy] process will be helping you to let go moment by moment of all the pain that's stored up inside of you. . . . The results of this process will be that there will be lightness at the end of the tunnel. You will feel powerful. You will feel strong. You will feel far more convinced that you are a good person, and that you deserve to be happy in your life. You will feel far more often than not that you are okay just the way you are. That's what's in the future for you . . . together . . . we're gonna keep plugging away at this, together we're gonna get you into your future that will feel very different from your present and will be very healed from your past. It will be filled with visions that you can't possibly even have right now. It'll be filled with accomplishments and dreams that you haven't had the chance to dream yet. You will feel about yourself ways that you didn't even know existed. And you're already inching your way there." These are powerful, motivating words to me. I came to this therapist not knowing where I would like to be, only that where I was, was not a good place. Every once in awhile I get a sense of what she was talking about. Just for an instant I feel strong, or I envision a tunnel with a light at the end, or I feel a release of some of the pain. At those moments I do sense an understanding of what it feels like to be *okay, good,* and, *in control.* At those moments I think of these words on her tape, and I think, Wow! So this is it! This is how it's going to be for me! And I know that I'm going to make it.

—Client X

As the client synthesizes new insights with new feelings and discovers that she has survived a great trauma, her desire to feel whole and strong flourishes. She may still doubt she is a good, worthwhile, and lovable person, but she is no longer convinced she is a bad, worthless, and horrible person. It is still difficult for her to cope with intense feelings and she is still unsure about what to do with them. She still feels confused about relationships but is getting comfortable with the idea that she has needs. She has more and more days when she feels good about herself and her sense of empowerment grows daily. This is a smoother stage of treatment, when the client makes more external, rather than internal, changes. She is flapping her wings preparing to leave the nest, sensing that therapy will be winding down. The client has a clearer sense of her own inner strength and is ready to infuse her life with new hope and new choices.

New Choices

By this time the client has developed a great deal of insight into her repetitious patterns of victimization. She perceives how her relationships, her self-image, and her life choices have perpetuated abusive dynamics. Her tolerance for these circumstances has diminished considerably. Although she has been scrutinizing her decisions throughout the therapy, she is more ready now to take new actions and she has already acquired many of the necessary skills. For instance, a client may have long accepted her demeaning position at work, but now she doesn't like how that feels. She notices that she feels helpless, ineffective, and criticized. By the end of a work day she feels drained of her power. She sees the connection to her family dynamics and comes to realize that she has had enough of those kinds of abusive situations. She has used her feelings and her insights to guide her toward new decision-making. She now understands that she has choices and she wants to make one that will leave her feeling empowered and good about herself. This may mean she becomes more assertive at her job or asks for a transfer. Or she may ultimately decide to make a plan to leave the job altogether. She may ask her therapist for advice on these matters. It is important for therapists who are treating survivors of childhood traumas to remember that these clients did not receive adequate life training. It may be useful to guide the client toward resources about job hunting or interviewing skills or how to write a resumé. The actual evaluation and decision-making, however, must be left to the client.

Relationships will be reexamined at this time. The client has now experienced one relationship within which she feels respected and validated. She will want to recreate this feeling elsewhere in her life. Although the therapeutic relationship cannot be duplicated, it has taught the client an enormous amount about healthy relating. She now knows how to express herself, ask for what she wants and needs, and how to set limits. These are some of the basic ingredients necessary for good relationships. The client will modify her behavior with her partner, friends, relatives, and children. The therapist needs to prepare her for their reactions. These people have come to expect certain kinds of duties and actions from the survivor and they will not all be happy to have the protocol change.

Elyse owned her own business in which she employed several people, including an apprentice. She had always been willing to be interrupted by her trainee for even the most trivial reasons. She felt she ought to be friendly and constantly accessible to him so that he could learn the trade. At some point in therapy Elyse decided that her time was extremely valuable and she needed to limit his interruptions.

Elyse: It has dawned on me that my apprentice bugs me all the time with ridiculous questions.

Therapist: What is "all the time"? Five times an hour?

Elyse: No. More like fifteen times an hour every hour of the day.

Therapist: Oh my gosh! How do you manage to get your own work done?

Elyse: That's just the problem. I'm way behind. I know I have to talk to him and set some limits. I know exactly what he'll say, too.

Therapist: What will he say?

Elyse: He'll tell me I'm not being nice. And besides, how can he learn the trade if I don't answer all his questions?

Therapist: What do you think about setting limits?

Elyse: If I don't do it I'll go crazy. I'm already really pissed off at just the sight of him. But I know now that the situation is under my control.

Therapist: So what do you feel you want to say to him?

Elyse: I want to tell him that I have to set some new guidelines . . . that he can only ask me questions once every hour for no more than 10 minutes.

Therapist: That sounds reasonable. How do you think he'll react?

Elyse: He'll be angry at me. He'll try to tell me that I've changed for the worse. That he liked me better the old way.

Therapist: Then what will you say?

Elyse: I'll tell him that these changes are important to me and that I expect him to abide by them.

Therapist: What about that liking-you-less stuff?

Elyse: It will make me feel really bad. Maybe this isn't so nice.

Therapist: Elyse, remember that no one likes to have the rules change halfway through the game. He's letting you know that he feels off guard. How do you think you'll stand up to that?

Elyse: I guess I just have to ignore that part, huh? I guess I can just say that I know best how to run this business and I hope he can appreciate that.

This conversation (and several others) prepared Elyse for her confrontation with her apprentice. She walked into their meeting feeling confident in herself and the position she had established. As she had predicted, her employee was unhappy and challenging but she maintained her position. He punished her by sulking and becoming hostile. Elyse remained firm, and after three weeks of her reiterating and enforcing her new policy, the apprentice continued to behave insolently. Elyse spoke with her therapist about the possibility of firing him because she could no longer tolerate having people around her who did not treat her with respect. Just as she was about to notify him that he must leave, he announced that he was quitting because he could not work under such "rigid" conditions. Elyse felt triumphant about maintaining her boundaries and was well prepared for the consequences.

The client's intimate relationship goes through many changes as the end of therapy nears. If she has been in a basically loving and supportive relationship, there is dramatic improvement in the quality of that connection. The healing client will have learned how to assess and express her own needs within a relationship context and she will take those skills home with her. Her primary relationship will need to be rebalanced to accommodate two individuals' needs instead of just one. This process deepens and enriches the client's love relationship. If she has been in a more abusive situation, that relationship will either go through remarkable changes or end. In some cases, couples treatment can be helpful in facilitating adjustments in the relationship.

The client is also ready to explore her sexuality on her own terms. She no longer feels like a sexual hostage. She wonders how it would feel to be aroused and sexually free within the context of a loving relationship. Her first step needs to be the appreciation and the joy of her own body. This task cannot occur until late in the therapy when all the negative associations have been washed away. She needs literally to embrace her body and feel it as an ally and a source of strength and pleasure, rather than as a traitorous villain that feels only pain or numbness. A step-by-step behavioral approach teaches the client how to develop a positive body image. Once this has been achieved, the treatment can address sexuality and intimacy issues. (For a more detailed discussion about relationships and sexuality during the course of treatment, see Chapter 6 on Intimate Relationships.)

Healing Rituals

The incest survivor usually develops an aversion to certain mundane daily routines and holiday gatherings. As old abusive associations are rooted out of the client, new and healthy rituals and celebrations need to be added to her life. Throughout the course of treatment the client will have shared the frightening episodes that accompanied bedtimes, birthdays, Christmas Eves, prom nights, or bath times. By this point in therapy, the client is ready to create new habits or break the macabre aura of holidays past.

For as far back as she can remember, Suzanne has hated Thanksgiving. Although her father drank heavily most days, his drinking was more uncontrollable on Thanksgiving. What always made matters worse was that the extended family was present, making Suzanne's embarrassment more severe. By the time the turkey was set upon the table, her father was so drunk that he couldn't carve the bird and in frustration would fling it out the apartment window into the street below. Every Thanksgiving meal consisted of stuffing, potatoes, vegetables, and all the other trimmings, but no turkey. Once the relatives had left and Suzanne had cleaned up the mess, her father would viciously accuse her of ruining their holiday. With her mother already passed-out, her father would rape Suzanne. Since leaving home she actively avoided celebrating Thanksgiving. As she was completing therapy, her therapist raised the possibility of creating her ideal Thanksgiving dinner. Suzanne fantasized out loud who she would invite, what food would be served, what beverages would and would not be available, and how she would like the evening to end. Finally feeling in control of the situation, Suzanne carefully planned for the upcoming holiday. She and her partner invited several of their closest friends plus Suzanne's brother, sister, and favorite cousin. No alcohol or TV were allowed—just interesting conversation, games, and gentle music. Suzanne offered a very meaningful prayer before she carved the turkey. It was a delightful success and prompted Suzanne to create many more healing rituals.

Once Molly left home, she never took a bath again. Whenever possible, she rented apartments only with stall showers—no bathtubs. When she was a child Molly's father fondled and molested her during her nightly bath. She promised herself that when she was old enough to leave home, she would only take showers. She was progressing well in her therapy and was developing a more positive body image. Her therapist asked her if she might consider taking a bath sometime. Molly's immediate reaction was "No way!" The therapist dropped the issue only to have Molly raise it two months later. Molly wondered if the therapist thought she was actually healed enough to take a bath. They discussed in detail what it would take for Molly to feel safe with that experience. Her requirements were to be home alone with all the doors locked, to have pleasant-smelling bubbles to submerge in, to have soothing music playing, and to have a few candles lit. With supportive encouragement from her therapist and the permission not to follow through (if she couldn't), Molly planned her bath. It took another month before she actually enacted her plan, but when she did she was very pleased with the results. Eventually, long bubble baths became Molly's reward to herself on particularly bad days.

There are countless opportunities to create healing rituals. Besides undoing the nightmarish associations of the past, many incest survivors find it curative to stage funerals for their lost and damaged childhoods, followed by a celebration of their new-found hopes. It is useful for the therapist to toss out a melange of suggestions to the client during this last phase of treatment. No two clients will create the same rituals. These are highly individualistic ceremonies. One survivor built a funeral pyre in her backyard where she burned pictures of her abuser, old painful mementos from all past abusive relationships, photos of herself as a frightened child, and a locket her abuser had given to her. The therapist, the client, and her partner stood silently watching the flames swallow up her past. Afterwards, all three made a champagne toast and took turns reading prepared statements affirming the client's health and well-being. Another survivor gathered old papers and pictures and privately sought an isolated wooded area outside of town. There she dug a hole, buried the items, refilled the hole, and planted a bush on top of the pile. When she was done she sang a hopeful and powerful song to herself at the top of her lungs alone in the woods. Another survivor collected all the family photos from her childhood and all the pictures from her adult life. She chronologically arranged all the pictures into two separate albums—one of her past and one of her present. When she was done, she put the most recent album in a prominent place in her living room for all to see. She wrapped the other album in tissue paper, put it in a storage box, and stored it in her basement. To her, this meant that she was no longer denying the past, but was consciously choosing to put it where she could still have access to it. These are just a few resourceful ideas clients have had about how to put the pain to rest symbolically. These rituals have a powerful impact on bringing closure to the incest trauma, and therapists need to be active in urging clients to pursue such celebrations.

Relaxation

With much of the burden lifted, the client is ready to learn how to play. Earlier in the therapy the client may have experimented with playful activities, but at this point there is greater safety to truly let loose. The therapist will need to describe a variety of childhood games, as the client may be quite unfamiliar with ordinary choices such as tag or hopscotch or jump-rope or stoop ball. Dr. Seuss, Shel Silverstein, Mercer Mayer, and A. A. Milne have written fantasies that will tickle a child's funny bone. Visits to the children's section of the library can help open up the child-client. (The author's personal favorite, which works wonders with incest clients, is *Eloise* by Kay Thompson.) Swinging on swings, hanging from monkey bars, sliding down slides, and spinning around merry-go-rounds offer the client long-forgotten moments of freedom. Learning to play, whether child-

or adult-style, is an essential aspect in building a balanced, healthy life for the survivor.

Termination

Before terminating treatment, two questions will surface for the client. Is it possible to heal fully from the incestuous experiences if the client has not confronted her abuser or nonprotectors, and is forgiveness necessary? Undoubtedly these issues will have been raised many times during the course of treatment but now that the client is preparing to end therapy, she feels pressed to resolve these questions. Each survivor will know best what her own particular resolution will look like. This will be filtered through her own unique experience, her family situation, her value system, her spiritual outlook, her educated anticipation of consequences, her inner strength, and her intuitive understandings. The appropriate therapeutic stance on these issues is one of nonjudgment. It is easy for the therapist to superimpose her or his belief system onto the client especially when it comes to the dilemma of forgiveness. The client needs a free, open space to find her own peace of mind. By the end of treatment her perceptions have been righted and she is more than capable of making the best decision. (Because the issues of abuser and family confrontation and forgiveness are so complex, there are separate sections addressing these concerns.)

And so the therapy comes to a close. This is a joyful and moving moment for both the client and the therapist. Most survivors will know when it is time to leave and initiate termination conversations. As in all other therapies, there should be a gradual weaning process of less frequent appointments. With incest survivors it is important to allow them a good deal of control over the ending process: when to end, how to end, and some sense of what will happen when it's over. This enables the client to come full circle from dependent victim to empowered individual. The therapist will need to reassure the client that the door is always open for future contacts; it is all right for the client to have needs again. An appropriate analogy is the retaining of an attorney. The client may need an attorney to facilitate her divorce. This is a long, arduous process that eventually ends. Sometime later she may need her attorney to look over a rental lease, so she makes an appointment or two. Later still, she may draw up her will. The point is, the client needs her attorney's guidance for different life events over a long period of time. A therapist to an incest survivor serves much the same function. An illness, a death, a birth, or a move may precipitate a need to touch base with the therapist. This always remains an option and should be clearly stated.

The process of ending therapy should include a review of all the work accomplished. The client and the therapist should express their own points of view about the progress that has been made. This is a good time for the therapist to remind the client how she was when she first walked in the office and how she is now upon leaving. These contrasts bolster the client's own sense of growth. Additionally, the therapist should point out what issues may still ignite the client. The goal here is to make the client human rather than perfect. If the client leaves treatment with the sense that she is now *fixed* never to return to her old ways, she is being set up for disappointment. Allowing for potential pitfalls acknowledges that certain issues are volatile, but are also manageable.

It is now appropriate for the therapist to share some of his or her emotional reactions to the horrible stories the client has revealed over the years. To have expressed these responses sooner would have impeded the treatment. The client will be grateful to know the therapist had very human reactions but did not reveal them at the time. Now the client can tolerate hearing how much the therapist admires her ability to have survived and the strength it has taken to proceed in the therapy. This is a warm and joyful ending. Both the therapist and the client are extremely aware of the great strides made and the hard work that has been accomplished. Both will feel proud of their perseverance and appreciate the resiliency of their relationship. This will have been a unique experience for them both. Judith Herman (1990) writes:

> I have often wondered why these patients keep seeking help despite repeated failures and disappointments. One might view this behavior as simply another repetition compulsion. Or, taking a more affirmative view, one might consider their persistence as a testimony to their virtues of determination and hope. Many of us who work with these patients have been inspired by their courage. Their endurance in the pursuit of treatment reflects a conviction, often unarticulated but nonetheless very powerful, that recovery can begin if only the right connection—between patient and caregiver, and between symptom and trauma—can be found. Our role in the healing process is to bear witness and thus to make it possible for the patient to bear a reality that cannot be borne in isolation. By our presence, we enable our patients to tell what has happened to them and to make sense out of the unspeakable events of the past. [p. 291]

4

Therapeutic Strategies

Incest survivors present many unique problems that are not present with such intensity in other populations. The severity of the early childhood trauma that is created as a result of sexual abuse can leave the individual with a wounded and hidden soul. The therapy attempts to heal and free the client from her dark corners. But along the path there are many encounters with her nightmares, self-loathing, emotional numbing alternating with emotional flooding, continued fears and mistrust, missed linkages, and clever—yet idiosyncratic—coping mechanisms. It is useful for the therapist to understand the particular meaning of some of these defenses as they appear in survivors and to be prepared to make very eclectic interventions. This chapter will discuss in greater detail the recurrent theme of self-destructive thoughts and actions, the therapeutic use of dissociation, creative intervention, and group treatment.

SELF-DESTRUCTIVE AND SUICIDAL BEHAVIORS

There is an unusually high occurrence of self-destructive and suicidal behaviors in adult incest survivors (Bass and Davis 1988). This is a constantly recurring problem in the psychotherapy and one that must be confronted boldly, yet sensitively, from the very beginning of treatment. During the early contracting sessions the therapist can let the client know that self-destructive thoughts and behaviors are common among incest survivors and that they will need to develop some plans for dealing with those moments. This invites the client to reveal her habits as she feels comfortable in the therapy, because she will already know that the therapist expects to deal with this. These behaviors are often very private and it may take some time before the client can share this information.

As the client discloses some of her destructive habits to the therapist, the first task will be to uncover the meaning and the purpose of the behavior(s).

After ten months of therapy Maxine shyly revealed to her therapist that she had a collection of broken glass that she sometimes used to cut into her upper arms. Although the therapist was shocked and saddened she asked Maxine, "Why do you keep these pieces of glass?" Maxine proceeded to offer an elaborate and insightful explanation stating that she had become so used to physical pain that she wasn't sure what else she was good for. When she had moments in her life that seemed confusing or empty, she would cut herself as a reassurance that she existed for some purpose. At other times she cut herself to control her emotions. If she felt angry or sad she would often become overwhelmed and need to put those feelings away. She discovered as a child that when she felt the pain of being raped she could make herself "go away" physically, emotionally, and mentally to a much lovelier place. Cutting herself as an adult still let her have that same *relief.* Maxine followed her explanation with a pointed question. "You won't ask me to give you my glass, will you? Because I won't give it away. It's mine and I won't let you have it." Resisting her urge to plead for this implement of self-destruction, the therapist responded, "No, I won't ask you to let me keep your glass. I understand it's yours. What I will ask you for, though, is to fight real hard not to use it on yourself. That will be difficult, I know. But I think you've experienced enough physical pain for several lifetimes and our job together is to help end that pain. I hope that, in time, you will feel less overwhelmed by all your feelings and no longer need to cope with them by hurting yourself." Maxine was greatly relieved and surprised to hear this. She had expected her therapist (like other therapists before her) to ask for the glass for safekeeping. She liked the control the therapist gave her while offering her hope that things would change. Not surprisingly, Maxine cut herself only minimally twice more after this and eventually threw away her glass collection.

This demonstrates the usefulness of approaching these behaviors from the client's meaning system rather than the more commonly used behavior modification methods. Once there is an understanding of the client's meaning, there are infinite possibilities for reframing the issues.

The next task for the therapist is to assess the lethality of the client's behavior. There is a whole range of destructive acts common to incest survivors (see following lists) and it is important to delineate the potential danger to the client. Certainly the ultimate goal is to eliminate the harmful behaviors entirely, but this will need to be accomplished slowly. The most destructive or life-threatening behaviors must be dealt with immediately. The less dangerous actions will be defused little by little over the course of the therapy.

The underlying psychology of these destructive behaviors reveals that the client is perpetuating the abuse that has become *normal* in her life experiences (Schetky 1990). Sexual, physical, and emotional abuse were steady fare in her childhood. Just because the abuser is no longer present to hurt her does not mean that she is now free. As a child her whole existence revolved around abuse: perceiving it, receiving it, avoiding it, comprehending it, internalizing it, anticipating it, feeling deserving of it. What could replace abuse as a central theme in the survivor's life, if abuse suddenly were no longer an issue? Seeking affection and love? Abused children don't develop a healthy notion about how to receive appropriate love, so they tend to recreate what they have always known. Would they look for success in their lives? These are people who have become convinced they don't deserve to succeed. A therapeutic balancing act develops. New central themes of self-worth must be built brick by brick so that the old abusive habits are no longer necessary for the client. It is very useful for the therapist to understand these behaviors as childhood carryovers rather than pathologically self-destructive tendencies.

Common Forms of Self-Destructive Behaviors

Incest survivors tend to exhibit destructive habits in five areas: physical pain or danger, addictions, sexual acting out, negative self talk, and suicidal ideation or actions.

Physical pain.   Adult incest survivors will often continue physically painful behaviors from childhood. If the child was raped, the adult may insert various objects into the vagina to recreate genital pain. If the child was burned, beaten, or scalded, the adult may burn herself with cigarettes, bang her head against the wall, or run her hands under boiling water. If the child was hurt sexually or physically on a regular basis for either being a good girl or a bad girl, the adult will punish herself as well for being good or bad. The adult may also tempt the fates by engaging in reckless or daring behaviors. This may include dangerous driving or drinking on a dare, consuming hazardous combinations or quantities alcohol, or dodging legalities.

Addictions.   Drugs, alcohol, cigarettes, and food offer incest survivors options for numbing themselves. Because they are so cut off from themselves physically, these clients do not have an accurate perception of when they have had enough to drink, smoke, or eat. As they ingest more and more, they become more distant from the source of their pain. Addictions become very attractive. Exercise can also develop into an addiction for some of these clients. It is an attempt to exorcise the demons. "If I sweat/run/swim/bike . . . enough, I will get it (the pain) all out of my system." Endorphin-produced highs also play a part in this.

Sexual acting out.   A great many incest survivors have experienced periods of promiscuity in their adulthood. Without exception they report that it was not about sex but rather about control and power. They used their sexuality to lure partners for an insignificant sexual encounter and then walked away. Generally these clients experienced neither pleasure nor pain from the sexual actions but did feel gratified about having such control over the situation. Some incest survivors will recreate sexually abusive relationships by gravitating toward partners who resemble their abusers. These are the women who eventually fall into the battered category and seriously endanger their lives. Still another form of sexual acting out is obsessional, abusive masturbation. This is the most transparent recreation of the incest experience.

Negative self talk.   The litany of self-denigrating thoughts an incest survivor can recite is gargantuan. "I'm such a stupid jerk . . . I'm a dumb asshole . . . I can't do anything right . . . I always screw things up . . . I'm fat and ugly . . . I'm good for nothing . . . I'm really a disgusting human being . . . If anybody really knew me, they would puke. . . ." It goes on and on. In part, she is parroting what she heard throughout her childhood and, in part, she has internalized these messages.

Suicidal ideation and actions.   Suicidal thoughts in the incest survivor are recurrent and fall into two categories: passive and active. The overwhelming majority of suicidal ideas are passive fantasies with one goal—to make the pain stop. An elaborate plan may be devised in the client's head without any intent to follow through. It serves the purpose of reassuring the client that if everything becomes unbearable, she has a scheme to end her misery. Interestingly enough, one reason why the suicide plan is so complicated is that the client does not want anyone to suffer from her death. It becomes very difficult to concoct a scenario where no one will feel guilty or sad. A passive death wish is not a lethal threat. It is an expression of pain becoming too great. The more active suicidal behaviors must be dealt with swiftly. Common suicidal attempts among incest survivors involve drugs or alcohol, car crashes, and wrist-slashing. These acts should be taken very seriously as truly self-annihilating wishes. Everything must be done to protect the client.

Therapeutic Approaches

During the initial contracting sessions with the client, the therapist should raise the issue of suicide. If the client claims this is irrelevant in her case, then the topic can be dropped. Many clients, however, will be very interested to learn that the therapist anticipates suicidal moments and that she or he has specific plans about how to handle them. This is an appropriate time to spell out customary procedures. The therapist needs to define emergency plans including telephone calls and hospitalization. It is important that the client is clear about whether the therapist can be called at home or the answering service or the clinic. Most clients will want to know which hospital the therapist prefers to use, and most will protest the whole idea of hospitalization. The therapist's firmness is critical here. If a therapist waffles at the client's threats about refusing to be hospitalized, there will be serious trouble. If that client does become dangerously suicidal, the therapist is either left totally responsible for her life or death (an impossible task for the therapist) or forced to commit the client to the hospital. Either situation will result in termination of the therapy and a major setback for the client. Instead, it behooves the therapist to state simply and firmly that "If you become dangerous to yourself, I will take every action necessary to have you hospitalized until you are no longer suicidal. I cannot be available to you twenty-four hours a day to prevent you from harming yourself. I will need help with that. If you do enter the hospital, I will continue to be your therapist and collaborate with the staff there, and stay as involved as possible while you are there." What is most reassuring to clients who are prone to suicidal ideations is that the therapist will not abandon her, that the hospital will be a healing and safe environment, and that the therapist will go to great lengths to insure her self-protection.

It has been important to me to know that suicidal feelings are sometimes a part of the incest recovery process. Early in my therapy with my current therapist we discussed these feelings. It was important for me to know what her reaction might be should I feel suicidal. She assured me that these are normal feelings, that she would be here for me, and help me through the times when I felt that way. She said that we had the option of setting up an appointment, or talking by telephone every day. She also said that I would have the option of entering a hospital if I chose to do so. She added that sometimes she recommends that clients go to a particular hospital in a nearby community. This facility allows her to be involved in the treatment by allowing her to continue meeting with her clients while they are hospitalized. The client makes the final decision on whether or not to admit herself into a hospital. As we were discussing suicidal feelings and treatment options my therapist appeared calm, confident, and reassuring.

I would like to attempt to explain, albeit in my layperson's language, what it means to me to know that my current therapist and I have a suicide plan. In the past, whenever I've felt suicidal, I experienced a feeling that everything in my life was totally out of control. But, now things are different, because I know that should I feel that way again, I have a plan of action to deal with these feelings. This knowledge serves to neutralize the helplessness. Having this plan available allows me to regain some control. I realize that no matter how bad things get, I always have this positive alternative. Thus, having a plan to deal with suicidal feelings serves to neutralize the very feelings for which the plan was invented.

—Client X

Long-term "no suicide" pacts are often met with resistance in incest recovery. Until growth and healing are more evident to the client, she will need to hold on to suicide as a viable option for escaping the unending pain. Shorter-term pacts can be effective, however. In incest treatment there are inevitable periods of much more intense anxiety, pain, and confusion. This can set off the suicidal thoughts. The therapist can ask the client for more time to work together to move through the awful spot. "I know talking about these memories is particularly painful for you and I understand why those suicidal thoughts are back. What I know from doing this work with other people is that if we work together very hard, you can get to the other side of this pain. You will feel very different than you do right now. But we will need some more time to get there. Could you agree not to take any destructive actions for, say, a month?" Most clients will agree to this short-term plan. The therapist is simultaneously offering understanding of the client's despair while planting hopefulness within the client.

Power and control are themes embedded within self-destructive tendencies. The client is saying, "If anyone else is going to hurt me, it's going to be *me*. Just you try and stop me." The therapist needs to recognize that control actually does rest with the client but she or he wants to avoid a possible suicide. "I accept that suicide is a choice you may want to make. I hope it's a choice you don't make. I fully accept that I have no control over your life-or-death decisions. I do hope that you will choose life and feel hopeful as a result of the work we are doing together." Not wrestling with who has control over the client's life has a tremendous impact on reducing any immediate danger. The stakes are raised when the client feels hurt or controlled.

Doris waited until the last five minutes of the session to tell her therapist that she was feeling fairly suicidal that week. "What's the use?" was the theme. She left the office stating that she wasn't comfortable saying anything else at that time but that she did not feel in immediate danger. When she appeared for her appointment the following week she was ready to say more.

Doris: I'm sorry about dropping a bomb last time. That wasn't really my intention. I was just very cautious about how you might respond. What I need to ask you is whether or not you would commit me if I talked openly about my suicidal and self-destructive feelings.

Therapist: No, I wouldn't. If you recall when we first began our work, I anticipated that you would have these feelings. If hospitalization becomes necessary, it will be voluntary.

Doris: So what would you say if I told you that I've been digging my nails into my fists, playing with knives, eating only junk, and imagining banging my head violently against the walls?

Therapist: I would ask you what is brewing that you feel is just about to let loose within you.

Doris:	I'm not sure. Sometimes I think it's just about feeling so worthless and alone.
Therapist:	How does physical pain help with those feelings?
Doris:	In a weird way, it keeps me hanging on and in other ways, it's just about self-punishment.
Therapist:	Can you picture a time when you would not feel so punitive?
Doris:	Not really. It all feels pretty hopeless to me.
Therapist:	What I can share with you from my experiences with other survivors is that these are typical feelings—painful though they may be. We are just a little way into our work together and I expect that you will have many moments when you will want to hurt yourself. Here's where I stand on that. I most certainly hope that you do not choose to harm yourself in any way, but I also understand that, for you, this is one avenue of control you have available. I do not have the desire nor the power to take that away from you. You are entitled to self-control. I urge you, however, to stay engaged in the treatment so that you can develop some healthier and more hopeful forms of control.
Doris:	I'm really relieved that you won't intrude into my choices. Right now I can't promise you that I won't hurt myself or that I can find some reason why it would matter whether I was alive or dead. But I guess I've already begun this therapy and I have a bit of trust in you, so it probably makes sense to wait and see what might be possible for me.

One creative technique for encouraging the client to nurture rather than to harm herself is the use of individualized audio tapes. (See Creative Interventions later in this chapter for more details.) These are tapes filled with affirmations, relaxation exercises, guided imagery, and soothing music that the therapist designs specifically for that particular client. During predictably rough moments in the treatment the therapist can advise the client to temper her self-destructive thoughts by replacing her old tapes with her new one. The "new tape" is the therapist speaking to the powerful survivor who has weathered many other storms and who can get through this one, too. Having the therapist's voice offer messages of hope, calm, and validation has a remarkable effect on deterring destructive thoughts and behaviors.

"The desire to hurt yourself is your way of picking up where your abuser left off." The client will recoil to hear herself identified with her tormentor. Reframing those behaviors in this light opens up new understanding for the client. She triumphed as a small and defenseless child by surviving the incest in the first place. Now she is an adult struggling with only the memories and feelings of that abuse, not the physical reality. If she gives in to her self-destructive tendencies she will have let him win after all those years of fighting back. Now is the time to be powerful and truly victorious, and the best way she can do that is to complete her therapy no matter how difficult it becomes. Appealing to the fighter, the survivor, the strong person who withstood all those childhood traumas is the most powerful way to guide the client toward healthy behaviors.

THERAPEUTIC UNDERSTANDING AND USE OF DISSOCIATION

Dissociation and denial are part and parcel of the experience of trauma. It is the human being's method for coping with extraordinary circumstances so that he or she can survive. In the treatment of incest survivors dissociation will be a prominent feature. The more completely this mechanism is understood within the context of the original trauma as well as continued coping with familiar stimuli, the better able the therapist is to work effectively to help the client resolve the stored impact of the abuse.

David Spiegel (1990) offers a concise and helpful approach when he writes:

> Trauma can be understood as the experience of being made into an object: the victim of someone else's rage, of nature's indifference, or of one's own physical or psychological limitations. Along with the pain and fear associated with rape, combat trauma, or natural disaster comes a marginally bearable sense of helplessness, a realization that one's own will and wishes become irrelevant to the course of events, leaving either a view of the self that is damaged; contaminated by the humiliation, pain, and fear that the event imposed; or a fragmented sense of self. There is an understandable desire to escape psychologically when one cannot escape physically. Since the literature on absorption has demonstrated that hypnotic-like dissociation experiences can occur in pleasant situations (e.g., at the movies), it would be strange indeed if individuals faced with overwhelming helplessness and fear did not utilize such resources to escape psychologically from events that are physically inescapable. The preexisting personality attempts to carry on as though nothing at all had happened. However, the need for the dissociation implies that pain and humiliation were, in fact, inflicted, and the person only partially reconsolidates, left with a sense that the real truth is the dissociated and warded-off self that was humiliated and damaged. . . . What may occur in response to trauma is a polarization of experience in which trauma victims alternate between intense, vivid, and painful memories and images associated with the traumatic experience, and a kind of pseudonormality in which they avoid memory by traumatic amnesia, others forms of dissociation, or repression or by a complex combination of these mechanisms with a consequent constriction in adaptive ability and the availability of the full range of affective response. [pp. 251–253]

Here Spiegel is normalizing the necessity for dissociation during trauma, deeming it a valuable resource for survival.

This is an appropriate therapeutic attitude when encountering dissociation in the incest survivor. In order to preserve any sense of self, the child sexual abuse victim withstood the physical and psychological damage by protecting her mind.

Most survivors describe the abuse as if they were observing it from afar, which is, in essence, what they did. Recalling the specific details of the abuse in the course of treatment will return the client to that dissociated state so that, in the retelling, she can withstand the pain, sadness, anger, and humiliation. It is the therapist's task to help the client to better integrate the two vantage points so that greater resolution can occur. Understanding that the continued dissociative episodes in a client's life are self-protective rather than pathological demonstrates the clinician's insight into the nature of dissociation. Rather than responding with alarm, the therapist must react with respect, gentleness, and engagement. Any other approach would jeopardize the client's well-being and call her sanity into question. Dissociation and denial are not crazy. They are necessary.

Each survivor will have her own idiosyncratic brand of dissociation so it is difficult to clearly categorize the possible manifestations (Kluft 1990). There is a spectrum, however, of minimal-to-dramatic presentations. Some clients will appear extremely passive during upsetting moments revealing no affect whatsoever. A client may be reporting a particularly horrifying childhood memory or even describing a present-day tragedy as if it were no big deal. This is one frequent version of dissociation with these clients. Other clients seem to have taken their passivity to greater lengths by perfecting their ability to seem *invisible* or *not present* during an interaction. Others have forgotten large chunks of time during their childhoods or need to be reminded by their partners that, for instance, they had painful knee surgery last year. More dramatic still are moments of catatonia or *freezing up* when certain associations are triggered. These clients stare blankly and become silent, appearing as if they no longer know where they are. Nearly all survivors who have not completed their recovery describe "not being present during sex." The associational cues here are obvious.

Self-destructive behaviors in incest survivors can also be explained as dissociation. For these women, physical pain can set off the distancing necessary to cope with overwhelming emotions. There is a paired response of physical pain to psychological escape. There are new investigations in the area of neurophysiology that suggest these behaviors of cutting, banging, or hitting release endorphins that create a euphoria (Schetky 1990). This phenomenon underscores the importance of therapeutic intervention to work through the trauma so that new and healthier coping mechanisms can replace these old associations. (For further discussion about self-destructive and suicidal intervention responses, see previous section in this chapter.)

There are four treatment strategies that can be powerful tools when working with dissociation in the therapeutic setting. What follows is a discussion and examples of encouraging the expression of affect, reframing, imagery, and active engagement. (For related examples, see the section on Creative Interventions in this chapter.)

Tracy learned by the time she was 5 years old that she could achieve greater control over her circumstances if she sucked in her strong feelings, toughened up, and went about her business. She had experienced ridicule when she protested or cried when her father molested her. She was able to develop a modicum of well-being if she could shut down her emotions. This control carried into adulthood.

Tracy: Every time I think about what my father did to me I just want to get so angry.
Therapist: What stops you?
Tracy: What good would it do? It's over and done with. I survived. I'm not doing too badly for myself. What's the big deal? All you therapists think we're all supposed to "express our feelings"—as if that's the only good choice.
Therapist: So you think holding in your anger is a better choice?
Tracy: Absolutely.
Therapist: The way I see it is that when you were a child, not expressing your feelings was the best choice available to you. It helped to protect your dignity and your privacy of thought. This was clever, Tracy, and I applaud your ability to have done that. But today in your life, that holding in has a different impact on you. Today it's giving you constant intestinal problems and lots of generalized symptoms of tension. I have no doubt that guarding your feelings still protects you sometimes, but it is now also taking a toll on you.
Tracy: I can tolerate the stomach pain. I'd rather do that than get all emotional about my past.
Therapist: I'm not suggesting that you let it rip. I'm urging you to pay attention to what is different about right now. Right now in your life you have power and control. Right now your tightness is making you ill. And right now, you have the help of someone who will respond appropriately to your feelings. Although it won't be pleasant, it will be a relief to let go of some of those feelings you've held in for so long.

By supporting the child-client's coping strategy while bringing it into the present tense for the adult-client, the therapist can gently persuade the client to begin to speak the feeling words. She needs to be reassured that she will not be met with the same experience of her past. Taking it in small doses allows the client to feel some control over the emotions and the process. This work must be slow and contained until such a time that the client becomes more comfortable in the affective realm.

Reframing the dissociative behavior can offer the client a new perspective on what has become a dysfunctional pattern. This is done in a nonjudgmental manner that encourages the disruption or examination of the troubling behavior.

Diana was molested so repeatedly over so many years she developed the notion that "If I can become absolutely perfect then my father will stop doing these dirty things to me." This set in motion hyperperfectionistic behaviors including dusting, redusting, and polishing the furniture, writing and rewriting her spelling lists countless times, rehearsing the same piano piece for hours, setting out to clean up the cat litter and cleaning the entire basement in the process, writing drafts of school papers dozens of times and then typing and retyping them until they looked just right. She rarely experienced exhaustion from her regimen, clearly getting fueled by anxiety-produced adrenalin. This perfectionism was still quite operative in adulthood. As an accountant in a large firm she often worked well into the evening, not only completing her work but redoing it and combing it obsessively for flaws. No amount of praise or financial compensation persuaded Diana that her work was competent. She was convinced that it was just "a matter of time before my boss discovers that I'm a total jerk." Lately she has been finding her compulsiveness disruptive in her home life.

Diana: My husband is really getting irritated about how late I come home from work. I keep trying to explain to him that I need to work these long hours for now because of the big account I'm working on. He complains that I always seem to have a big project I'm working on and that he never gets to see me anymore. I just can't seem to make him understand.

Therapist: How are you feeling toward your husband these days?

Diana: (flatly) Well, I love him, of course.

Therapist: Are you interested in spending more time with him?

Diana: Yes and no. Yes because I love him and sort of miss him, but no because I always feel like he wants something from me. Like I always have to satisfy some desire or another. And I don't necessarily mean sex either. It's just that he wants to play or go to the movies or just cuddle up watching TV. A lot of times I'd just rather be working.

Therapist: Might it be possible that you prefer working because you don't have to deal with your or your husband's feelings? Are you more comfortable being productive than you are being expressive?

Diana: Well, when I'm being productive I'm not having any feelings, except maybe a bit of anxiety that I'm not doing a good enough job.

Therapist: I get the sense that you believe that if only you got everything done perfectly then everything would be wonderful—your job, your marriage, yourself. Things would be safe and easy.

Diana: That's exactly what I think. That's why I have to work so hard and cover all my bases. If I miss something then everything could just come tumbling down.

Therapist: Diana, I think it would be important for you to understand this perfectionism from another angle. When you were a little girl and your father was molesting you all the time, your world was out of your control. Bad things always happened to you and you were sure that it was because you were bad. That is how children think. In order to cope with that sense you capitalized on your strengths. Those skills were your competence, your endurance, and your attention to detail. You developed the notion that the path to being good and therefore

having good things happen to you was to become a perfect little girl.
For you that meant housecleaning, babysitting, and schoolwork had
to be done without any mistakes. Mistakes, to you, meant something
bad would happen. Can you hear how you still believe that today?

Diana: Yes. But it's true. I know it's true. I am bad.

Therapist: Actually, the truth is that you are good, but that your father did bad
things to you because of his own problems. You have maintained your
beliefs to protect yourself from acknowledging that your father was
bad. If you realized that your father was bad then you might conclude
that he wasn't capable of loving you and that would have been worst
of all to admit. It has been safer for you to place the onus on yourself.
The real problem is that in your life today your obsessions can get out
of hand and they interfere with your ability to stay emotionally
connected to your husband. It may be time to take a second look at
your long-held assumptions.

Imagery that clients are able to access in their dissociative states provide the
therapist with an entry pass. The place a client needs to go to "space out" is a
necessity but it can also become a resource for approaching her feelings. If the
therapist can visualize this place without intruding on it, the session can continue
uncovering affect while the client protects herself. Eventually the dissociation
will drop off and the client will speak of feelings in a more connected manner.

Gloria had the habit of "spacing out" during her therapy sessions. It could happen in
the middle of a sentence or after a poignant question from her therapist. Rather than
allowing the silence to persist, the therapist asked Gloria, "Where have you gone to?"
Gloria was able to describe a floating sensation that took her "nowhere." The therapist
urged her to explain what "nowhere" looked and felt like. "Tell me what color it is.
What sounds do you hear? What sensation do you have while you are there? What
images does it create?" Eventually Gloria was able to describe a place filled with light
and humming that brought her a sense of calm. It felt distant from the present setting
in the office but she was able to call herself back into the moment when she chose.
Together the therapist and Gloria began to understand this as her particular haven
that she needed to enter whenever the material was too loaded. Gloria named it "The
Light." The therapist became adept at identifying whenever Gloria would enter "The
Light" and eventually addressed her in that space. "I know that my question pulled
you into "The Light." It's okay that you are there. From that nice, safe spot can you
respond to my question? I will repeat it for you now."

The most dramatic episodes of dissociation can occur in the therapy setting
with survivors who were severely sexually, physically, and emotionally abused
over a prolonged period of time. When painful memories emerge—and there are
so many of them—dissociation will inevitably occur. For these clients the
manifestation is more pronounced, and they appear less present, more withdrawn, and more regressed. Spontaneous age regression is a common presentation.

When the therapist inquired about Martha's father during the earlier phases of her therapy, Martha would often make such a thorough transformation at the sound of his name that the therapist wondered if she was observing the appearance of an *alter*. She began to assess for Multiple Personality Disorder and realized Martha did not fit the profile. Although she did not immediately eliminate the possibility of MPD, the therapist was puzzled about what was occurring and how best to respond to it. With the help of a supervisor, the next time Martha withdrew the therapist tried the following intervention.

Therapist:	Martha, do you know where you are right now?
Martha:	Yes, I'm in your office.
Therapist:	Are you feeling frightened?
Martha:	(No response. She is sitting rigidly with her hands under her thighs, her shoulders hunched up and her eyes staring widely but blankly ahead, past the therapist.)
Therapist:	I see that you needed to go away, Martha. I must have said something to trigger that. But I don't want you to go too far away. If you do, we'll lose contact and then it will be difficult for me to help you. Do you still want my help?
Martha:	Yes.
Therapist:	Then we need to find a way to stay connected while you are away. Can you tell me how old you feel right now?
Martha:	Eight years old. I know I'm an adult sitting here but I feel 8 years old.
Therapist:	I understand. You're sort of in two places at once. Is that okay with you?
Martha:	I do this all the time. Of course it's okay.
Therapist:	Is there any room there for me to join you? Or do you need to be there alone?
Martha:	I'm usually alone but I guess you can come here if you want to.
Therapist:	How about if I pull my chair closer to yours and just hold your hands while we talk?
Martha:	Okay. (She slides her hands out from under herself and offers them to the therapist without making eye contact. She is a little bit less tense.)
Therapist:	Martha, tell me what you can about being 8 years old.
Martha:	(A wave of panic passes through her and her eyes begin to dart around the room as if she is seeing images projected onto the walls.) It's happening.
Therapist:	What's happening, Martha? Is your father here?
Martha:	(with terror) YES! He's coming to get me. He's going to touch me. He's going to make me put it in my mouth (gag response).
Therapist:	I'm right here with you. It's okay to keep talking. I'll lead you all the way through this. Go ahead.
Martha:	I can't breathe. I'm going to die. Oh God, it's all over my face. I hate it. (As she is describing this, she rocks back and forth, squeezing the therapist's hands.)

Therapist: Is he gone now?
Martha: Yes. I feel sick.
Therapist: Do you need to vomit?
Martha: No, it's passing now.
Therapist: I know that it's horrible to remember these things. I feel honored that you let me be with you while you relived that moment. How do you feel right now and where are you?
Martha: I think I feel relieved that I finally told someone. It's all so disgusting. I guess I'm coming back now.
Therapist: Take whatever time you need to journey back to this moment. I will hold your hands and be right here waiting for you.
Martha: (As she reenters the present reality, she looks at the therapist) Do you think I'm terrible?
Therapist: Oh no! I think you were and are very brave. You did the best you could possibly do to survive such terrible experiences. I'm sad that you had to suffer so much.

By constantly repeating Martha's name and by holding her hands the therapist kept the connection with present reality and to the therapeutically safe relationship. This allowed Martha to go further into the affective realm than ever before. Usually she would retreat into a kind of catatonia and remain there until it was safe to return. It was useful for the therapist to engage Martha at the earlier age level while remaining in touch with the adult. This kept Martha grounded while giving her permission to dissociate.

The therapist became the "enlightened witness" (Miller 1990b) to validate the client's reality. These episodes can happen repeatedly and provide moments of catharsis for the client. Once the therapist and the client establish an effective mechanism for staying in touch during these times, the dissociation can allow the client to release what has been stored for so long.

Using dissociation rather than squelching it will become an ongoing aspect of incest treatment. It is important for the therapist to be prepared to work effectively and respectfully with this defense. (For an extensive, detailed, and systematic Ericksonian approach to dissociation in incest work, see Dolan 1991.)

CREATIVE INTERVENTIONS

In order to accomplish the goals of incest recovery, the therapist and the client need to be as creative and expansive as possible. Talking goes a very long way in repairing the damage but it is not enough. The therapist needs to allow the client to *experience* new feelings and understandings. Much of this can be done within the safety and confines of the well-defined therapeutic relationship. What follows is an extensive description of various unusual interventions that offer powerful healing for incest clients. It is not meant to be a finite list but rather a sampling of different approaches. Some therapists will be very uncomfortable with some of these ideas and therefore should exercise caution when trying to duplicate these methods. For others, this will allow some creative license in this work. Either way, there are specific ethical guidelines to consider before trying unfamiliar interventions.

On many occasions a therapist who is treating an incest survivor will happen upon unusual treatment ideas. For instance, it may occur to the therapist that the child-client could benefit a great deal from having a story read to her at bedtime. It might not be particularly radical to suggest that the client's partner read to her at night, but it would be quite another matter if the therapist thought it would be very powerful to read the story into an audiotape for the client. This raises questions about boundaries and appropriateness; yet the idea keeps surfacing for the therapist. Something instinctive nags at her or him that this would be useful. If the therapist has not had much experience in these kinds of interventions, it would be helpful to receive some supervision before proceeding. A skilled supervisor can separate treatment potential from overinvolvement. Creating a powerful yet unusual experience for a client must be centered around the client's needs only and must exist within the limits of the client–therapist relationship. If an experienced supervisor does not feel the intervention is appropriate then the notion must be dropped. There is a gray area when assessing the potential value of out-of-the-ordinary methods, but good common sense, solid clinical expertise, and a well-boundaried therapist can minimize the possibility of inappropriate interventions.

In order for the therapist to become receptive to creative ideas for healing, he or she must open all the senses. The therapist must hear the specific language and words the client chooses. The therapist must be observant about the client's body language and facial expressions. The therapist must learn to sense when the client "goes away" and find out where that place is. What is *not* visible or known is as important as what *is* obvious in the client's presentation. Being able to stay in touch with the child and the adult residing within the client is a very clever task for the therapist, one that can bear much fruit. Moving out of ordinary modes of perception can dramatically alter a therapeutic moment.

Therapeutically Rich Questions

The bulk of therapeutic skill lies in being able to ask just the right question in just the right manner at just the right time. The therapist guides the client towards greater openness setting the stage for a tremendous revelation. It is not uncommon in incest treatment for many well-placed questions to lead to dead ends. Memories are repressed. Protective layers bury feelings and clients truthfully respond, "I don't know" to therapeutic queries. One thing to remember is that for some clients, the abuse occurred preverbally or before sophisticated language and cognitive development. Their worlds were perceived visually, tactilely, and auditorily. It makes sense, then, to question these clients from those points of view. "What color is the room?" "How small are you?" "What do you smell?" These types of questions can jar old memories at the developmental level that they were stored. It is difficult for many of these clients to respond to "How did you feel when that happened?" because they shut off whatever they were emotionally or physically feeling at the moment of the abuse in order to cope. Eventually they may be able to retrieve those thoughts and feelings, but they will need to approach them in a remedial fashion.

Within every adult exists a small child that is loving, strong, and competent as well as vulnerable, frightened, and needy. Drawing out that child is essential work for an incest survivor but getting to her can be very tricky. Most survivors have buried and hidden that inner self and have no intention of ever sharing it with anyone. That self is a small child who was badly hurt and now exists where no one else can touch her. Even though a client may describe that "true self" as bad, stupid, ugly, or weak, the therapist knows that at the very core of this adult rests a beautiful and powerful child who is a pivotal resource for healing. But how can that child be revealed?

After sharing a particularly vivid memory of being raped by her father, Lynn turned to her therapist with saucer eyes and exclaimed, "He's going to get me. He can still hurt me. I'm still not safe from him." The therapist was aware that Lynn was not at that moment a 29-year-old woman but a small abused child. The therapist asked, "How old are you now?"

Lynn:	(in a child's voice) Ten. I'm 10 years old.
Therapist:	What room are you in?
Lynn:	My bedroom. My bedroom. It's always in my bedroom.
Therapist:	Has your father left?
Lynn:	Yeah. He got what he wanted. Now he'll leave me alone for the rest of the night.
Therapist:	Where are you in your room?
Lynn:	On the bed. Curled up in the corner.
Therapist:	What do you do now?
Lynn:	I don't cry. I don't cry. I'm tough. I can take care of myself. I go to the bathroom and wash myself. No one can know what happened. I don't look at myself when I clean myself off. I just take care of business.
Therapist:	What do you do now that you're back in your room and it's over.
Lynn:	I'm scared to go to sleep. I'm not really safe yet.
Therapist:	What will make you safe?
Lynn:	Me. Just me.
Therapist:	I don't understand.

Lynn:	I used to be okay. I used to be able to feel safe. But I don't now. He took that away.
Therapist:	What did he take away?
Lynn:	Me. ME! Don't you get it?
Therapist:	Do you remember You?
Lynn:	Yeah.
Therapist:	Can you describe You?
Lynn:	What do you mean?
Therapist:	Your father made your little girl go away but you still remember her. Can you introduce me to your little girl? What's her name?
Lynn:	Lynnee, of course!
Therapist:	And what is Lynnee wearing?
Lynn:	(smiles) Her red shirt. That's her favorite. She feels good in her red shirt.
Therapist:	Mmm. That sounds nice. What else is she wearing?
Lynn:	Play pants. You know, after school pants that she can get dirty.
Therapist:	Is she wearing sneakers?
Lynn:	How did you know? Yeah. She has her sneakers on.
Therapist:	What does her hair look like?
Lynn:	It's kind of long. In braids. It looks pretty.
Therapist:	Lynnee sounds like a lovely girl. What does she like to do?
Lynn:	Mostly she likes to play. She likes to play baseball 'cause she's really good at it. The boys even let her play with them 'cause she's so good. Most kids like her. She's fun to be with.
Therapist:	It sounds to me like Lynnee is still with you. That she's not gone at all. She's just hiding.
Lynn:	(smiles) You're pretty smart. I never told anyone that Lynnee is still with me. I make everyone believe I'm just big and tough. Lynnee's my secret. I have to keep her secret or else my dad will get her for sure.
Therapist:	I think it's wonderful that you've protected Lynnee so well all these years. She needed you to do that. But you know what? I think it might be safe for her to come out and play again.

This is an example of the kind of exploring that can occur on other levels of consciousness or from more regressed states. These are usually spontaneous moments when a client has used a particular set of words or sat in a particular position that can clue a therapist into another part of the client's world. Opening up these other doors creates infinite possibilities. Continuing Lynn's story, she was able to retrieve that playful and joyous child within during her depressed or scary moments. Eventually she integrated the child and adult and stopped referring to her smaller self in the third person. Likewise the therapist was able to call up the child when it seemed therapeutically wise. Lynn as child became an invaluable resource.

Another form of questioning that can remove blockages is the use of imagery. When a client is unable to answer such direct questions as "What does that make you feel/think/remember. . . ?" or "What do you do with those feelings?" a different angle may work better. "Where in your body is that feeling stored?" "Describe the image that you get when you think about your father/your anger/your body. . . ." "If you were to paint a picture of the very core of you, what would it look like?" "Show me how you think. When such-and-such happens, you think what? And your next thought is what?" "Where in your body is there a peaceful place? What do you need to do to get there?" "If that sensation were a sound or a kind of music, what would it sound like?" Using all five senses and visualizations can tap other forms of expression that may be more accessible to clients.

Relaxation and Meditation

Although few graduate schools specifically train therapists in methods of progressive relaxation, yoga meditation, and deep and focused breathing, these are all generally acceptable means toward wellness. It is difficult to imagine treating incest clients and never teaching any of these self-regulatory skills for the reduction of stress and anxiety. Not only do these clients need to learn some new skills for living, but the therapy will need to be paced so that the clients do not become overwhelmed. Without question, many therapy sessions will raise unbearable feelings for the client. Once revealed, the client will need to learn how to have some degree of control over the intensity and duration of the feelings. Relaxation techniques are extremely effective.

During a session when a client is experiencing oppressive fears and a desire to stay in control, a therapist can teach deep breathing. The client is instructed to lie down with her arms at her side, palms turned upward. Her legs should not be touching and any binding clothing should be loosened. Her head and shoulders should be flat against the floor or couch and her eyes should be shut. The therapist offers these instructions:

> I want you to simply follow the sound of my voice and do as I instruct you. You will be breathing deeply beginning with your diaphragm, moving up through your rib cage, filling your lungs and up through your nostrils. When you exhale you will force the air out of your mouth, feel your lungs and your diaphragm deflate. Place your hand on your diaphragm so I'm sure you know where we will start. Good. Now rest your hand at your side again. I'm going to slowly count to 6 for the inhale and 6 for the exhale. All you need to do is focus on the sound of my voice and the air moving through your body. Are you ready? Okay. Beginning with your diaphragm, inhale 2–3–4–5–6. And through your mouth, exhale 2–3–4–5–6. And again, 1–2–3–4–5–6 and exhale 2–3–4–5–6.

This continues for approximately five minutes and then the therapist can ask the client how she is feeling. If the client is more relaxed and feeling more control, then she has achieved the goal. If she is still tense and anxious, the therapist can inquire about the trouble spots. Any adjustments should be made and the process should be repeated until the client gets the hang of it. This is the basis for more extensive relaxation or meditative states.

If the client is receptive, the therapist can also teach progressive relaxation. Essentially this is a guided exercise incorporating deep breathing with the releasing of muscular tension throughout the body. Again, the client is instructed to follow the sound of the therapist's voice slowly urging the departure of all tension. Equally effective is combining the deep breathing with mantra repetition to bring about a state of deep meditation. It is valuable to ask the client for an appropriate mantra, whether it is a phrase or a word or a sound that would help create a peaceful association.

Incest clients are very worried about losing control in general and, in particular, emotionally. Teaching relaxation techniques is very useful for these clients because it offers regulation of intensity and self-sufficiency. These are all exercises the client can do alone whenever it becomes necessary. The end result is very powerful.

Imagery

Guided visualizations and the creation of metaphors have become standard methodologies in psychotherapy. They offer different languages for self-expression as well as symbolic representations of reality. These are especially meaningful vehicles for incest treatment (Gawain 1978, Groves 1987).

A therapist listening very closely will hear the client's own imagery. Particular words or metaphors are used repeatedly. Sometimes the vocabulary is borrowed from the client's profession or avocation. For instance, a client may speak of the incest as she would her garden. "It's like there is a beautiful vegetable patch that has been overrun with weeds. Hungry rabbits attacked the garden every night, leaving the food half-eaten and rotting on the vine." A garden can then be used continuously as a way to speak both of the damage as well as the healing. The treatment will weed the garden, put up fencing to keep out the animals, and the vegetables will fully ripen to be picked when the client so desires. Images that can be both haunting and triumphant are filled with rich symbolism that the client can mentally return to time and time again. It becomes an engrossing tale that begs the client to read on and find out how the heroine prevails.

It is helpful to discover the client's imagery for the very pit of her being or her little girl or her spirit or whatever else she may call her strong inner self. Most clients have carried images within themselves for years. They range from the mystical to the mythical to the heroic to the aesthetic to the mundane—Prince Valiant, Superwoman, Artemis, the Goddess, the Warrior, the Princess, Earth

Mother, a Lioness, the Sea. Encouraging a client to speak from that personification lends her power and the opportunity to enlarge that part of herself. The therapist's unconditional acceptance of this image validates the client's sense of inner strength. At difficult therapeutic moments the therapist can inquire "How would the Princess respond to this situation?" thus appealing to the client's own wisdom and inner resources.

Combined with deep relaxation techniques, imagery provides healing serenity. While guiding the client through a breathing exercise, the therapist can interrupt to ask what image arises on the inhale and exhale. If none occurs for the client the therapist may suggest one.

> Suffering an acute anxiety attack during a session, Sarah requested that the therapist help her calm down. Instruction was given in deep breathing and Sarah began to relax but was still agitated. When asked where the problem was, Sarah said she felt her middle tighten up on the exhale. It felt scary. The therapist asked her if there was a visual image that accompanied the feeling. No. "Is there any recurring picture in your mind that brings you a peaceful feeling?" Sarah proceeded to describe her deep affection for lavender lilacs and how she could create time-lapsed photography in her mind's eye. At first she would see the closed lilac buds and then imagine them opening up as in a fast film. This provided the therapist with the perfect image! She instructed Sarah to return to the deep breathing, adding to it a visualization of that lilac cluster opening up on the inhale and taking a still photo on the exhale—just like a camera. This seemed to work well so the therapist added the smell of lilac to the image. With several deep breaths Sarah had achieved a controlled and relaxed state, using the smell and sight of the lilacs. This was something she was able to return to whenever she needed it. The pairing of the visual image of the lilac and the deep breathing was a potent combination.

Reparative Visualization—Mariah

Reparative visualization is a highly specialized technique that does not work for all clients or all therapists. When it can be used successfully, the client has a remarkable, almost magical, healing experience.

> Mariah was an exceptionally resourceful and innovative client (see Preface and Chapter 1) who was able to recount her childhood experiences as if she were actually transported in time and space. The ego boundaries would fall away and she *was* the child being abused. As she told what was happening to her she became terrified.

Therapist: Where is your father now?
Mariah: He's coming up the stairs. I can hear the light switch click on. I can hear his footsteps on the stairs. I can see the light in the hallway. I can't get away. There's no use. Everyone else is sleeping. There's no one to help me.

(She is hunched over in the corner of the couch holding herself.)

Therapist: What is happening now?

Mariah: He's standing over my bed. He's unbuttoning his shirt. Oh, God. No! No! I don't want this to happen.

Therapist: Tell him you want him to go away. Tell him to leave you alone.

Mariah: I can't.

Therapist: Just try it.

Mariah: (in a small voice) Don't Daddy. Please don't. He doesn't hear me. He's still getting undressed. Stop him! Someone stop him.

Therapist: (realizing that Mariah needs a safe adult to intervene) I'll stop him. I'm right here and I won't let him hurt you. I'll protect you. (to the father in a loud voice) Get out of here! Leave Mariah alone! I won't let you touch her or hurt her. Get out of this room right now!

Mariah: He's mad at you. He's going to get you too. He's not leaving.

Therapist: (to father) I said get out of here and I meant it. You won't be hurting Mariah and you won't be hurting me. If you don't leave this second I will call the police.

Mariah: He left! You did it. No one ever did that for me before. No one ever came to get him out of my room . . . (sobbing)

Not many clients can relive those moments as sharply as Mariah and yet this illustrates a unique and spontaneous therapeutic intervention. By inserting herself in the remembrance, the therapist offered Mariah the protection she never received in her childhood. This created a curative image. Mariah realized that she was too small to have successfully warded off her father by herself, thus ending her sense of responsibility for the incest. She also got in touch with her deep sense of betrayal by her mother who never gave her what an unafraid, sober, and protective adult should have given. Rather than stating to the therapist, "I wish you had been my mother," Mariah remarked, "I really wish that you *had* been there to protect me." "So do I," replied the therapist.

Writing

Journal writing is recommended by many therapists these days to facilitate the therapeutic process. This enables the client to stay focused on expressing and expelling all the thoughts and feelings that whirl around inside. Bass and Davis (1988) have outlined a detailed writing program for incest survivors. It is the best guide available. Their premise is to encourage clients to write about their experiences of childhood and healing as a path toward recovery. Innumerable clients have been helped by their suggestions. Within individual therapy it is the client's choice as to whether or not any writings will be shared with the therapist. It can never be made an expectation by the therapist. It is important for the client to feel that her journal is private and can remain so; otherwise she will fear a familiar sense of intrusion.

Letter writing is a dynamic tool for the client. To be able to say, without interruption, everything she has ever wanted to say to certain individuals is very freeing. The majority of these letters are never sent but the impact remains the same. Some letters will be carefully crafted and eventually sent. The therapist must help the client anticipate the probable responses (or nonresponses) so that she is not left defenseless.

The creation of a fairy tale by the client and/or the therapist weaves a rich tapestry. Characters emerge, challenges arise, victories follow defeats, and the heroine continues on her quest. Not only is the imagery insightful but this particular kind of writing allows the client to write her own triumphant ending. The therapist can write a tale when a client seems unusually stuck. The story can lead the client down a different trail away from the thorny path. If the therapist knows what kind of literature or period in history the client is attracted to, then the story can speak in that voice. Fairy tales and myths are so archetypal that the symbolism the client selects can be very revealing.

There are certain moments during the course of treatment when it could be healing for the therapist to write something to the client. As the therapist is preparing for a vacation, the client is getting anxious. A short note promising to return is tangible reassurance to the client that she need not worry. And if she does get panicky while the therapist is away, she can pull out her note and reread it and feel comforted. If the client is planning a trip out of town to see her family, the therapist can write a note of encouragement to be packed in her suitcase. If there has been an extended period of turbulence in the client's life, the therapist can write a note acknowledging how hard things have been, but how much faith she or he has in the client to pull through it all. These brief written words are concrete reminders to the client that the therapist is there for her in spirit even when they are apart.

Personalized Audio Tapes

The sound of the therapist's voice can be hypnotically soothing and supportive for the incest client. It is the coupling of the phrases of encouragement and the caring tone of voice that provides such a unique experience. The client is more accustomed to harsh and critical judgments from those around her or from herself so the therapeutic rapport is very uplifting and new. Audio tapes are a clever way of infusing the client's world with calming positive messages (Wallas 1985).

The therapist has wide latitude when creating a tape for any particular client. If the client is prone to anxiety attacks, the tape can be a guided progressive relaxation. If the client has trouble giving herself kind messages, the therapist can talk positively to the client affirming her strong inner self. If the client is reluctant to be playful and takes life too seriously, the tape can be filled with silly poems, songs, and stories. The goal of these tapes is to provide the client with an individualized program for growth and healing. The tape must be specific to the client's needs and used during particularly rough moments. Three elements make these tapes especially powerful: the sound of the therapist's voice, soothing or uplifting music, and affirming instructions to the client.

Audio tapes that can be bought in a store may be useful for an incest client, but hearing the therapist's own voice guiding the client is infinitely more personal and powerful. To hear the caring, nurturing, and reassuring tone in the therapist's voice helps a client know that the therapist truly believes her recovery is possible. Most incest clients need to hear the same messages or insights frequently repeated. Being able to hear it right from the horse's mouth over and over again whenever needed is very comforting for the client. Besides, it means a great deal to the client that the therapist would take the time to create such a gift.

Music can be very transporting. It can turn bad moods into good moods and tense moments into mellow ones. Selecting appropriate music for these tapes combines a bit of guess work and a bit of instinct. Much of the New Age music is intended to calm rattled nerves and some of it is quite effective. It is useful to spend time previewing various artists and experiencing the music's impact before making any purchases. Some music is too atonal to feel soothing. Certain soloists are lush and satisfying. Classical and certain jazz selections can also provide just the right feeling for these tapes. Many clients report that Women's Music is very empowering for them. Regardless of the musical category, the selection should convey through music what the therapist is trying to say in words. The talking combined with the music creates a complete association for the client.

Affirmations, hopefulness, encouragement, and supportiveness need to be addressed in the spoken sections of the tape. These can be selections from literature or poetry, guided visualizations, story telling, or the repetition of crucial therapeutic insights. It is very helpful for the client to hear in many different ways on many different occasions the same consistent message. She spent a good portion of her life being brainwashed about how undeserving and unlovable she was. This kind of tape can reprogram her thinking towards the positive end of the spectrum.

One unusually creative idea for these audio tapes is to make something for the small child who did not receive ordinary kinds of care. Many incest survivors don't remember being tucked safely into bed at night or having a bedtime story read or a lullaby sung. A therapist can record a tape filled with these kinds of activities. He or she can read children's storybooks or fairy tales and record a lullaby or two. The most powerful result is making the nighttime safe again.

There are so many creative ideas if the therapist considers the use of personalized audio tapes. Asking clients what they would ideally love to hear on a tape can inform the therapist's choices. It is extremely potent for a client to receive such a gift of ongoing support from the therapist. This way the client can have the therapist available whenever she needs without feeling compelled to phone during every difficult moment between sessions.

Other Forms of Creative Expression

Although psychotherapy is primarily focused on the verbal expression of self, other creative forms can be especially fruitful. Art, music, dance, writing, and drama all provide expansive possibilities. This can be particularly poignant for the incest survivor. Many abused children were verbally silenced, thus leaving them to develop with some articulation problems. They have come to feel intimidated by language, yet filled with much that needs expressing. Therapists can encourage other forms of expression for these clients during or outside the therapy sessions. Without acquiring other credentials in music, art, or movement therapy, a creative therapist can open up new avenues for the client. Some possibilities include voice lessons, art classes, music composition, poetry writing, sculpting, acting or role-playing, and dancing. These kinds of activities can encourage the client to discover a more accessible means of communication. The products of these endeavors are quite dramatic, powerful, and healing.

Children's Play

Many incest survivors have either forgotten how or were rarely allowed to play as children. Even such simple things as coloring books are not remembered. One goal in the healing process is to become carefree and playful, but this is often something that must be taught to these clients. The popular T-shirts that claim "It's Never Too Late to Have a Happy Childhood" are correct. Incest clients need to be urged to play *like* a child and to play *with* a child.

Therapists who treat many incest survivors need to fill their storage closets with soap bubbles, bubble gum, coloring books, large boxes of crayons, comic books, and balls and jacks. As a client shows embarrassment about walking into a store to buy any of these items, the therapist can produce a present for her to take home. It can be a very curious, yet delightful, moment. As the client gets more comfortable with the notion of being more childlike, the therapist can recommend trips to the toy store, children's bookstores, and a playground. These are activities the client can do alone or with friends but the focus needs to be on the client's playfulness and pleasure.

If a client does not have children of her own, at some point it is important for her to spend time with children of various ages. Not only does she need to be reminded of how small and dependent children really are, but she also needs to enter their world of play. Trips to the zoo, the circus, or the playground are wondrous experiences for children. A client needs to plan several of these outings in hopes of reawakening that child within herself. In addition, offering protection and nurturance to children can help a client give that which she never received. There is a soothing, yet sad feeling, that comes over the incest survivor who tucks a child into bed at night and gives a kiss on the forehead. But these are important opportunities.

Although this does not relate specifically to children's play, some clients have expressed their need to give to other children in some unusual ways what they never got. Some incest survivors donate their money, time, or professional expertise to children's causes such as the Children's Defense Fund or Shelter Associations. They feel they are optimizing other children's chance for a happier childhood.

Rage Work

The emergence of rage is inevitable in incest treatment. Rage is the long-suppressed response to the abuse. In the course of therapy it will become safe to finally unload these feelings. How that is conducted is something each therapist must consider before ever arriving at that point. A great deal can be accomplished through talking directly to the therapist or through more Gestalt methods of double- or empty-chairing, when a client verbalizes thoughts and feelings in a dialogue with an inanimate object that symbolizes an aspect of self or the perpetrator. This may be quite adequate for many clients. But for others it may not be enough either because the anger is so frighteningly repressed or because it is so overwhelmingly powerful. The therapist is quite certain of the necessity of the expulsion of the rage, yet may need to resort to more unusual methods for urging it to the surface.

There are several strict guidelines to follow whenever coaxing the client to allow her rage to explode. The therapist must always ensure the physical and emotional safety of the client, taking the process very slowly, offering a longer session, never doing anything without the client's consent, never proceeding without feeling fully in control of the situation, and never prodding anger before teaching relaxation or self-regulatory techniques. In order for the client to feel safe enough to proceed, there must always be a counterbalance. If the client is agitated, the therapist must be calm. If the client wants to race through her feelings, the therapist must apply the brakes. If the client feels out of control, the therapist must be unwavering. If there is an eruption of rage, it must be followed by peacefulness. If the therapist does not feel confident in offering these safeguards, then talking must suffice.

Incest clients know all too well the destructive nature of anger. They are terrified of turning into their abusers and attempt to hold all their anger inside. This, of course, backfires at some point and needs to be turned into a healthier expression of these feelings. A client will need to learn a great deal about appropriate ways to release anger and the therapist will need to do much of that teaching. It is important for the client to be assured that no matter how her rage explodes that the therapist will see to it that nobody is hurt in any way. She will inquire as to the therapist's methods for handling those moments and the therapist needs to be ready with an answer.

Once the anger starts to flow the client feels an urgency to get it over as quickly as possible. If this happens too quickly, the client becomes hopelessly overwhelmed to the point of dysfunction. This will only validate her worst fantasy. Residual rage from incest does not come up only once and then is finished. It comes in waves repeatedly over a long period of time until it is sufficiently purged. This understanding helps the client to know that each moment of rage will be just one spurt of many. It cannot or should not go any faster. The therapist can offer reassurance that she or he will move to shut it down if the client seems too overwhelmed. This kind of control is a great relief to the client.

A client will often announce that she has been feeling a build-up of angry feelings that she needs to release. The therapist can then arrange for a marathon session with the client. These are appointments when the office building is relatively empty, when there are no other clients scheduled, and when there are no specific time constraints. These conditions give greater allowance to the client to explore her feelings fully without the sensation that she will have to close everything down before the next client appears.

Absolutely everything that occurs within these sessions must have the full consent of the client. If the therapist thinks that pounding pillows would be useful, the client must give permission. If the therapist feels that playing the role of the abuser would be helpful, the client must agree. The client must have full control over the choice of methods while the therapist must have full control over the process. If the client becomes totally immersed in smacking a tennis racquet against a cushion to the point of beginning to swing the racquet at other objects around the room, the therapist must firmly intervene. If the client makes a move to harm herself, the therapist must be able to prevent that. These divisions of responsibility for control need to be stated explicitly before the session begins.

It would be irresponsible and very poor judgment to encourage incest clients to express their rage before teaching them how to bring themselves under control. As already mentioned, relaxation exercises that the client can perform for herself allow her to regulate emotional intensity. It may be important in the course of one of these "anger sessions" for the therapist to guide the client toward deep breathing and relaxation, but the client will also need to be able to do this alone when she remembers the session later. It is not recommended to uncover a client's rage before she is quite comfortable with self-regulatory exercises.

Once these guidelines are established the client and therapist can join together to create a safe experience for the client. These sessions generally begin with the client sharing her recurring angry thoughts. Under these protective circumstances the therapist can encourage her to go deeper into her memories and feelings. At some point in this process the client will exhibit greater agitation. This can be in the form of screaming or yelling, making a fist, pacing, jumping out of her seat, or body contortions. If comfortable with this idea, the therapist can use any of these body clues to give the client permission to scream louder or pound cushions or stamp feet or move about the room. The physical release is very powerful and the therapist must be braced to keep things safe. The most intense explosion will not last for much more than 10–20 minutes. Afterwards, the client is usually very drained emotionally and physically. A period of time to debrief the client is useful. This allows her to ask any questions she may have about her experience or memories and to integrate some insights. A serenity often overcomes the client that can last for several weeks. It is easy to understand how empowering and freeing these marathon sessions can be.

Once Bea had revealed many of her incest experiences to her therapist, her numbing began to relax; over several weeks' time she experienced a build-up of anger towards her stepfather although she was very reluctant to express it. The therapist suggested an extended session and Bea agreed to give it a try.

Bea:	I don't know if this is going to work.
Therapist:	What concerns do you have?
Bea:	I'll lose control. I never lose control. It would only get me in trouble.
Therapist:	What would happen if you were to lose control right now?
Bea:	I'd get so angry I wouldn't be able to stop. I'd turn into him.
Therapist:	I know your stepfather could fly into a rage but this is different in that your feelings are focused but will not harm anyone. All we're going to attempt is a safe release of what is pent up inside.
Bea:	What if I go wild—really lose it?
Therapist:	I will do all I can to contain things to a manageable level.
Bea:	So what am I supposed to do?
Therapist:	Why don't you just share your current angry thoughts with me?
Bea:	I just keep getting these recurring flashes. I see my stepfather waving my mother out the door on her bowling night. I used to be so scared. I'd beg my mother not to go. I'd tell her I was sick and needed her. She just ignored me. Then the panic would really set in because I knew what was next. He would have already had a few beers and no matter how hard I tried to hide from him, it was no use.

Therapist:	In those images, can you recall how small you were?
Bea:	That's exactly what's been occurring to me lately! How small I was! The size of my niece. She's 6 years old.

(As she is getting in touch with this, Bea folds her legs under and curls up tightly—becoming small.)

Therapist: Stay with that image of yourself. Now picture your stepfather standing near you but not touching you.

Bea: NO! NO!

Therapist: Keep screaming the words out loud that you used to hear inside your head.

Bea: GET AWAY FROM ME! GO AWAY! LEAVE ME ALONE!

(Bea begins to shake and her fists clench.)

Therapist: Keep going. Say more.

Bea: I HATE YOU! YOU DISGUST ME! YOU HURT ME! I HATE YOU! I HATE YOU!

(The therapist places a plush cushion next to Bea.)

Therapist: There is a pillow next to you, Bea. Try pounding your fists on it while you continue yelling.

(Bea hesitates, rocking herself, trying to stay in control.)

It's okay to release these feelings. I will be here if you need me.

Bea: I hate him so much for what he did to me!

(She reaches for the pillow and places her fists on top. Slowly, at first, and then gaining force, Bea pounds her fists into the pillow.)

NO! NO! YOU BASTARD! YOU ASSHOLE! I WISH YOU WERE DEAD!

(This continues for about 3–5 minutes. Bea stops and then sobs.)

Therapist: Yes, there are tears, too. Rage and sadness have been stored inside you. It is healthy to release this.

Bea: (after awhile) I've never let myself do anything like this before.

Therapist: How does it feel?

Bea: Better. I get to feeling so tight I can hardly breathe. It's weird but I feel sort of relaxed now.

Therapist: That's what can happen when you stop applying force to contain intense emotions. There will be other times when you will feel that build-up. Hopefully, now you understand that you can let go without getting out of control or hurt.

Some clients will not want to reveal the intensity of their rage in front of anyone, not even the therapist. It is the therapist's responsibility to suggest safe outlets for the client. Several suggestions can be offered in hopes that the client will discover some method that works for her. All options should be physical in nature yet physically harmless. Common techniques include angry letter-writing, pounding pillows or beds with fists or racquets, the use of punching bags and racquet sports, yelling, crying, art work, dancing, and swinging bats.

The major rule of thumb in providing more creative forms for the client's expression of rage is safety first. The therapist needs to exhibit a great deal of control and tolerance when dealing with intense emotions. These clients will sense in a minute if the therapist is uneasy or overwhelmed. It is far more productive for the therapist to honestly describe her or his level of comfort with the expression of strong feelings and allow things to develop from there.

Replacements

As described in previous chapters, incest survivors have a highly developed code of behavior. There are many ritualistic habits the client has come to use to protect or take care of herself. These behaviors include self-destructive tendencies, deprivation habits, and affective control. Put altogether these actions form the client's sense of security in her world. To dismantle these habits too quickly leaves the client undefended and truly helpless. Another approach to draw the client away from these unhealthy routines is to slowly *replace* one habit with another.

Every night Jane curled into a tense fetal position in one corner of her bed to protect herself from painful intrusion. Eventually she was able to fall asleep but there were many nightmarish interruptions. On her therapist's recommendation, Jane bought herself a very soft and very cuddly teddy bear. At bedtime she wrapped herself around this most harmless of companions and over a period of time was able to physically relax as she fell asleep. Sometime later the nightmares stopped.

Whenever the anger inside of her built up to a dangerous point, Estelle would bang her head against the wall. She explained to her therapist that this released the anger and made her focus on the fact that her head hurt, thus distracting her from her heartache. The therapist suggested that Estelle put four pillows against the wall before she felt the urge to hit her head the next time. Estelle complied and reported that she had still appreciated the physical release of the motion but did not suffer any pain. After three more head-banging episodes Estelle told her therapist she was ready to talk about her anger.

Cassandra suffered prolonged bouts of depression. Quite by accident she shared with her therapist that she always had music playing in her home. Asked to describe her favorite kind of music, Cassandra replied, "The more woeful the aria, the more compelling." Together they explored what other types of music Cassandra enjoyed and the therapist suggested she listen exclusively to her collection of old Motown hits. After one week Cassandra felt the depression lifting. After two weeks she was actually feeling well. On the third week she went back to her opera records and began to feel low again. Cassandra became very astute about how music could alter her mood and became very conscious of her selections.

As a way to deflect any strong negative feelings towards others, Tara used a special piece of jagged glass to cut into her thigh until she drew blood. She claimed this made her feel better since she no longer felt angry at the other person and, besides, she couldn't feel any physical pain anyway. She hadn't experienced physical pain in years. Of course, her therapist was alarmed at this destructive behavior but knew that Tara would not part with her glass. While shopping one day, the therapist's eye caught several baskets full of polished stones and crystals. They were shiny and smooth and she immediately thought of Tara. She studied the stones carefully and finally selected a perfectly smooth green one. At their next session the therapist handed the stone to Tara saying, "I know that you are filled with lots of intense feelings these days and they are hard for you to control. I know that makes you want to take out your piece of glass and cut yourself. I am really hoping that you won't do that. But I was thinking that if you found yourself reaching for your glass, you might pick up this stone instead. It is all smooth with no sharp edges to hurt you. This way you could still have something shiny and glassy that you can hold in your hand and even press against your thigh without hurting yourself." Tara deeply understood the therapist's actions and appreciated the respect she received. Tara only cut into herself once more. Eventually she threw away the piece of glass and kept her green stone in a special place.

These clients have developed habits that enable them to control their responses to horrendous circumstances. The therapy raises the memories and feelings surrounding those episodes. It stands to reason, then, that they would employ old, familiar strategies. The problem, however, is that these behaviors are harmful and dysfunctional. The notion of creative replacement allows these clients to sustain a containment habit while transforming the behavior into something pleasant and nurturing. These are creative treatment opportunities for the therapist and delightfully healing moments for the client.

Rituals

So many life milestones were uncelebrated or spoiled for incest survivors—missed birthdays, horrendous Christmas Eves, ignored graduations. Although many incest survivors make a big deal out of their loved ones' special occasions, they have come to abhor or fear any fuss being made over them. Holidays or rituals are filled with trauma. During the latter phases in treatment, the therapist will suggest the creation of new rituals in the client's life. These ceremonies include undoing past damage, celebrating what was previously uncelebrated, and symbolically rejoicing in growth. The client and the therapist can work together to create many transforming occasions (Imber-Black et al. 1988).

There is hardly an incest survivor who does not have a negative association to a particular holiday, time of year, life event, or family gathering. During the course of therapy she will usually share some of these painful memories. At that point the therapist can plant the seed for some future ceremony. "You might want to think about how you would ideally like to spend your next birthday. Maybe this will be the year when you can finally celebrate it." Although the client may initially resist the idea, she will undoubtedly entertain the thought. When she is ready, she will usually ask, "What exactly did you mean when you said I should think about how I'd like to celebrate my birthday?" From that point the two can discuss all the client's fantasies and devise a plan to make it a reality. Unacknowledged awards, milestones, and events can be celebrated as well. It's never too late to have a party (decorated cake and all) to mark a client's high school graduation or placement on the honor roll or appointment as first clarinet. The new ritual breaks the spell of the old one.

Instead of ignored or damaged occasions, new rituals can be created to symbolize the client's healing and growth. These ceremonies need attention to detail to optimize their curative powers. A client's spiritual or philosophical belief system usually underlies any plan. As she nears the end of her therapy, a client may desire a funeral for her lost childhood. The therapist can guide her to consider what actions, words, symbols, people, and setting would feel powerful. The very process of creating the ritual can also serve to bring closure to the therapy. Many clients have chosen to bury the past ritualistically while planting something living for the future. These ceremonies often include significant people to witness the client's emergence. Both the process and the completion of these symbolic rituals provide the client with an inspiring experience.

Touch

Touching clients is a loaded issue that raises many ethical concerns. In general most accepted forms of psychotherapy strongly discourage therapists from ever touching their clients, deeming it never appropriate. At the other end of the spectrum are therapies completely based on hugs and constant demonstrations of physical affection that claim there can be no healing without touch. Touch is a very volatile issue for all incest survivors and it is one that will be discussed throughout treatment. So the question arises if it can ever be appropriate or curative for a therapist to touch an incest client? The answer is Yes with many stipulations.

An incest survivor experiences all forms of touch as sexual or unsafe. This suggests that it would never be prudent for a therapist to even slightly touch a client on her way out the door, until there has been an enormous amount of trust established. It also suggests that the client will have much to learn about safe touch, safe people, the difference between sexual touch and nurturant touch, how to have control over who touches her, and what pleasures touch can bring. For the most part the therapist will be talking about all these issues rather than offering demonstrations. There are some moments during the course of treatment, however, where a safe experience with the therapist can be exceptionally healing for the client. For instance, a client may be reimmersed in a very painful memory and telling the therapist how badly she had wished someone could have been there for her. The therapist can extend a hand and offer to be here now during this moment of retelling. While holding the therapist's hand the client may be able to move all the way through the traumatic thought. Or a client may be sobbing about the death of her grandmother who was the only safe adult in her childhood. She may be remembering how she did not allow herself to cry at the funeral. As the client is crying now, the therapist can gently dab at the streaming tears with a tissue, thus validating the client's right to her tears. At other times a client may specifically ask the therapist for a hug. If both the therapist and the client understand the meaning of the hug, and the therapist is comfortable with the idea, then a hug can increase the sense of safety the client feels. These are the poignant human moments in the therapy where the therapist can become a caring adult responding as if the person was not a client. Within the context of a well-boundaried and trusting relationship the client will experience these occasions as very special and warm.

There are some general guidelines to observe when considering any physical contact with an incest survivor. Most importantly, touch should be used sparingly and only with the client's permission. The therapist should only offer touch that is caring or nurturing, much as one would behave with a child. The gestures should be simple and generally brief as in a gentle hug or a pat on the shoulder or the grasp of a hand. The contact should be verbally initiated by the client. "It would help me feel safer if you could hold me for a moment." Unless the client is in a deeply regressed state and the therapist feels that touch would be appropriate, the therapist should not be the one to initiate contact. Even in that regressed state, the therapist must ask for permission to touch the client. There will be moments after a particularly moving session when a therapist will want to hug the client as she leaves the office. This is more for the therapist's sake than the client's and should not be offered. Any physical contact must be requested by the client, comfortable for the therapist, and discussed to clarify intent and meaning. Touching should be infrequent in order to maintain appropriate boundaries. When used too often, the roles become too blurred. As most incest clients will not make continuous requests for physical contact, this might never become a concern. If the therapist is uneasy with any physical gestures, she or he must express this to the client and eliminate it as a therapeutic possibility.

The huge majority of long-term psychotherapies for incest survivors will be conducted through ongoing verbal interactions using everyday language. This will be productive and curative. By drawing on other creative resources inside and outside of the therapy room, the healing process can become rich and varied. For therapists who are comfortable exploring other senses, languages, and actions, the unusual intervention can create a powerfully new and rewarding experience for the client. It is a unique opportunity for a client to actually have a transforming experience within the safety of the therapeutic relationship.

GROUP TREATMENT

No discussion about incest treatment is complete without examining the potential usefulness of group therapy. With the rapid increase in self-help and twelve-step groups for nearly every malady, incest recovery groups are cropping up everywhere. These groups range from leaderless self-help programs, to educational presentations, to support groups, to long-term in-depth treatment. A group can offer a client a very different kind of experience than individual therapy. Whether that is a positive or negative force all depends on the nature and quality of the group. Overall, groups need to be approached as *adjunctive treatment* rather than the primary treatment of choice. (For another view see Sgroi and Bunk 1988.) As has been made clear previously, the one-to-one client–therapist relationship is the essential vehicle for healing from incest. This intense connection cannot be developed within the context of group therapy. This is not to say that groups have no place in incest treatment.

Short-term focused incest recovery groups offer two benefits to the client: breaking through the isolation and learning new information about incest and its victims. Being able to tell her story and listening to others without the skies opening up or the earth crumbling below is a powerful opportunity for the client. Saying the words out loud and finding that she is not the only one who experienced such traumas helps the client feel less isolated and more connected to the rest of the world. It is one thing to tell one therapist about the incest privately and quite another to tell a dozen people who nod knowingly, which is energizing and empowering.

Most short-term groups are facilitated by a mental health professional whose role is to provide a structure for the participants to tell their stories safely and to educate them about the phenomenon of incest. Brief talks are given about why some adults sexually abuse children, what the consequences are for the child, who is actually responsible for the abuse, why adult survivors continue to feel a sense of helplessness and doom, what the dysfunctional family patterns look like, and what it takes to fully recover from the trauma. Most group leaders will make it very clear that individual therapy can be most useful in repairing the damage. For many survivors, these talks are the first information they've ever heard about sexual abuse. It can be very enlightening and even overwhelming. Many people attend several meetings of the group and then need to leave in order to digest this new point of view. In time, most of these same people will take another step toward their recovery.

These focused groups provide an extremely important educational function for adult incest survivors who are just beginning to uncover their pasts. They may not be ready to launch into intensive psychotherapy but they are preparing themselves to start a healing process. Finding out that there are so many other survivors and being able to identify as both victim and survivor of incest is a bold first step. It would be very short-sighted, however, to see these groups as therapy of any kind. The purpose is essentially educational and exploratory.

Longer-term psychotherapy groups dealing with incest issues are a complicated matter. The stated goal of these groups is to provide an opportunity and an atmosphere for full recovery from the childhood traumas. Can this truly occur in a group context? Is this an optimal experience for a client? Are intensive group settings too charged for an incest survivor? Can a skilled group leader adequately monitor all the complicated dynamics among the members? A more detailed examination of these issues is necessary.

Therapy groups can provide some valuable lessons for incest survivors. As in the focused groups, clients can come out of their isolation and secrecy by sharing their stories with each other. Because there is more time in a long-term group, clients can go into much more detail about their reactions and feelings about the incest. Over time, each group member can become more comfortable speaking of their horrors and feel less split off from their pasts. A tone of safety and confidentiality is established to facilitate this openness. The support and empathy offered among group members is healing and empowering.

Beyond sharing stories, there are countless learning opportunities for group members. Incest survivors often need information they never received in childhood. This can range from life skills, to how relationships work, to problem-solving approaches, to explanations of emotions. The group leader contributes rational ideas on a steady basis helping the members to reshape their perceptions. Participants are often very surprised that others see the world in similarly distorted ways. These misconceptions can even provide moments of levity in the group sessions.

In any psychotherapy group, the interactions among members recreate familiar patterns from their pasts. This is certainly true in an incest group. Clients project their family members onto various individuals within the group and reenact positive and negative relational habits. With the guidance of a skilled group leader, the client has a chance to resolve old conflicts and learn new ways of relating. This can be risky and painful work but group encouragement can help it along (Courtois 1988). In a more creative light, group psychodrama techniques can energize this kind of work and make it more compelling and dynamic for the group.

Many clients have fears about becoming too dependent upon any one individual, as would occur within individual therapy. Group treatment offers a less intense connection to a therapist and more opportunities for peer relatedness. This is an appealing option for many. Authority figures are approached with great skepticism and trust may be more likely with other survivors. The therapist is perceived more as a guide than a primary healer.

The major benefits of an ongoing psychotherapy incest-recovery group are telling the story, learning new life and relationship skills, projectively working through unresolved relationships, and forming a less dependent relationship with a therapist. It is also important to examine the drawbacks of a group therapy experience, because these well-intentioned groups can often also become overwhelming for clients and therapists.

When there is one incest survivor in the room and she is sharing her painful memories, her sentences are punctuated with "It really wasn't that bad" and "I'm probably exaggerating." When there are several survivors in the room sharing their stories a ranking system emerges. "Well, at least it wasn't my father who abused me." "I wasn't penetrated so I shouldn't be complaining about anything." "I shouldn't even be here. What happened to you was incest. I was just fondled." After hearing or reading other accounts of incestuous experiences, many clients will minimize the damage they have incurred. It becomes very difficult to alter those perceptions in a roomful of other survivors. If one woman was repeatedly raped for thirteen years and another woman was molested only once as a child, the latter will feel guilty for "not getting over it." Although a therapist can repeat a thousand times that all childhood sexual abuse leaves scars no matter how infrequently or frequently it occurred, clients will have a hard time validating that statement. So, potentially, there can be greater denial and minimization when a group of women share their stories.

As had been already stated, incest survivors have trouble understanding one-to-one relationships. Multiply that by seven or eight and these clients experience overwhelming confusion. Add to that the projective identification that naturally occurs within groups and there is a huge tangled web. How is it possible for the therapist(s) and clients to sort all this out? How can boundaries be established in multiple relationships among people who do not understand how to form appropriate boundaries? In short, how can a group *not* recreate dysfunctional family patterns? The responsibility for this task certainly belongs to the therapist(s) but it may be an impossible feat. The therapist would need to move into a more pivotal/parental role as the leader to establish norms and order within the group. This would lead to sibling rivalries that may or may not get worked through. In the end, too much responsibility has been placed in the hands of the therapist for effective group treatment. At best, the group could be an environment to act out previously forbidden feelings. At worst, the clients can become entrenched in the same familiar roles and dynamics of their families. Because of this relationship complexity, only the most skilled and confident group therapists should even consider conducting incest treatment groups.

It is customary for group leaders to recommend concurrent individual therapy for the group members. This appears to be an ideal balance where a client can derive the benefits from both methods (Courtois 1988). But this, too, can backfire. Once the therapeutic relationship is well established with the individual therapist, the client desires more separate attention. This is not possible within the group. The client experiences the clarity of the one-on-one relationship and begins to feel more and more uncomfortable with the chaos in the group. With coaching and collaboration between the two therapists, the client can make repeated attempts at boundary setting in her relationships within the group. If the other clients are not responsive, however, the old abusive dynamic is revisited. She can be chastised and verbally assaulted by the other members, leaving her, once again, to doubt her rightness to say no. At some point the client will usually struggle with a decision to leave the group and concentrate on individual therapy. This is fraught with reminiscent feelings of guilt, disloyalty, and self-doubt. It is often a healthy sign when a client decides to remove herself from a chaotic or unproductive and painful group experience. In an unplanned way this can have a very therapeutic result—to be able to leave that which is unhealthy.

There is little question that the needed depth of repair from incest requires a one-to-one therapeutic experience. There are still many questions about the relative value of groups in this recovery process. Most clients report that supportive, educational, and focused groups are very useful in a limited way. Conversely, a great many clients who are also exploring individual treatment report that therapy groups are confusing, upsetting, and minimally productive in the healing process. This seems to imply that incest survivors need a highly specialized kind of group psychotherapy. The current state of the art of group-work does not adequately address the complex needs of this client population. Until such time when an innovative strategy appears on the scene, group treatment can only be viewed as adjunctive to primary individual therapy.

5

Dealing with the Family Today

Most adult incest survivors are still in contact with their families. Their roles in their families are so integrated into their beings that the thought of disentangling from the morass is simply a passing fantasy. As the client heals from her incestuous experiences, developing a new sense of herself and her family dynamics, issues surrounding her present-day relationships to her family come into focus. The basic dilemma she faces is whether she can maintain a position of strength and health in the face of continued family dysfunction. To better understand this quandary, an overview of incestuous family dynamics will be useful.

Calof (1987) offers an extensive list of problems that are most prevalent in incestuous families. They can be loosely categorized into three areas of dysfunction: collective denial, parental and marital troubles, and aspects of a closed system. Through the pervasive use of denial, parents and children join together in distorting reality to present an "everything is fine" facade both privately and publicly. The presence of various forms of abuse within the family is hidden and denied. This is done to such an extreme that children are forced to mistrust their own perceptions of reality. Both parents bring many problems to the dynamics of incest. They are usually the product of inadequate or abusive parenting themselves and therefore function poorly, erratically, or abusively with their children. The parents are hypercritical of the children, assaulting them with messages that they are bad, unwanted, or stupid. The marriage is often highly dysfunctional emotionally and sexually, leaving an avenue open to triangulate the child into the marital dynamics. Abusive families are closed systems that are not apt to let members leave nor invite new resources into the environment. This leads to social isolation from peers and extended family, frequent moves, and an intolerance for differences or individuality. These families are often highly moralistic as well as void of appropriate displays of affection. Calof notes that the child-victim internalizes this family structure and suggests that the goal of treatment with the adult survivor is to externalize the family structure so that she can create a healthy and well-boundaried sense of self.

Denise Gelinas (1988) focuses her attention more acutely on relational disturbances within the incestuous family. She points out that the child-victim becomes parentified in order to take care of the "depleted and avoidant mother" and the "emotionally and sexually demanding father" (p. 28). Her studies have revealed that men who sexually abuse their daughters marry women who can tend to their unmet needs to be mothered. In turn, women who marry this type of man are usually abuse survivors themselves and therefore have been trained in the art of caretaking. By the time children (especially daughters) come along this woman is too drained to care for her husband *and* child. Her parenting becomes inconsistent and she avoids her husband's needs. Having his wife's attention directed elsewhere, the husband seeks caring from his daughter. The child learns early that her needs will not be met and that her role is to care for her parents and often her siblings.

This is the only reality this child knows. She grows into adulthood understanding herself and relationships through these distortions. She is extremely self-sufficient, independent, responsible, and caring. She does not understand how to participate in a mutually caring relationship or to comprehend that she has needs. In the course of therapy, the denial and dynamics get unraveled. As the client develops a more empowered sense of herself and externalizes the dysfunction, she wants to create a new role for herself within her family. But this is tricky.

Speaking synergistically, if one member of a group makes a positive change there is a ripple effect. Although the group may initially protest, new behaviors will eventually settle in. This simply does not occur within incestuous families because the entrenchment in the denial, deception, and dysfunction is too great. The family members (especially the parents) have years of investment in their version of reality. If the client begins to take less responsibility for her parents, she will be criticized for being selfish. If she chooses to avoid a holiday gathering, it will be talked about for months. If she does not cower in her father's presence, he will escalate his intimidation tactics. The daughter's changes will be seen as a threat to the family's homeostasis.

Because of these continued abusive dynamics, a confrontation with the abuser or other family members must be carefully evaluated during treatment. The likelihood of a recapitulation of the abuse is inevitable. Although there is a movement afoot for survivors to confront their abusers as an avenue towards empowerment and healing (Bass and Davis 1988), this needs to be approached with greater trepidation. Each client and therapist must engage in lengthy conversations to assess the wisdom of a confrontation for that particular client with her particular family. It is safer to generalize that confrontation will lead to further abuse and loss for the client than to generalize that confrontation will offer a healing experience. This is not to say that the client should continue to keep the incest a secret throughout her family, or to remain engaged in dysfunctional patterns of relating, or to dismiss the potential advantages of a family confrontation. The treatment goals for the adult survivor making decisions about her present relationships to her family are to no longer feel threatened by her perpetrator and to create a new identity and role for herself as a member of this group. These goals are achieved as the therapy proceeds, but the client will need guidance when it comes to interacting with her family.

Each survivor faces different dilemmas depending on who her abuser was, who did not protect her, who she was protecting, and who her allies were. Because each scenario creates slightly different dynamics a separate look at the most common circumstances is warranted.

FATHERS AND STEPFATHERS AS PERPETRATORS

The victim's loyalty toward her father is a particularly delicate area. Despite initial appearances, incest victims do have a great deal of loyalty toward the offender, and there are some good reasons for this. During the family's development, the father is usually the primary relational resource for the daughter. The mother often appears distant, unavailable, and depleted. The father, on the other hand, is relationally pursuant, and although he does sexually abuse his daughter, whatever attention and affection she receives usually originates with him. Also, she is tacitly taught by the family to take care of her father in many ways, and this sense of responsibility usually adds to her loyalty toward him. [Gelinas 1988, p. 37]

The adult survivor remains caught in this position of caretaking with intermittent appropriate affection from her father. For a therapist to suggest some kind of disruption in this relationship would be asking the client to do something she is not psychologically capable of doing. "But if I let go of my father there won't be anyone in my family who pays any attention to me. The rest of them just ignore me unless I let them down in some way," the client laments. Although the client can now acknowledge the incest and its ramifications for her, loving and abuse are intertwined in her relationship to her father.

Justine continued to have regular contact with her family. She attended holiday gatherings, spoke on the phone, and periodically visited with her parents. In the course of her therapy she became more aware of the lack of safety she felt in these situations. Additionally, her rage at her father and mother was surfacing. Christmas was approaching, and she wondered how she could possibly go through the same old motions.

Justine: There's no way I'll be able to sit at the same table with my father and pretend anymore that nothing happened.

Therapist: What do you imagine will happen for you this Christmas if you go to your parents' home?

Justine: I can't even picture it. I'd rather not go at all.

Therapist: Okay. What about that as one option?

Justine: Oh sure! I don't go home. Everyone yells at me, they tell me how I'm ruining the holiday for everyone and I get to hear about it until next Christmas. I *have* to go.

Therapist: "Have to" is a pretty strong statement. Maybe you can look at the options of going or not going and weigh them. You don't sound as if either one is a great choice right now so I wonder which one you feel is the lesser of two evils.

Justine: I just don't think I'm ready to make the decision to stay away. My head tells me that would be good for me but the rest of my being can't imagine doing that.

Therapist: So maybe it's best to think about how you can best protect yourself from feeling small, intimidated, or trapped while you are there. For this year, for where you are right now in your work, it sounds like you need to make the decision to go home for Christmas. So let's think about how you can give yourself some room to move.

Justine: Well, I can ignore my dad.

Therapist: Is that realistic?

Justine: Kind of. If there are enough other people around, I wouldn't have to be alone with him.

Therapist: Yes, not being alone with him would be a great idea. How can you make that happen?

Justine: Well, I can play with my nieces and nephews the whole time. And maybe I can bring my best friend with me and ask her to stay close by me.

Therapist: Terrific ideas. I would suggest that you give your friend the assignment of being like a body guard. If you knew that you could prevent being alone with your father, does going home feel any different?

Justine: Yeah, a bit. It makes me less anxious to think about it. Like maybe I can go and enjoy the kids instead of being at my father's beck and call.

Therapist: And if, for some reason, things get out of hand, what will you do?

Justine: I want to say that I would leave but I think that would be hard for me. It's my job to keep the peace.

Therapist: Maybe this can be another assignment for your friend. Ask her to judge when the situation is no longer safe enough and escort you out of there.

Justine: Yeah, I think I can do that.

That Christmas day turned out to be very interesting for Justine. She did everything that she and her therapist had discussed, and she found that she actually enjoyed being with her nieces and nephews and did not feel conflicted about attending to them rather than to her father. This experience moved her treatment along because she realized that she *did* have options, that it did not have to be an either-or process, that she could get some of her own needs met within her family, and that she could remain more individuated in their midst. This was very powerful for Justine and it opened up a new avenue of thought for her. Eventually she became more clear that she could act on her own behalf and the repercussions would not be disastrous.

The therapist needs to appreciate the emotionally intricate connections for the survivor in her family. She may feel hateful toward her abuser but continue to feel protective of her mother and siblings. She may desire to confront or to avoid her abuser but she cannot figure out how to do this without upsetting other family members. It is useful for the therapist to step away from either-or thinking while strategizing with the client and to move into a brainstorming mode instead. This frees the client to think beyond two untenable choices as well as learning an important life skill. To survive, the child developed rigid thought patterns. The adult needs to learn how to think more expansively.

Only Ariel's husband knew that her stepfather had sexually abused her from the ages of 9 to 18. She felt she had sufficiently buried any impact the abuse had on her until she began experiencing anxiety attacks for no apparent reason. In the initial interview with a therapist, Ariel wondered aloud if her stepfather's impending death had anything to do with these attacks. When asked how she felt about her stepfather, Ariel replied that she hated his guts and looked forward to his death because then she would finally be free from her abuser. She shared with the therapist that she had never talked about the incest with anyone in the family—especially not her mother. She felt that her mother would fall apart or have no idea how to deal with the information, and she simply could not do that to her mother. She described her mother as extremely dependent upon her husband and very upset about his declining health. Ariel identified herself as her mother's caretaker, advising her about matters of money, family, and work. She felt she was the mother and her mother was the child. As her stepfather's death approached she felt conflicted about what to do.

Ariel:	I know my mother expects me to come visit her while *he* is in the hospital. She counts on me to take care of matters. She's already asked me how to make funeral arrangements.
Therapist:	What do you want to do? Would you like to go and help your mother now?
Ariel:	You know, before I started this therapy it wouldn't even have been a question. I would have gone there to take care of her and just tried to ignore him as much as possible. But now, the thought of even seeing him makes my stomach turn. And I feel so guilty about *wanting* him to die. I just can't imagine how I'd handle this emotionally.

Therapist: So it sounds like it would be too difficult for you to go and take care of your mother right now.

Ariel: Oh, God, I guess that's what I'm saying but I feel so terrible about that.

Therapist: What's so awful?

Ariel: It would be the first time in forty-one years that I haven't taken care of my mother. I don't know if I can handle that. I don't know if she can handle that.

Therapist: How do you think your mother would respond if you said, "I know you could use my help right now but this isn't a good time for me to leave town."

Ariel: That sounds so cold!

Therapist: Okay. What sounds better?

Ariel: I could say, "Mom, I know you need help now but you'll also need help when he dies. I really can't come there twice. We can't afford that. You know, there's nothing I can really do while he's lying in the hospital. But I can help take care of the funeral and what to do after he dies. How about if I wait to come there until it's all over?"

Therapist: Sounds good to me. How does it feel for you?

Ariel: Better. I think I can manage that one. This way I'm still taking care of mom, but I'm protecting myself from having to deal with such loaded feelings if I had to see him.

In this case Ariel felt strongly that it would only hurt her mother and siblings if she revealed the incest. Interestingly enough, during the time following the funeral, one of Ariel's sisters took her aside and shared that she was so relieved that their stepfather was finally dead. Shocked, Ariel inquired why. Her sister said, "Because he was disgusting. Not only did he beat the crap out of all of us but he molested me for years!" Ariel burst into tears and shared her own secret with her sister. They talked for hours and both of them concurred that telling their mother was a bad idea. For each of them, it was comfort enough to have shared their wounds with each other and they were content to continue protecting their mother.

GRANDFATHERS AND UNCLES AS PERPETRATORS

When the abuser is someone outside of the nuclear family, the adult survivor has more options for protection. It is easier to avoid a grandfather or an uncle except during the occasional large family gatherings. These events are attended by many relatives and only occur a few times each year. It is not as difficult to feel safe.

The family dynamics are different if the perpetrator is a grandfather or an uncle. It is usually safe to assume that the grandfather abused his own daughter(s) or other grandchildren. He is probably a pedophile who has sought out young children for many years. The dilemma for the adult survivor centers around knowing that if she were to expose her grandfather, she would likely touch her mother's past as well. Often, she feels too protective of her mother to take this risk. She may choose to talk to siblings or cousins in hopes of finding an ally somewhere in the family. This can be a powerful option.

> At family gatherings, Mara began to notice that one of her cousins appeared to avoid her grandfather as actively as she did. She began to suspect that her cousin had been molested by him too. With the support of her therapist, Mara mustered up courage to approach her cousin after a Thanksgiving feast. She began by taking small risks to feel out her cousin's response. First, Mara commented that their grandfather was getting on in years and she was imagining the family without him. Her cousin responded by saying she had also considered that same possibility. Mara went on to say that in some ways she thought she'd feel relieved when he died because she had always felt tense around him. Her cousin replied, "Yeah, I know what you mean." Little by little, Mara inched her way toward disclosing to her cousin that she was in therapy, in part to deal with some of the tensions she felt within the family. Her cousin's face lit up as she discovered she had a kindred spirit in Mara. Soon they were off for a walk by themselves sharing perceptions and stories about their experiences with their grandfather. Eventually they both got up the nerve to describe the molestations they had suffered and how they were recovering from the trauma. Mara never expected to find such a "gift" within her extended family and the impact of her shared connection with her cousin has had long-lasting and far-reaching consequences in her therapy.

Similar dynamics are present when an uncle is the molester. There are complicated multigenerational relationships that the client can assume include several abusive ones. If an uncle is abusing a niece, he is probably also abusing his own children or other nieces and nephews. He probably has a history of trauma in his own childhood that is likely to be evident in his siblings' lives as well. For the victim to confront the perpetrator, she must be aware that she is blowing the whistle on the entire extended family. She would be raising pain or denial in nearly every family member. Many survivors of this form of incest simply choose to avoid their uncles.

> As a young boy Jerry was sexually abused by his maternal uncle on several occasions. Although he protested to his parents that he did not want to visit at his aunt and uncle's home, his cries were ignored. His adolescence was unusually difficult and he acted out through alcohol, delinquency, and truancy. He married at a young age and became a father soon thereafter. The responsibilities became unbearable for Jerry and he began a self-destructive decline. Fortunately, the woman he married was loyal, patient, and firm. With her help, Jerry was able to turn his circumstances around and begin to thrive. As part of his recovery process Jerry decided to completely avoid his uncle. He was no longer powerless to protect himself or his family. Although he was pressured by his parents to attend extended family gatherings, Jerry and his wife stood their ground. The only explanation he offered was, "I don't like Uncle John and I never

want to see him again." Since they were not a communicative family, Jerry's parents never asked any questions. A younger brother, however, was curious. Why did Jerry dislike Uncle John? Had Uncle John done something bad? Jerry answered honestly. "When I was a kid he used to take me in their basement and force me to perform oral sex on him. I hate his guts for what he did." This news did not shock his brother. Instead, it confirmed his suspicions about their uncle and allowed the brother to offer support to Jerry.

As discussed previously, the goal for the client is to arrive at a point of safety and power and clear boundaries when dealing with the abuser now. There are countless strategies for achieving this without forcing an "either confront the abuser or not" bind. Therapists need to be creative and encourage clients to enact changes that satisfy these goals.

SIBLINGS AS PERPETRATORS

Sibling incest is dynamically very different from the previously discussed scenarios. For one, the similarity in ages between the perpetrator and the victim gives the appearance of a more consensual or peer relationship. Secondly, sibling incest implies a lack of adequate parental supervision and a reenactment of parent–child abuse. Thirdly, the victim of sibling abuse is more apt to view the incest as "no big deal" or more like ordinary developmental sexual exploration. The therapist will need to address all of these issues.

The most relevant question the therapist needs to raise repeatedly with the client is whether on not she felt coerced into sexual encounters with her sibling. Did the client want to be sexual with her sibling? Did she initiate such contact? Did she feel threatened, humiliated, or frightened by her sibling? Did the abuse leave her feeling terrible about herself? Survivors will answer these questions by emphatically stating that they never wanted any sexual contact with their brothers or sisters and that they feel guilt and shame as a result. Once the client becomes clear that there was a power imbalance in the relationship, the therapist can describe this as the primary underlying element of abuse.

Where there is sibling sexual abuse, there is dysfunction in the parents. Many survivors have suspected that their siblings were being abused by their parents. This understanding does not make them feel better about their own trauma but it offers insight about the "why me" question. To see the whole family system as troubled makes the client feel less singled-out for mistreatment. This becomes the springboard for acknowledging the parents' inadequacies. The survivor has always been confused about why her parents didn't protect her or supervise the children better. The chaos and misbehavior have always seemed obvious to the survivor, but her parents' lack of response has made her feel crazy or overly sensitive. Seeing her parents as troubled and inappropriate fills out the picture for her.

Because the perpetrator is not an older adult, the survivor of sibling abuse has a tendency to minimize the damage. The therapist needs to keep reframing this as an issue of power rather than one of age. One way to help the client with this is to describe an equivalent scene where the client is the more powerful actor. "Picture yourself as 7 years old and your sister as 4. You've been playing together nicely even though you've been a bit bossy. Your bossiness gets a bit out of control when you suggest to your sister that it would be fun to pretend that she has been a bad baby and needs to be locked up in the closet. Your sister protests and cries and says she doesn't want to play anymore. Instead of respecting her pleas, you grab her by the arm, ignore her screaming, and lock her in the closet. Would you say that you abused your position as the older sister? Would you say that you forced your plan on your little sister? Would you say that your sister would never suffer as a result of your coercion?" Most clients are horrified when they imagine themselves being the aggressor, but they get the point that any abuse of power—be it age or size or position—will have lasting negative consequences for the victim.

Knowing how to behave with siblings in adulthood presents the survivor with many concerns. It is not unusual for the power imbalance to still be present in the relationship so the reenactment of abusive behaviors is a very real possibility. The client will struggle with attempts to equalize the dynamics. Depending on the level of persistent threat the client still feels from her sibling, she is more likely to frame her decision as an either-or situation. Because of the similarity in ages, the client may feel powerful enough as an adult to confront her brother or sister. She may decide it is necessary to do so in order to protect her own children or her nieces and nephews. It may also be easier to gain the support of her partner who may view siblings as more "dispensable" than parents. In lieu of a confrontation, the client may decide to avoid her sibling indefinitely. The therapist's role in this process is to facilitate a solution that brings a sense of power to the client.

It took nearly a year of therapy before Sally began to make sense of her relationship with her sister. She had always felt so intimidated by her sister but at the same time had a strong desire to be close to her. In describing recent phone calls, Sally spoke of the harshness and cruelty of her sister's comments. Over a long period of time, the therapist prodded Sally to talk more about when they were small children. Eventually Sally was able to remember the terror she had felt in the presence of her sister. Her sister would force her way into Sally's bed, hold her down, threaten her until she was silenced, and insist that Sally sexually stimulate her. Any time that Sally could free herself and run to her parents, she was admonished for tattling on her sister. Her parents insisted that the sisters work out their problems on their own. With difficulty, Sally was finally able to label her sister's behavior as incestuous.

As adults, Sally and her sister lived in different cities but tried to arrange frequent visits. As her sister's visit neared, Sally's anxiety peaked.

Sally: Everytime I think about my sister in my one-bedroom apartment I want to gag. I feel suffocated just thinking about it.

Therapist: Speak some more about that feeling.

Sally: It's like she invades the entire space. She's everywhere and there's no place for me to run to. It's physical. It's verbal. It's emotional.

Therapist: (with a slight chuckle) You don't still have any doubts about this being incest, do you?

Sally: (smiles) No, I guess not. But what do I do now?

Therapist: Let's start with ideal. Ideally, what would you like right now with your sister?

Sally: Not to see her!

Therapist: Okay. Let's talk about that. Could you ask your sister not to come for a visit?

Sally: Not without an explanation.

Therapist: What kind of explanation are you prepared to offer at this time?

Sally: I don't know if I could actually do this but what I'd love to say is, "You know, you were cruel to me when we were kids. You sexually, verbally, and physically abused me. You had no concern for my feelings. And not much has changed since then. Although there is no sexual violation at this time, you have hit me and screamed at me as recently as six months ago. Like the guy in the movie said—I'm angry as hell and I'm not going to take it anymore!!"

Therapist: Sounds like a good speech to me. Is that something you could actually say?

Sally: You know, to hear myself say all this out loud feels pretty good. It doesn't feel as difficult as I thought it would.

Therapist: What do you feel is at stake? What would you lose if you leveled with your sister?

Sally: That's just it. I don't think there's anything to lose. Only power to be gained. I really think I have had it with her treatment of me.

After several more conversations and role plays with her therapist, Sally did phone her sister to confront her about the abuse and to tell her to stay away until such time that her sister faced her problems. Her sister denied the allegations, called Sally crazy, insisted that she had been reading too much "feminist bullshit," and that the therapist Sally was seeing was obviously a quack. Sally stood firm and changed her behavior with her sister. She no longer allowed any form of abuse and got very good at hanging up the phone on her. After a year passed, Sally's sister finally began to acknowledge that she had problems but that she loved Sally and wanted to work things out. Once her sister was settled in her own therapy, Sally invited her for a visit with the stipulation that she attend several therapy sessions with Sally.

Stacy had never repressed the details of her incest experiences with her brother. As they grew into adulthood and ventured out on their own, she put as much distance as possible between them. This was more problematic at holidays since they were the only two children in the family. While she was in college, she never went home for a holiday without a friend or lover in tow. She was determined never to be alone in the house if her brother was also visiting. Her parents would nag her about not keeping in better contact with her brother. "You know, Rob always complains about how you never return his phone calls or respond to his letters." Stacy chose to remain silent around her parents. In time, both Rob and Stacy married and had children. This made matters more complicated for Stacy. She adored her two nieces and was frightened for their safety. She wanted all the children to be close as cousins but she couldn't tolerate being in her brother's presence. With the support of her husband, Stacy made some decisions.

Each summer Stacy invited her nieces to visit for two weeks. Rob and his wife were happy for the break and the girls were delighted to spend time with their cousins. While her nieces were in her home, Stacy gave of her love in many generous ways. The girls came to feel very close to their aunt and they would often call or write to her during the year. During the summer vacations Stacy would talk to the girls about safety and trust and love. In essence, she offered instructions to her nieces about how to protect themselves if their father was inappropriate with them. She reinforced the idea that she would always love them and care for them in any ways they might need her. She felt the most powerful healing she could do for herself was to protect her nieces as best as she was able. Although Stacy decided not to directly confront her brother, she felt empowered to play an active and important role in her nieces' development.

SIBLINGS AS PROTECTORS

It is rare in abusive families for only one child to be harmed. Although physical and emotional abuse usually occur openly in these families, sexual abuse happens in secret. So siblings generally know they are all in the same boat except when it comes to incest. Most therapists have heard countless stories about children intervening when a father is beating a mother or a younger sibling, even at the expense of getting hurt themselves. With incest, this protection looks different.

For the oldest daughter who is being sexually abused by her father, she is doing everything she can to protect her younger sisters from the same fate. She mothers her sister(s) in nurturing yet strict ways. As a young girl herself, she is trying to explain without actually explaining that her sister is in danger and needs to be careful. "Now go to your room and stay there until I tell you to come out" can be a cryptic warning that Dad is coming home and she'll deal with him so that her sister is safe. Because there is inadequate parenting in these families, the older daughter attempts to raise her younger siblings—an impossible task for someone so young, without any role models, but a job she will attempt anyway.

Although she may not be able to articulate this at the time, the oldest daughter is wildly conflicted about leaving home. On one hand she wants nothing more than to get away from her abuser, but on the other hand she is petrified that he will move on to her younger sisters. She has kept herself intact partly by parenting her siblings. She has invested a great deal in the idea of "I can handle this but she can't, so I'll sacrifice myself." To leave her sisters behind brings on unbearable guilt. Sometimes the oldest child will delay her leaving until she can take her siblings with her. Other times the survivor will shut down all emotional attachments to her siblings in order to save herself. She cannot tolerate the conflict.

Years later, when that oldest daughter is in therapy recovering from the consequences of incest, her heavy sense of guilt and responsibility for the lives of her siblings surfaces. She still has deep feelings of affection, protection, and attachment for her siblings. This will be an important part of her healing. The goals for a survivor in these circumstances are to grant adult status to her siblings and relinquish her role as parent, to address her issues around "survivor guilt," to gain a new perspective about the unrealistic expectations she had about being able to save them, and to establish a new kind of rapport with them.

Marie was not buying her therapist's point about the impossibility of her saving her two younger sisters from their father's sexual abuse. She was insistent that "If I hadn't left home until they were older, none of this would have happened. I'd already figured out how to cope with my father's behavior. They were too young, too fragile. They needed me to stay there." Her anguish was accentuated by the fact that she had lost contact with her sisters while she was away at college. Marie was convinced that her sisters now resented her for not taking better care of them and abandoning them. Every direction the therapist turned, Marie put up a barrier so the therapist tried a different tack.

Therapist: I want you to recall being 15 years old. Picture yourself entering 10th grade. By this time, your mother was totally unavailable to you. You were in charge of most of the household chores and taking care of your sisters. Your older brother had already left for college so his absence made it even easier for your father to get you alone, because you were moved into your brother's room. The summer before 10th grade was when your father escalated the abuse to include penetration. Remember how frightened you were of getting pregnant? While all this was happening, you were pulling straight A's at school and you were active in scouting. Got the picture?

Marie: Yes.

Therapist: Now picture your sisters. At that point Jody was 11 and Carrie was 9. They shared a room and basically minded your orders. They looked up to you and thought you were beautiful. They didn't know what was

	going on with your father and you, but they periodically said they were jealous of how much attention Daddy gave you. Remember you told them it was just because you were more grown up?
Marie:	Yes, I remember. They were so precious. I didn't want them to get hurt in any way.
Therapist:	Now I want you to focus on being 15 years old. You weren't old enough to drive a car, write a check, have a confidential appointment with a doctor or a counselor. You had no rights but you carried a very heavy burden. Don't forget that we're talking about 1963. Long before child abuse was spoken about anywhere and long before protective services were accessible. How could a 15-year-old have protected her sisters from the abuse she could not protect herself from?
Marie:	But I was able to handle it.
Therapist:	Yes, you coped with it. But you were 7 years old when it began. Did anyone protect you?
Marie:	No.
Therapist:	Who should have protected you?
Marie:	My mother. And my father never should have done it in the first place.
Therapist:	Right. Your parents were responsible for protecting and appropriately caring for you. It was their job not to harm you. How come it was their job to protect you, but it was your job to protect your sisters? Why wasn't it also your parents' responsibility to take care of your sisters?

This effectively stopped Marie in her tracks. The more the therapist was able to get Marie in touch with the child victim, the less guilty she felt for leaving her sisters.

When it becomes the role of the oldest child to care for the younger ones, it is easy for her to lose sight of the parents' responsibility. She is attempting to make a better life for her siblings by providing for them what was denied her: safety and love. If the client is able to move past her guilt, she opens up the possibility of building healthy alliances with her siblings that can be *mutually* satisfying.

Older brothers are often able to physically protect their younger siblings from abuse. Even if the incest was never discussed, a sister can experience the safety of her brother's presence. She may feel angry, resentful, and frightened when he leaves home. No matter how often she tells herself that it is normal for him to leave home, her loneliness and fear can be inconsolable. He may also harbor worries and guilt about his departure. This may create distance in their relationship for a period of time. As adults, it can be very healing for them to reunite. The therapist needs to listen for threads of a client's attachment to her more protective siblings and encourage a reconnection to them.

Siblings are often the most powerful and constant resources for the abused child and the recovering adult. They often have some degree of shared experiences and shared perceptions. They can affirm each other's realities and dispel the sensation of craziness. In many instances, siblings will speak openly about the incest and other forms of abuse within the family. This is a rich opportunity. The therapist must not overlook these potential connections for the client.

MOTHERS AS PERPETRATORS

The first relationship in life is with mother. It is a primitive and instinctive connection. It is a relationship filled with potential and power for both mother and child. Within an incestuous family, the mother's role, as either perpetrator or nonprotector, has a confusing and compounding impact on the child. The therapy will eventually wind its way around to addressing issues related to the client's mother. These are sensitive dilemmas entangled within a cultural and familial context that need to be unraveled.

Women in this society are expected to be nurturant, affectionate, kind, and protective. Mothers are expected to be all these things to the nth degree. The brainwashing is so extensive that "inadequate" mothers feel guilty if they do not behave in all these loving ways, and children defend their inappropriate mothers. Denial is pervasive where there is insufficient mothering. Conversely, when this "defective" mother is revealed, the rage and contempt hurled her way is endless. Fathers are not subject to the same kind of scrutiny. When a father is found guilty of child sexual abuse, there is an outcry of disgust accompanied by a lenient punishment. When a mother is accused of a similar offense, she is deemed less than human (unnatural) and beyond repair. Because of these attitudes, it is often difficult for a client to uncover her memories or feelings about her mother's role around the incest. She, too, believes "it just couldn't be possible" that her mother was overtly abusive or unprotective. The client's defenses are reinforced by the society.

It is important for therapists to remain aware of the severity of dysfunction within incestuous families. Sexual abuse does not occur in a vacuum. It occurs in the context of alcoholism, mental illness, chronic physical illness, severe loss, reenactment of the parents' pasts, or marital dysfunction. The abusive mother is struggling with her own psyche and past much as an abusive father is similarly disturbed. She is inappropriately and unconsciously acting out deep-seated problems. Because mothers are so pivotal—even mythic—in families, abused children attribute fantastic qualities to them. Up to the moment of acceptance, clients who were sexually abused by their mothers are *absolutely* sure they were *not* abused by their mothers. These extreme perceptions eventually evoke extreme feelings.

Mothers who sexually abuse their children have almost always been victims of the same crime themselves. If they have not overtly dealt with the realities of their own childhood abuse, they are at risk to recreate their abusers' role. Their children become the recipients of either their unresolved rage or their unmet needs. The pattern of maternal sexual abuse generally falls into two categories: aggressively sadistic sexual harm or intrusive affection that eventually becomes sexualized (Courtois 1988). In most cases the child copes by massive repression and denial. When that child matures and enters psychotherapy, it is rarely to resolve issues surrounding maternal sexual abuse. The adult generally enters treatment because of current relationship concerns.

Michael was a 28-year-old graduate student when he entered therapy. His presenting problem was the aftermath of a confusing breakup with his girlfriend of two years. His girlfriend had been struggling with anorexia and bulimia throughout their relationship and this had an impact on their dynamics. Michael had grown weary of taking care of his girlfriend and she had likewise decided she could not tolerate her dependence. Eight months after the fact, Michael was still confused about what had happened in the relationship, why it hadn't worked, and what implications this had for any future relationships. The therapy focused rather quickly on Michael's family history. His parents had divorced when he was 9 years old, and he lived with his mother and younger sister thereafter. He maintained contact with his father although emotional distance set in. Michael's mother was an alcoholic who had a penchant for physically abusive lovers who were also alcoholic. She rarely went grocery shopping or maintained the household. She worked sporadically and counted on Michael and his sister to be self-sufficient and resourceful. In the therapy sessions Michael would express anger and disappointment with his mother. He identified the cause of his discontent as her alcoholism. He described in elaborate detail the countless rages he flew into during his adolescence. "My mother was so unreasonable and irresponsible that we would just blow up at each other. I would get so angry that I broke several phones, smashed my dresser and shoved my fist through my bedroom door. I always had to go for a walk and cool off after these fights. Often I'd end up at my dad's house. Things were more ordered and sane there."

As Michael recounted these rages, the therapist pressed for more details about the antecedents. Over the course of six months, little by little, Michael revealed a great deal about daily life within his family. He matter-of-factly described his mother's constant attention to his developing physique. "I have the most handsome man for a son. All my friends think you are such a hunk." Several times a week his mother would be bedridden with any number of complaints—hangovers, depression, loneliness, wounds from abusive boyfriends. She would ask Michael to massage her back as she lay nearly naked in her bed. On the days when she was up and about, she wandered through the house in suggestive lingerie. She made a habit of brushing against Michael and engaging him in sexually explicit conversations. Over time Michael became aware that this was not appropriate behavior for a mother with her teenage son. It was in the course of these discussions with his therapist that Michael made the connection between his mother's seductive behavior and the resultant rages. Eventually he labeled his relationship with his mother as incestuous and worked hard in treatment to understand how this was affecting his current relationships with women.

Sheryl entered therapy at the age of 21 to deal with her social isolation. Eventually the treatment focused on her family of origin to uncover clues about her interpersonal disconnectedness. Her most intimate relationship was with her 19-year-old sister, and beyond that Sheryl did not have much to tell about her family. There was a void in her memory about her past and a vagueness about the characters of her parents. The therapist suggested inviting the sister to join Sheryl for several sessions. Whereas Sheryl presented so flatly most of the time, in the presence of her sister she came alive. Her sister had many memories and impressions that she shared including the bizarre behavior of their mother. When Sheryl pressed for more details her sister responded, "Don't you remember how mom used to pull you out of bed in the middle of the night?" With much help from her sister, Sheryl eventually pieced together her memories about the sexual abuse she suffered and how it related to her present circumstances. The two sisters had known since childhood that their mother had been raped by their uncle because they had witnessed it. Although they never spoke to their mother about this, they assumed this was not a one-time occurrence. By the time Sheryl was 10 years old, her mother was maniacally dragging her out of her bed in the middle of the night in plain view of her sister and despite Sheryl's protests. She was taken into the kitchen where her mother removed Sheryl's night clothes and inserted various kitchen gadgets into her vagina. After two more years of treatment, Sheryl still had moments of disbelief about the incest.

The discovery of maternal sexual abuse in the course of therapy is a shock for the client. Not only is there the trauma of the emergence of repressed material and how that information rewrites the client's history, but there is the most profound betrayal to face. "How could my mother have done such a terrible thing? What was so wrong with me that my own mother would want to harm me? I knew she wasn't too wild about me but why did she have to abuse me?" If there was never an adequate attachment to the father, the sense of abandonment is immobilizing for the client. She feels like the unwanted child who would have been better off never having been born. This creates some delicate treatment concerns.

When treating a client who was sexually abused by her (or his) mother the therapist must move slowly and gently. The defenses the child had to build are formidable and it would be a mistake to attempt to mow them down. As the client begins to feel a sense of inner strength and self-confidence, small challenges can be made to open up her perceptions and memories about her mother. Initially both the client and the therapist will only have hunches that something went terribly wrong in the relationship with the mother. It will not emerge as a distinct picture of abuse but rather like a scene in a mystery. Little clues here and there just won't seem to add up. There will be missing pieces and dreamlike sensations. The client and the therapist must become detectives.

After the sessions with Sheryl's sister, the therapist began a different line of questioning with Sheryl.

Therapist:	When you think about being a small girl, what is your sense of your relationship to your mother?
Sheryl:	I don't know. Kind of typical. She ran the household. I did what she asked. I got into trouble sometimes for picking on my sister.
Therapist:	When you got in trouble, what happened?
Sheryl:	Mom usually was really angry and had a fit.
Therapist:	Had a fit. What does that mean?
Sheryl:	You know, screamed, yelled, smacked. She'd storm out of the room and scream how awful we were and how sorry she was she ever had kids.
Therapist:	What kinds of things did you do to evoke such rage?
Sheryl:	Really bad stuff. (pause) Like I'd tease my sister until she cried. Then she'd tell Mom what I'd done. I was simply rotten.
Therapist:	Why do you think you were rotten?
Sheryl:	Well, can you think of anything more vicious than making your own sister cry? My mom was right for being so angry.
Therapist:	Do you realize that siblings often tease each other? It's part of most normal relationships between sisters. It's one way siblings express their jealousies.
Sheryl:	Even so, I was cruel. I deserved what I got.
Therapist:	Does it ever occur to you that your mother's rage was excessive?
Sheryl:	Not really. She was angry a lot of the time. And I'm sure she had every right to be. We weren't the best kids all the time.
Therapist:	Even so, it sounds like your mother was a walking time bomb ready to explode at any arbitrary moment.
Sheryl:	My sister would agree with you. That's just what she's always said.
Therapist:	And how would you characterize your mother?
Sheryl:	As kind of normal—like what other moms must be like.
Therapist:	Have you ever had any other notions about your mother?
Sheryl:	Not really. Except that I've always had this recurring dream about my mother. I've had it for as long as I can remember. It's not always a sleeping kind of dream. Sometimes it's more like a waking kind of dream.
Therapist:	Can you describe it?
Sheryl:	Well, the usual pattern is that I am teeny-tiny and quite frightened. It usually takes place in the house I grew up in. I'm in danger and I'm trying to run or hide. I usually wake up just as this looming, dark, huge presence is about to attack me. It leaves me feeling panicked and breathless.
Therapist:	And who is that presence?
Sheryl:	I can't see the face but ever since I was little I always called that presence the "mom monster."

Sheryl and her therapist worked with the imagery of the "mom monster" for many months. Through the use of guided visualizations Sheryl was able to fill out her description of the monster. The therapist became certain that this was Sheryl's creative method for coping with the abuse she suffered from her mother. Eventually Sheryl retrieved enough memories to piece together her own version of the sexual abuse her sister had suspected. Although parts of her remembrances were thinly veiled in her sensations of the presence or in imagery of the "mom monster," Sheryl became clear about the reality of her childhood abuse.

Metaphors and imagery are useful techniques for unearthing information about maternal sexual abuse. These methods allow the client to maintain whatever distance she needs and the pictures offer a more indirect route into the heart of her reality. Therapeutically the imagery can be very rich and can give the therapist many possible avenues for exploration.

When the mother has been the abuser and the therapist is a woman, gender may present some obstacles. The client may have greater-than-usual difficulty developing a sense of trust in the therapist. This can, in fact, create a hypothesis that there was damage in the relationship to the mother. When this is the case, the female therapist must strive to establish a slightly more distant yet warm therapeutic stance. This dynamic would also suggest that any touching—no matter how casual—would not be advisable. Dealing with maternal incest issues will be slow work for any therapist; with a female therapist it may go even slower.

MOTHERS AS NONPROTECTORS

The word *nonprotector* is used here to describe a mother who does not prevent or rescue her child from the incest. Nonprotector implies that the mother was either unaware, unable, unavailable, or unwilling to protect the child. There are many possible scenarios for the mother of a child who was sexually victimized. In many cases the incest secret is so hidden by both the perpetrator and the child, who may have been threatened to remain silent, that the mother simply has no way of finding out. Incest is committed under extremely secretive circumstances. Another common reason for a mother to be unaware that anything is amiss pertains to her own mental or physical health. Alcoholic, drug-dependent, mentally ill, physically ill, chronically depressed, or absent mothers are so absorbed in their own realities they don't perceive much else around them. Other mothers will not heed their child's protests. "I'm scared of Grandpa. He hurts me," is scoffed at or minimized. "Now don't be silly, honey. Grandpa wouldn't do anything to hurt you." In other families the mother may have a *sense* that something is wrong but is too defensive, horrified, dependent, or frightened to confront the situation. She *chooses* to remain ignorant of the truth. In some cases the mother may actually be quite aware of the incest but chooses to sacrifice her child for her own protection. In many instances it is the child who actively shields the mother from the truth. If the child perceives the mother as overcome by problems, such as physical ailments or spouse abuse, she may cover up her own troubles to protect her mother's fragility. Whatever the specific scenario may be, the end result for the child is that she experiences her mother as unavailable to help or rescue her.

As has been mentioned earlier, the child's response to the incest is one of total traumatization. Her world is filled with dangers and fears that she must find ways to cope with. Her relationship with her mother will not be immune from these difficulties. The child will not have the cognitive sophistication required to assess her mother's role in the incest accurately. If a mother is unaware or unresponsive to the child's plight, the child will conclude that things are as they should be. Her father is entitled to this sexual activity and her mother condones it. The child believes she deserves this treatment because she is bad or wicked and that her mother concurs in this belief. With this resolution, the child cannot perceive the mother as an ally. If the child tries to speak of the abuse and the mother discredits the child's story, the child is left wondering if she has made all this up or why her mother doesn't believe her. The lack of response by a mother renders an abused child completely powerless. She struggles to protect herself as best she can on her own as she accepts what must be her destiny.

It is difficult to imagine the profound state of terror that is the abused child's existence. So, it is even more difficult to imagine that traumatized child turning to another adult within the family system and revealing the incest. Family life is convoluted and unsafe for this child and she has already learned that adults who are supposed to be loving can hurt her. Rarely does a child risk further harm and humiliation by turning to her mother for help, for mother is part of the problem. Even if her mother could or would be supportive and protective, the child will usually not plead for help directly. The dysfunctional dynamics will often eliminate this option in the child's mind.

Somewhere in the midst of treatment Phase III, the Emotional Flood (see Chapter 3), the client's feelings about her mother's lack of protection will surface. This is extremely painful work and must be approached carefully and slowly. As the client is grieving and raging about the incest, it can be also overwhelming to face the betrayal or abandonment of her mother. The therapist must use a heavy hand here in the therapeutic pace. It is best to table the client's work about the mother until there is an emotional clearing. If, in the middle of her rage at her abuser, the client blurts out, "And where was my mother!? Why didn't she protect me?", the therapist can gently respond, "That is something we will need to look at eventually. For now, let's stay focused on your grandfather." Few clients will resist this suggestion.

Once there is an opportune moment in the therapy to raise issues about the client's mother, the therapist can expect a fair degree of resistance. The client may offer excuses or rationalizations about her mother's nonprotective role. She may habitually change the subject or express anger at the therapist for raising the topic. It is important not to blast through this barrier. When the client is prepared to address these concerns, she will. Periodically planting a seed, such as "You must be very angry at your mother" or "I wonder where your mother was in all of this," can prod the feelings.

Once the client's feelings about her mother's role do emerge, treatment will become very intense. The depth of the client's pain is unlike what she feels about her abuser. Whereas a client is likely to scream and cry all at once about her losses associated with the incest, she is more apt to sob and moan like a wounded animal about her sense of loss with her mother. She will have reached the bottom of a seemingly bottomless pit of despair, isolation, and abandonment. Every fiber of her being will ache and she will believe that she will never recover from this pain. The therapist's job is simply to be a witness to her grief and to offer whatever comfort possible.

As difficult as it is for the client to get in touch with her deep sense of loss, acknowledging her anger toward her mother will be even harder. The client fears that expressing that anger will eliminate all hopes that her mother ever loved her or ever will. The therapist needs to be reassuring that it is safe to open up those feelings in the office. In time, usually very late in the treatment, a client will be able to release some of her rage (justified or not) at her mother. One problem in this process is that sometimes a client will displace anger at the incest perpetrator onto her mother. Suddenly, Mom becomes the villain because she did not prevent the incest. She is seen as the true culprit and the abuser becomes merely a clever manipulator. The therapist must watch out for this and be persistent in keeping the client clear about who committed the crime. The mother may have been involved, but she did not commit the crime.

In the same way that the therapist dealt with the perpetrator, it is useful to take a family systems approach with the client about her mother's position in the family functioning. Learning about the mother's family of origin, her parents, and her marriage can give the client some much-needed perspective. This picture is for clarification rather than justification. The intent is not to get the mother off the hook, but rather to offer some hypotheses about why she may have taken the position she did in the family. This allows the client to interrupt her self-blaming to see the bigger picture.

After much thought, Janine decided to tell her mother about the incest she had experienced with her father and grandfather. She had arrived at a point in her therapy where she felt stronger and safer. Both of her abusers had been dead for many years and Janine was trying hard to be less guarded with her mother. Even though her mother continued to struggle with alcoholism, Janine felt there was absolutely no hope for any kind of relationship with her mother unless she was open about the incest. With a lot of help from her therapist, Janine prepared to write her mother a letter and anticipated a negative or passive response. She was clear that her purpose in writing the letter was for her own personal growth, and any secondary gains she might receive regarding her relationship to her mother would just be a bonus. Here is Janine's letter to her mother:

Mom,
  There's something I want to, need to tell you. I was sexually abused by Grandpa Al and Dad as a kid. I'm telling you now because I don't want to keep the secret any longer. The incest has affected my life and you need to know that. It's part of what makes me who I am. I'm doing this for me—to let the past go. I want to tell you because I want more from our relationship—not less—and to get more, you need to know who I am, what has happened to me that makes me who I am.
  I don't know if you were aware of the abuse and denied it because it was too atrocious to be true. I know I denied it. I began having memories of Grandpa Al about ten to twelve years ago with more memories coming and then memories about Dad— harder for me and you to deal with, I'm sure. And you may say 'I don't believe it, it couldn't have happened' but it did. I remember, and the visceral, auditory, and visual memories and pictures don't lie. There have been times and still are times when I don't want to believe it. Because I can't believe someone I love—who loved me—my parent whom I trusted could abuse and violate me for his gratification. That he thought he was more important when I, as a parent, know I would do anything to keep my children alive and safe—even if it meant my death to do it. And so I have lived my life afraid, feeling worthless, powerless, crazy; I never trusted, knew, or expressed feelings and felt like a block of wood. I tried to act like I thought people would if they were having what I supposed was the appropriate feeling for the occasion. I have had friends, lovers to whom I've never been able to feel the closeness, intimacy I could have, should have been able to feel. More important, I've not known me—not loved me. No matter how perfect I tried to be, it was never enough. And so I bring this up now. The incest occurred, from as much as I can figure, from age 4 to 14 (?)—twenty to thirty years ago. I bring this up now because it has and will always be a part of me. I'm learning to grow—to feel whole. And part of that for me means cutting through the denial, telling the secret, not carrying it myself.
  I need to tell you because you were there—whether you know about it or believe it—you were there. What I want from you is to acknowledge that it did happen and that it has had an effect on me. My fantasy is that you'll say, "God, I'm sorry honey. I didn't know it was happening. I wish I had known so that I could have stopped it." Why couldn't or didn't I tell you? I guess I didn't think you'd believe it. I do recall when Grandpa Al had come in some morning and I ran downstairs crying and you didn't try to find out why but only yelled for me to get back in bed. And I know that children don't just say "my grandfather raped me." They act out their fears through their behavior—my terror of sirens, the social worker. . . .
  And now I want to move on but that means giving up the fantasy of my parents and that means telling the secret, as scary as that is, because I can't resolve my relationship with you until you, at least, know it happened. What happens after this is unpredictable. You may deny, you may withdraw, you may try to understand and be support-

ive, you may get angry and attack me, because I've attacked your denial or your fears. But from here the path is honest. I can be clear, honest, and open and there is a chance for us then.

It took two weeks before Janine received a phone call from her mother. She simply stated that she had read the letter but offered no response. Janine asked if they could sit down together and talk and her mother agreed. Janine's mother admitted that it was certainly possible that she was sexually abused by her grandfather and father but that she did not know anything about it at the time. In addition, she had no interest in discussing it further. It had all happened a long time ago, both men were dead, and she preferred to avoid the entire topic. When Janine declared that such a position meant that their relationship would be extremely limited, her mother replied, "That's fine with me." Although the outcome was disappointing, Janine was not sorry that she had written the letter. She was relieved to tell the secret and to be honest with her mother. She no longer felt obligated to protect her mother or to cater to her needs. She established a less entangled relationship with her mother that caused a mixture of relief and sadness. But from here on, Janine was dealing with reality.

Needless to say, mothers play a critical role in all families. They are almost always the primary emotional attachment for the children. In incestuous families, whether the mother is the abuser or the nonprotector, the adult survivor will have complicated and primitive feelings to explore about her or his mother. The therapist must be especially gentle in this work and trust the client's ability eventually to reach down to the very pit of herself and pull out her deepest feelings of abandonment, loss, and betrayal.

GUIDELINES FOR FAMILY INTERVENTIONS WITHIN THE THERAPEUTIC SETTING

It is more the exception than the rule for an adult incest survivor to choose to confront her abuser or other family members. During the course of therapy most survivors will eventually experience a sense of empowerment and healthy separation from their dysfunctional families. Many feel that this is sufficient. But other survivors will decide to talk openly about the incest with various family members. One option is to have these family interactions occur within the confines of the therapeutic setting. These can prove to be pivotal sessions for the client, so careful preparation and some specific guidelines can be useful. The therapist will play a very active role in the preparation, execution, and aftermath of these meetings.

Intervention Guidelines

1. The therapist needs to engage the client in a meticulous process of goal clarification for these sessions. The client must be certain that she needs to have these family conversations for her own personal growth rather than in hopes of finding validation or acceptance. Her motives must be related to her treatment goals. If the client expects that her abuser or other family members will drop to their knees with remorse, embrace her wholeheartedly, and offer the appropriate affection she never received, she is setting herself up for a huge fall. It is the therapist's responsibility to uncover any hidden agendas that may sabotage the client's plan.

2. In addition to preparing the client for what might occur *during* the family sessions, the therapist needs to help the client anticipate the *aftermath*. In most cases, a family will experience a period of crisis characterized by intense and ambivalent feelings. The client will be in the hot seat, and various members will either accuse or support her. She will alternate between moments of euphoria and disappointment. In a relatively short period of time (1–6 months), the commotion will die down and it will be business as usual within the family. One of the few exceptions to this is ongoing support from siblings. Otherwise, most dysfunctional families will resume their ordinary dynamics. It is extremely rare for parents or families to enter therapy after an incest disclosure so many years after the fact. The client must be prepared for this reality.

3. The client should invite only one family member at a time to only one session. She needs to start with the most supportive member first. Were the entire family to descend upon her, the client would be overwhelmed and she would feel powerless. Group denial is more likely with everyone present as well. Having a nonprotective mother and an abusive father present during the same session will present too intense a triangulation and the client will undoubtedly lose out. The mother's loyalty will be too split and she will most likely support her husband. Limiting the invitation to only one session ensures that the therapy belongs to the client rather than expanding to include others in any ongoing way.

4. Once the family member has accepted an invitation, the therapist and client need several sessions to prepare for the meeting. It is useful for the client to write down a list of what she wants to say and role play it many times with the therapist. The therapist should assume a particularly resistant stance in the role plays to prepare the client for the worst. The client needs to rid

herself of any hopeful expectations. She needs to feel centered in her need to expel the secret for her own growth and internal integration.

5. The family session should be scheduled so that the client and therapist can meet together later that same day or early the following day. The need to debrief and reconnect individually with the therapist will be very great for the client.

6. The therapist needs to help the client anticipate how she or he will conduct the session and where the therapist's allegiance will lie. There should be no surprises for the client when it comes to the therapist's behavior.

7. The therapist must always be the one to control and guide the family session. He or she begins, focuses, and concludes the meeting with the primary purpose always in mind: this family member has been invited to the session so that the client may do a piece of work. The session is not intended to be therapy for anyone else nor is it an opportunity for absolution. The family member is present so that the client may finally reveal the truth in a controlled and safe environment. Anything else positive that may occur in the course of the session is simply icing on the cake for the client.

8. During the session, the therapist needs to be especially aware of the potential for triangulation and do everything to avoid that dynamic. As much as possible, the therapist must allow the client to speak for herself. If, for instance, a mother seems to have missed a point the daughter was saying, the therapist can intervene by suggesting that the client repeat it rather than having the therapist paraphrase her remark. The therapist's role is to facilitate conversation within the family rather than actively to partic-ipate in it. Moreover, the therapist's support of the client needs to be made explicit at the beginning of the meeting.

9. If any family member requests continued access to the therapist, this must be denied. One unspoken fear many clients have about these family inter-ventions is that privacy or confidentiality will be broken. The therapist must reassure the client that no further contact will be made with the family unless the client makes such a request.

10. During the debriefing session that follows the intervention, the therapist needs to allow the client lots of room to express whatever has been raised. There will usually be a wide range of feelings that simply need to be aired. She may feel strange returning to the office still sensing her family's

presence. She may feel big and small all at one time. She may not have liked everything the therapist did. She may accuse the therapist of being too unsympathetic toward her relative. Whatever the feelings may be, the therapist should not challenge them at this point. The client has just experienced a scene where there wasn't quite enough room for everything she feels and thinks. To clear the air of this constriction, the session needs to be expansive for the client. In addition, the therapist should offer any corroborating perspectives with the client. The client will be glad to know that she had things figured out accurately.

11. Above all else, these family sessions and the debriefing that follows must not recreate any of the original dysfunctional dynamics. The therapist must take a great deal of care to prevent this.

As the client heals in the course of her therapy, she will confront many dilemmas about how she now wants to interact with her family. All along the way there may be small changes she can make but the reorganization of most of these family relationships does not occur until later in the treatment. From a position of strength and clarity, the survivor will discover the most viable solutions for her own family constellation. The therapist must have an appreciation for the depth of the client's attachments (positive and negative) to her family and be confident that the client will arrive at her own meaningful conclusions. If both the therapist and the client suspend either-or thinking, creative brainstorming can occur. From a wider range of options, the client can then make empowering choices.

6

Intimate Relationships

Incest survivors have profound confusion around issues of intimacy and sexuality. Cruelly and prematurely forced into the world of adult relationships, their understandings about love, sex, affection, and closeness are tainted and twisted. The decision to enter psychotherapy is a decision to unravel these distortions.

Before she enters treatment, an incest survivor has little information and few experiences with healthy adult relationships. To her way of thinking, relationships are built around another individual's needs and her role is to accommodate them. She is devoid of needs or feelings, having learned long ago that they were of little importance. Sexuality is understood in terms of power; she is to submit to another person's desires. She does not understand sexual responses and she will usually cut off or dissociate from them. Love and sex are intertwined. If she is loved, then that person will want to be sexual with her. If that person does not want sex, then she is not loved. She does not understand what clear boundaries are in a relationship so she is susceptible to invasions, exploitation, unreasonable caretaking, or excessive submissiveness. Before entering therapy, the survivor has usually experienced several dysfunctional relationships that have re-created this confused pattern and/or abusive behaviors.

During the course of her therapy, the client's learning about healthy relationships will increase exponentially. As has been discussed up to this point, the client will experience a healthy and well-boundaried relationship with the therapist that will allow her to explore her thoughts, feelings, and needs. She will want to replicate this in her primary relationship. She will want to feel the wholeness, competence, and worth that she has developed. If her relationship does not make her feel good about herself or perpetuates a sense of confusion, she will make changes to modify the situation. As her healing progresses, she will desire a sexually functional and fully intimate relationship with her partner.

This metamorphosis within the primary relationship will be very bumpy. Whenever one individual within a couple experiences intensive growth and the other does not, the relationship will be jarred from its previous homeostasis. Incest recovery creates dramatic changes for the survivor and her partner will be forced to adapt. This process can be periodically troublesome but, ultimately, wonderfully transforming.

The role of the therapist in facilitating the client's growth in areas of intimacy and sexuality resembles that of a teacher. The client has so many things to learn about healthy relationships and sexuality that the therapist can be a knowledge-able educator and guide. It may be appropriate for the therapist to recommend other resources to the couple, such as books, groups, or couples therapy. Just as a teacher would, the therapist needs to track the development of the client's relationship and urge her to take new risks. All during the treatment the therapist must stay aware of the unfolding dynamics in the primary relationship so that small changes and interventions can take place all along. If the client or her partner are waiting until healing is complete before adjusting their relation-ship, they will end up in trouble. The therapist is in an ideal position to regularly raise issues around the functioning of the relationship and to coach the client to bring her new awarenesses home.

What follows is an overview of the most common and recurrent themes that are raised in the course of incest treatment in the areas of intimate relationships and sexuality. It is not the scope of this book to treat these subjects in detail. For more in-depth discussion of these topics refer to Graber (1991) and Maltz (1991). Both these books offer a wealth of valuable information and insight for clients and therapists.

PARTNERS

An incest survivor will often enter psychotherapy as a result of a current relationship. She will have arrived at a point in her life when she is aware that her primary relationship is an abusive one, needing to gather the strength to leave it, or perhaps aware that it *is* a supportive one, and wanting to be healthy enough to maintain it. There is something about her present adult relationship that either recreates her destructive past or soothes enough of her pain to provide a sense of safety. In either case, the survivor has become cognizant of the consequences of her earlier abuse and she is ready to move beyond them. Therapy will have a huge impact on the intimate relationship; therefore a closer look at these dynamics is warranted.

Incest survivors have had limited opportunities to fully develop a strong ego identity. Instead their personalities are organized around assessing other people's feelings, needs, and behaviors. This means that a survivor will enter an intimate relationship focused on her partner. She will invest her energy and emotion in making her partner happy and satisfied. Were she to be drawn toward an abusive person, she would find herself right back where she started. She would behave as that small child desparately seeking the love and acceptance of an important person and concluding that if she did not feel that love, it was because she was unlovable. She would, once again, be victimized by a domineering force. Her dependency and low self-esteem help re-create the abusive dynamics. She may stay in this kind of relationship for a very long time as she has no concept that this is anything other than as it should be. She does not know that she is valuable and does not deserve to be mistreated emotionally, psychologically, sexually, or physically. The survivor in an abusive relationship may never seek treatment or only when her children are harmed. She may never have developed or held onto enough inner strength to fight her way out.

Conversely, there are those survivors who are determined to find one human being who is essentially safe and loving. Often they are drawn to people who are basically solid with a propensity toward caretaking. Paradoxically, the partner is often attracted to the survivor not because of her vulnerability but because of her quiet strength and fierce determination. They join together in a mutual effort to shield the survivor from further harm. The partner takes over life tasks that frighten or challenge the survivor, thus diminishing her power. All this is couched in tenderness and protectiveness. These relationships can be maintained for a long time before trouble surfaces. Over a period of time the survivor feels secure in the comfort of the relationship and this allows her to take new risks. As she strives for greater competence or independence, the relationship is rocked.

The destructive or the comforting relationship is founded on the same premises. The survivor is seen by both partners as fragile, incomplete, needy, and dependent, but she is also viewed as persistent, loyal, competent, and tough. How these dichotomies are handled depends on the relationship dynamics. An abusive individual will try to break the spirit and gain control of a strong person. A caretaker will protect and coddle the vulnerabilities. In any event, the survivor is not a whole person. She does not enter the relationship with positive self-esteem and a balance between her strengths and weaknesses. She is susceptible to seeing herself as her partner defines her. This will be an incomplete image that establishes an imbalance in the relationship. The survivor is half a person and the partner is complete. This is harmonious for each of them. Therapy will, of course, upset this balance.

In the case of an abusive primary relationship, the therapy will eventually focus on what the client needs to do about it. Generally speaking, the healthier the client becomes, the less tolerant she will be of any form of abuse. If her partner is unwilling to get help for his or her own problems, the client usually chooses to leave the relationship. This is the ultimate demonstration of integration and healing. The therapist can offer support and guidance without pushing the client to leave before she is ready. The client will need her ego strengths reinforced at every step. Leaving will be a great challenge to the survivor.

A supportive and tender relationship will actually be more complicated for the client to transform. The dynamics are more subtle. On the most obvious level the client feels loved and cared for, yet a sense of helplessness persists. She feels emotionally supported by her partner but this leaves her feeling dependent. Whenever she expresses greater self-reliance she senses her partner's upset. This is very confusing and will only get more confusing over the course of therapy. The partner will be forced to deal with a more complete person than the one she or he fell in love with. The rules will be changed and the partner will feel out of control. This was not the original bargain they made. Helping the survivor anticipate the possible changes therapy will bring can go a long way toward facilitating the metamorphosis of the relationship.

The therapist needs to be appraised of the issues that will undoubtedly surface in the primary relationship with consideration for both the client and her partner. What follows is a description of how the primary relationship will be affected by the therapy.

Confusion in the Primary Relationship

Riding out the ups and downs during the course of treatment will keep the partner feeling perplexed. At one moment the client will ask to be comforted and in the next she might ask to be left alone. What was helpful yesterday may not be so today. There is no way for the partner to predict the changing moods and needs of the client safely. The client will be learning about emotions and needs and how to express them but that will be inconsistent for a while. To say that a survivor's partner will need to be patient during this process is an understatement.

The client will become a study in contradictions within her intimate relationship. She will simultaneously desire closeness and distance, dependence and independence, acceptance and rejection, and familiarity and change from her partner. These are her attempts at sorting out many of her interpersonal dilemmas. Do the old habits serve her well? Will this partner be like her abuser? Will she be the victim again? Can she experiment with new feelings or behaviors? As she moves through these issues in treatment she will act on or act out what she is discovering. Eventually this falls into a more consistent pattern as the client finds those behaviors that work best for her now. In the meantime, her partner will feel off balance, as the footing seems to change so rapidly and frequently.

There is a tendency among partners of incest survivors to want to protect their loved ones from any further pain. They may even feel uncomfortable or frightened by the outpouring of those feelings. During therapy the client will be in touch with many sad and painful emotions that she may eventually share with her partner. The subdued affect of the survivor may have been very attractive to her partner at the beginning of their relationship, so this shift will be disconcerting. If the partner cannot adequately tolerate the client's feelings, the client will close herself off and be confirmed in her earliest conviction that "it doesn't pay to say what's on my mind."

If there has been an imbalance around relative neediness of the two individuals, therapy will cause the client to attempt to equalize this. Oftentimes partners of incest survivors are rescuers. When the client no longer wants to be rescued the relationship will need to adapt. Partners can feel "put out of a job" and identify their anxiety as "worry about my spouse" rather than their own discomfort. Unless the partner is able to take responsibility for adjusting to new roles, the client will receive the message that she needs to be cautious, is taking on too many risks, may not succeed, or is still fragile. Hearing these pessimistic warnings creates tension and confusion in the relationship. The partner needs to be urged to clarify his or her own issues of dependence, independence, intimacy, and separation; otherwise the confusion becomes overwhelming to the point of crisis.

Although it is a normal human response to want to seize control in a complicated or tense situation, if a partner does this too much everyone will lose. The partner will feel helpless because these efforts will not necessarily work, and the client will feel angry if she does not have more impact. If there is a side to err on, it is better for the partner to do too little rather than too much. Incest survivors are used to taking care of themselves and others. They don't expect the generosity of their partners and may even feel uncomfortable with it. Were the partner to become excessive with worry and caretaking, the client will react in anger or rejection. It is best, if there is a moment of great confusion, for the partner to inquire, "Can you tell me what is going on? Is there anything I can do?" If the client cannot give a very clear answer the partner can reply, "Whenever you feel like talking let me know. In the meantime I will go about my business. I'll wait for you to ask for whatever you need from me." The client will feel reassured by this type of response and the partner can feel that she or he has reached out sufficiently.

Significant Changes in the Primary Relationship

This is a good news–bad news situation. The good news is that the client will learn what loving and intimacy are truly about and she will have that to offer her partner. This will deepen and intensify the relationship, and the partner will receive a richer quality of communication and loving. The bad news is that the process of arriving at that point is not always wonderful. Additionally, the partner may need to learn more about his or her own issues around love and intimacy, and may be challenged to stretch beyond the point of complacency.

There will be such profound growth on the client's part that many of the initial understandings that formed the basis of the relationship will need to be reexamined. The identity, roles, tasks, and disposition of the client will no longer suit her. She will be forging a healthier, more integrated self. Both the client and the partner may feel frightened by this transformation. Will the client still want to be with her mate? Will the relationship have enough room for growth? Can the partner tolerate the new rules? Will the partner love this "new" person? Can the relationship be elastic enough to include two healthy individuals or will one of them always need to be more fragile? There is no rule book to predict the outcome to any of these questions. There certainly are risks involved.

One particularly upsetting dynamic that surfaces during this process is the projection onto the partner of the abuser. As is true in all intimate adult relationships, there is a re-creation of parts of the child's relationship to the parents. This can be especially volatile for the incest survivor. Quite to her surprise the partner can suddenly remind her of her abuser. It may happen because of a manner of speaking or behaviors or simply because of the intimate connection. This will usually provoke fear or anger and a recapitulation of the client's childhood response. It is disruptive to the functioning of the relationship. The client will need help from the therapist in separating the abuser from the partner.

Judy reported to her therapist that while she and her husband, David, made love earlier that week she suddenly had a flashback. David had whispered an endearment into her ear just as he inserted his penis into her vagina. This triggered a memory of her stepfather calling her "his special pumpkin" as he raped her. When this occurred, Judy lost a clear sense of reality and screamed at David to stop. Understandably, David was very startled but respected her wishes. Judy and her therapist discussed the flashback in detail, and she was able to release the memory and surrounding feelings. She had a clearer understanding of the differences between an act of aggression and an act of love. The therapist urged Judy to speak openly with her husband about what had happened and how they could deal with it if it were to occur again. In addition, the therapist suggested that there was a high probability that sex could set off more flashbacks and that an effective way of coping would be for Judy to say "stop," open her eyes, reorient to the present environment, and see her husband next to her. If she was unable to proceed sexually at that moment, that was fine.

Because there is so much change during the treatment, the partner may experience a sense of loss about the way things used to be. She or he may feel rejected or no longer needed. The more directly those sad and painful feelings can be expressed, the easier the two people can approach them. It is when that loss gets translated into "I want you to be the way you were when you didn't feel so strong," that the relationship will suffer.

The Partner's Jealousy of the Therapist

When treatment begins, most partners are relieved and supportive. They feel less worried about the client's well-being now that professional help is on the scene. As the therapeutic relationship is cemented the partner may feel left out or replaced. Whereas he or she used to be the focal point of all sharing for the client, the therapist has now assumed a very prominent place. The client may share less with her partner or defer to the therapist. "I've already talked to my therapist about that. I don't feel like saying anymore," or "My therapist says it's normal for me to shut down when such-and-such happens." The triangulation can be upsetting and disruptive to the partner. Although the therapist may be temporarily pivotal to the client's emotional well-being, the partner is still the primary connection in the client's life. The jealousy is understandable but the therapist is not going to replace the partner. As long as the therapist continuously urges the client to stay open to her partner, jealousy should be minimal.

The Partner and the Survivor's Abusive Family

As the client faces and works through the aftermath of the incest, she will make new decisions about interacting with her family. She may choose to confront her abuser or nonprotector. She may decide to avoid family gatherings. She may desire protection from her family. Any of these decisions will affect the partner's relationships to the client's family. Additionally, as the past becomes more revealed to the client and she shares that with her partner, some new decisions may follow as well.

Partners of incest survivors are deeply pained to learn about the abuse their loved ones suffered in childhood. If the abuser is still alive, the partner can find it difficult being in his presence. Many partners wonder why the client has anything to do with her family and often urge a total cutoff. Conversely, other partners are so disturbed about the incest they have a reaction formation and insist on maintaining contact with the survivor's family. It is reasonable for the partner to have a variety of responses to the abuser and the family, but it is often difficult for the client to cope with those feelings. They become too entangled with her own feelings and she will often revert to defending her family. It is useful for the partner to deal with his or her more intense emotions about the client's family with someone other than the client. Whenever possible, the partner needs to support the client's position and decision-making.

The partner has a particularly acute vantage point that can be helpful for the client. If the partner accompanies the client to a family gathering, she or he can often perceive what the client cannot see because of her own defenses. The partner can report that "Your father was so verbally negative with you and your mother, it just made me cringe." This may be a surprise to the client. She is so accustomed to this kind of interaction that she accepts it as the status quo rather than something harmful. The partner's perspective can lend new insights to the client that she can bring into the therapy.

The Couple's Sexual Relationship

During the course of treatment the client will be dealing with highly charged sexual material. She will be learning about her own sexuality as well as developing ideas about what is healthy and normal. She will be facing the shameful context within which she was introduced to the realm of adult sexuality. At times this work will cause her to avoid all sexual encounters. Her partner will feel those consequences. There will be periods when the client simply cannot feel safe enough to be sexually available. Her partner may simultaneously feel compassion and anger. Undoubtedly he or she will understand the origin of the client's sensitivity and, at the same time, experience the unpleasantness of not having sexual needs met.

There is a balance that needs to be approached here. On one hand, the client's need not to be sexual at times must be respected. On the other hand, the partner's needs must not be entirely ignored. If the couple simply agrees not to be sexual indefinitely, there will be trouble down the road. If there is a mutual consensus to have an asexual relationship, it becomes difficult to introduce sexuality sometime later. Sexual intimacy has been defined as too dangerous. One midpoint that can be comfortable for both is maintaining a physically affectionate connection that is nonsexual. The client will often require more cuddles and hugs that feel safe and warm and protective. Although this will not be sexually gratifying, it is better than complete physical distance. Verbally communicating about both of their needs will also continue a more intimate connection. Even if they are imperfect in meeting each other's needs, they are at least aware of them. It is important for the therapist to urge the client to perceive her partner's sexual needs so that the client does not lull herself into the creation of an asexual mate. Full recovery includes a sexually functional relationship and this should never be too far away from the client's thinking.

The Client's Therapy and the Partner's Repressed History
of Incest or Abuse

It is not uncommon for partners of incest survivors to reevaluate their pasts and suddenly become aware of incestuous or abusive dynamics in their own families.

What had seemed "ordinary" may now be seen as harmful. The client's work on clarifying the family functioning teaches the partner new perspectives. If a partner becomes aware of damaging memories, therapy for him or her would be recommended.

During the course of treatment the client will ask the therapist many questions about her primary relationship. As the therapist is not treating the partner, she or he will need to offer generic responses about common relationship struggles and healthy dynamics. The emphasis must be on the client's experience and evaluation of her intimate relationship rather than on the therapist's assessment. The first area of concern is whether or not the client feels safe in her relationship.

If the client describes her partner as being verbally, physically, psychologically, or sexually abusive, the therapist will need to help the client express the feelings she has in this relationship. The more cognizant she becomes of her pain, the more likely she will decide to leave the relationship. The therapist must be careful not to push too hard unless it is apparent that the client is in immediate physical danger. The client is so accustomed to mistreatment that she will need help identifying cruel behaviors. The therapist can coach the client to set limits and ask for what she needs from her partner. If the client receives little satisfaction over a significant period of time, she must consider leaving the relationship. The therapist's role is to support the client's reasoned (as opposed to impulsive) decision-making.

If the primary relationship is essentially loving and supportive, the therapist needs to encourage the client to share as much of her story as possible with her partner. The therapist must be mindful of the potential for triangulation and attempt to minimize it. By urging the client to keep an open communication with her partner, the therapist is emphasizing the importance of that relationship. There will be times when the client is not willing or able to share certain information with her partner. This is acceptable as long as there is the mention that "maybe some day you will be able to tell your partner about this." As much as possible, the therapist must encourage the client to share her growth and change, as it is occurring, with her partner. Otherwise, the relationship will be in serious trouble toward the end of treatment.

Throughout treatment the therapist needs to bring the partner's needs into the picture. The client's current context is as important as her past context. Discovering what patterns the incest has left with her, she is also learning new habits. These must include balanced relationships where both adults have needs and work together to meet them. The partner will be taxed quite a bit during the healing process and his or her needs ought not be forgotten. Even if the client is now unable to address her partner's needs, they must be part of the scheme.

There will be moments when a client will deliver a request to the therapist from her partner. "My husband wants to know if he can speak with you about my progress or how he can help." "My lover wants to know if you think we should be in couples treatment." These remarks should be reflected back to the client. "Do you want me to speak to your husband?" "Do you feel you need to be in couples treatment?" The client is very adept at addressing these issues. She usually knows exactly what she wants to do. The therapist can just take the client's lead. If the client gives the therapist permission to speak to her partner, they need to discuss the parameters of that conversation. The client's privacy and confidentiality must be honored.

WHEN IS COUPLES TREATMENT RECOMMENDED?

If a therapist were to take a purist family systems approach, an incest survivor who was in a committed relationship would be encouraged to commence treatment together with her partner. Since the incest is undoubtedly affecting the marriage, the issue is framed as a family concern. From this treatment bias the recommendation makes sense, but in actuality it does not work. A survivor beginning recovery in couples therapy achieves only minimal progress. The reunification of the self largely occurs in the context of a one-on-one therapeutic relationship. The survivor must have the privacy of this prescribed relationship to relive her shame, sadness, rage, humiliation, and loss. To encourage her to attempt this in the presence of her partner is asking too much. She will not be able to explore the depths of her reality in couples treatment.

As the client enters the latter phases of individual treatment, some couples treatment may be useful to help the couple adjust to all the changes. As has been discussed, the wholeness of the client alters the fundamental agreements the relationship was based on, and that will put the couple through some rough times. They may feel that an objective third party would be helpful. Under these circumstances, couples treatment can, indeed, be extremely useful.

In lieu of engaging in couples therapy, the client can receive individual coaching from the therapist. This is a technique used by family therapists who treat individuals from a systems perspective (Carter and Orfanidis 1976). In essence it is like the football coach calling in the play from the sidelines. The therapist makes a suggestion to the client about a particular relationship dilemma that she can take home with her. Hopefully the play will gain yardage for the couple and they can move further down the playing field.

As Maureen progressed in her therapy, she began to experience many intense feelings. At times she was overwhelmed with sadness and grief. Her therapist had encouraged her to share those moments with her lover by talking about the sources of her sadness and asking to be held and comforted. She did just that but it turned out less than satisfying. Maureen's lover, Heather, was unable to tolerate the intensity of emotion for more than a few minutes. As she listened to Maureen and held her, Heather became tense and wooden. Soon after she said that it probably wasn't a good idea for Maureen to "get so wrapped up in all this sadness" and maybe they'd be better off if they played a vigorous game of tennis. Maureen was disappointed and asked her therapist what to do next.

Maureen: I don't think I knew before recently that Heather has such trouble with feelings but, now that I think about it, she always stuffs her own feelings away too. I finally get to a point where I can experience feelings and now she's of no use to me. I guess I just won't be able to talk to her about this stuff.

Therapist: I wouldn't recommend that. She needs to stay informed about what is evolving within you.

Maureen: Well, how can I do that if she can't tolerate it?

Therapist: Maybe you have to take smaller steps with Heather. And make it an exercise in mutuality. For instance, you're in the middle of this grief process. What if you sat Heather down at a relaxing moment, say after a nice dinner, and raised the topic of loss and grief in a neutral way? Like you could say, "This therapy is really dredging up all kinds of sadness for me. It sure gets intense sometimes. It gets me to thinking about how my family never dealt with sadness. What did your family do when your grandmother died? Did people cry or talk about how devastating her death was?" In other words, bring Heather into the conversation and see if she can open up a little bit too.

Maureen: I know her. She'll say two brief sentences and try to change the topic.

Therapist: Demonstrate how you could respond to bring it back.

Maureen: I guess I could say, "I know you don't love talking about feelings but I think we both need to learn how to do this. I worry about both of us— that we'll give ourselves ulcers if we keep swallowing everything we feel. Would you be willing to spend more time talking about how we both learned to deal with our feelings?"

Therapist: How do you think she'd respond to that?

Maureen: (laughs) She'd probably say I've been talking to you too much!! But then she'd probably give it a try.

Maureen did go home and tried this approach. Heather was unusually open and talkative. Tears came to her eyes when she spoke about her grandmother's death. Maureen was able to offer support and encouragement and explain to Heather that she wanted more moments like this for each of them. Although Heather never initiated these conversations, she became fairly cooperative in listening, talking, and comforting.

Under no circumstances should a therapist recommend couples treatment in an abusive relationship. The abuser must be referred for appropriate treatment while the victim pursues individual therapy. If the time arrives when the abuser has made sufficient progress, couples treatment can be cautiously approached as an adjunct to individual work.

As the primary treatment of choice, couples therapy is contraindicated. As adjunctive work towards the end of the survivor's individual treatment, couples therapy can be a useful resource in aiding the adjustments within the relationship.

Incest treatment will have a profound impact on the client's primary relationship. Moving from a fragmented individual with low self-esteem to becoming an integrated and worthy person will change the entire landscape of the relationship. There will be a transformed person needing to find new ways to connect with her partner. However, there will also be a partner looking for remnants of that former self. The relationship will be challenged to establish new outer limits and achieve a new balance. As trying as this will be for the client, the demands on the partner are equally significant.

SEXUALITY

No recovery from the scarring of childhood incest would be complete without the adult survivor developing a positive and healthy sense of her own sexuality. As a child she was introduced prematurely, inappropriately, and often cruelly into the world of adult sexuality. She was not allowed the opportunity to discover and explore her own sexual feelings gradually. What the child learned about sex was filled with terror, distortions, confusion, loss of power and control, humiliation, and shame. The child has grown up linking inappropriate sexual advances with being loved. She will bring these notions into her intimate adult relationships. Additionally, although the survivor is often repulsed by adult sexuality she also feels that her purpose in life is to sexually pleasure all who request it. This dichotomy has the potential to lead to self-loathing. All of this convoluted learning will be challenged in the therapy and eventually the client will emerge with a clearer and saner view of her own sexuality.

As the therapy winds down the client will be filled with hundreds of questions about normal sexuality. Her questions will range from biology to sexual orientation and everything in between. There are three areas of fundamental learning that will help the client establish a healthy sense of sexuality: physiology, sexual development, and body image and appreciation. The therapist can provide answers to some basic questions, direct the client toward appropriate reading and medical attention, and offer intervention strategies. Sexuality is not something the therapist will need to raise. When she is ready, the client will present her concerns. As she integrates all her new learning over the course of treatment, her motivation to feel sexually healed will naturally emerge. This usually occurs during the last phase of therapy.

Whereas the client would have felt too embarrassed earlier in the treatment to ask the therapist some basic questions about physiology, she will certainly ask at this point. In essence, she is seeking the information that a good parent would have shared with a child. She will want to know about menstruation, what causes cramping, what vaginal discharge is about, why one breast is larger than the other, what the gynecologist is checking for, and the name of that instrument she uses. Some survivors may have searched medical textbooks to find answers to their questions, but many others will have avoided gathering any written or verbal information related to their bodies. If the therapist feels adequately informed she or he can address each question but may also suggest reading a basic consumer text such as *Our Bodies, Ourselves* (1979) or a visit to a sensitive gynecologist. Again, the therapist's responses here can be those of a parent.

The client will need to learn about sexual responses, sexual development, normal sexual behaviors, and the differences between male and female sexuality. It is not necessary to prescribe any technical reading in this area (such as Masters and Johnson); instead the therapist can answer some basic questions and then guide the client toward her own self-awareness about her likes and dislikes, bodily sensations, and values and attitudes. The client will ask questions about masturbation, various sex acts, sexual fantasies, sexual orientation, celibacy, and sexual development in childhood. As long as the therapist does not offer value judgments, she or he can offer explanations to these queries. It is very important for the therapist to steer clear of anything other than factual information about sexual development. Most survivors were instructed in sexual attitudes by their abusers. "It is a father's duty. . . . It's wrong for boys to do this to you. . . . You will only enjoy this with me. . . . I'm going to teach you everything a woman needs to know about pleasing a man. . . . Little girls are very seductive and irresistible. . . ." The new learning must be filled with accurate information that can be assimilated into the client's own experiences.

Most incest survivors harbor very negative and distorted body images. They have come to feel betrayed by their bodies and cut off from any appreciation or sensations. In order to develop a positive attitude toward sexuality, the client will need to work hard to establish a loving feeling toward her body. This is impossible to approach until the client has a powerful and affirming sense of herself. Earlier in treatment the client feels that her body epitomizes everything that is bad and wrong with her. She sees herself as fat or ugly or gross or disgusting or dirty. As she becomes confident that she is lovable and that she did not cause the incest, she is ready to embrace her body as an ally and as a source of pleasure. The therapist can suggest exercises in body awareness and appreciation that could include athletic activities, dancing, massage, self-touch, long baths, or sensual experiences. If the client can develop a positive body image, sexual pleasure is just around the corner.

In addition to learning about sexuality in the physical realm, the client needs to integrate this into the context of a caring relationship. One of the best resources for clients and their partners is Maltz and Holman's *Incest and Sexuality* (1987). This book describes the necessary ingredients for a healthy intimate relationship and how to achieve that when one or both partners have suffered from incest. It is a sensitive and simple book that, in particular, addresses the issues of mutual consent, trust building, open communication, and the establishment of healthy boundaries (see also Maltz 1991).

SEXUAL ORIENTATION

Many incest survivors will grapple with questions about sexual orientation and this will be part of their sexual discovery and healing. Almost without exception, women who were sexually abused as children by men will wonder if they wouldn't feel more sexually comfortable with other women. They have struggled with such negative experiences of male sexuality that they feel profoundly confused. The therapist needs to grant permission and safety for the client to raise all her questions and concerns.

One thing is certain: incest does not determine one's sexual orientation. In fact, incest interrupts ordinary sexual development to the point where the adolescent is often cut off from her own sexual feelings and desires. Puberty is usually a time when a teenager notices her attractions and arousals to her peers—male or female. Experimentation follows, and eventually the young woman senses her tendency toward same-sex or opposite-sex relationships. For incest survivors, this may not unfold so naturally because sex is a painful and shameful subject. Although she may make a choice about sexually relating to men and/or women, the survivor may still be unsure about her truest sexual orientation.

It is important for the therapist to approach these questions openly and without homophobia. This is the client's opportunity to go back to a missed developmental stage, and she needs to know within her soul that she has freely and rightly chosen the gender best suited to her. The therapist's role is to be the witness to this process rather than the judge.

Sexual healing for the incest survivor has a very optimistic prognosis. When approached carefully, slowly, and bit by bit, the client can embrace her own sexuality and rejoice in the pleasure it brings her. This will enhance her ongoing relationship and elevate it to a new level of intimacy. Once this is accomplished, the client is usually ready to terminate therapy.

7

Forgiveness

The *American Heritage Dictionary* defines the concept "to forgive" as "to excuse for a fault or offense; to pardon; to renounce anger or resentment against; to absolve from payment." Synonyms listed are "excuse, condone . . . to pass over an offense and to free the offender from the consequences of it." Judeo-Christian doctrine avers that "to err is human; to forgive, divine." People who can forgive the wrongdoings of others are considered spiritually enlightened and worthy of the highest esteem. To be unforgiving is viewed as harboring unnecessary resentment, as in holding a grudge. American society places a high value on forgiveness and many incest survivors feel the pressure to forgive their assailants. What are the implications of such a request?

TO FORGIVE OR NOT TO FORGIVE

An incest survivor is urged to absolve the perpetrator of his crime, let go of the anger she feels toward him, release him from suffering any consequences of his actions, and to move on with her life. There is a popular notion that if a survivor does not forgive her abuser then she will be stuck, unable to recover fully from her wounds and steeped in perpetual anger. Does this make sense? Is this healthy for the client? Are other crime victims similarly pressured?

When someone has been the victim of a random and senseless attack, such as robbery, assault, or "wilding," there is no emphasis placed on forgiving the assailant. In this society a criminal is expected to be tried for the crime, to be

149

publicly identified as having committed the act, to receive a just punishment, including possible financial restitution to the victim or prison time, and to be rehabilitated before reentering the community. The more heinous the crime, the more contempt the society feels for the individual. Although some victims or their families have found it within themselves to forgive their attackers, this is not the focus of the resolution to the situation. The focus is on justice and making the guilty party pay for the consequences of the actions. It is unlikely that survivors of the Holocaust, terrorist hostages, or families of murder victims will ever be pressured to forgive their captors or destroyers. It is acceptable for them to stay angry and to not offer absolution for acts that are so clearly irrational and evil. Yet incest survivors are urged to understand their abusers and forgive them even when there is no acknowledged culpability for their crimes.

It would seem that asking the survivor to forgive the perpetrator is asking her to continue to take responsibility for something that does not belong to her. As a molested child she felt responsible for creating the incest experience. The adult did not say to her, "I'm sorry for abusing you last night. I wasn't appropriately taking care of my own needs." Instead, he conveyed, "This is your fault. I'd control myself if you weren't so beautiful/stubborn/bad/seductive. . . ." Many years after the fact most abusers hope and pray the incest is forgotten by the now-adult. He still does not come forward to apologize, take responsibility, or acknowledge that it even occurred. Even when confronted, the abuser rarely validates the victim. And it is in this context that the survivor grapples with the notion of forgiveness. It is certainly crazy-making and counterproductive to treatment goals to encourage the client to excuse the harmful behaviors of her abuser.

Adults who commit incestuous acts are not seen as criminals. They are seen as fathers, grandfathers, uncles, brothers, mothers, stepfathers. The family position is emphasized rather than the destructive nature of their actions. They are seen as troubled individuals worthy of compassion, although the act of sexually molesting a child is viewed with horror and disgust. The person and the action are viewed separately. This is not true of most crimes. Those who kill are called murderers. Those who loot are called robbers. Those who sexually attack adults are called rapists. Those who sexually molest children at random are called pedophiles or child molesters. But those who sexually molest children within their families are called fathers, stepfathers, grandfathers, and so on. The victim is asked to understand that her father was abused by his father who was abused by his father before him and therefore he "just couldn't help himself." But the client *has* made the decision to help herself. If she could take the responsibility to face the devastation the abuse caused, why didn't her father? This contrast in choices does not propel the client toward forgiveness, but instead makes the issue a total puzzle. For the survivor, responsibility and forgiveness are inextricably bound. Were the abuser to take responsibility for his actions, forgiveness might be a possibility. Then there would be justice. Then there would be validation. Then there would be remorse. Then the responsibility would fall on the appropriate shoulders. And this could lead to forgiveness.

HEALTHY AND UNHEALTHY REASONS TO FORGIVE

In the absence of admission of guilt by the abuser, what are the psychologically healthy reasons for a client to forgive? Over the course of her life, a client may have developed a spiritual or moral belief system that includes forgiveness of others' wrongdoings. If she has adequately expressed and resolved her anger about the abuse she may feel it would be compatible with her belief system to absolve her abuser. However, if this occurs prematurely it would represent an avoidance of experiencing her most intense feelings. If it occurs in the last phases of treatment, the client may feel liberated or cleansed.

If the assailant has acknowledged the incest, expressed remorse, and entered treatment the client is in a good position to truly heal the relationship. Discussion of the events and the abuser's taking responsibility for past and present behaviors optimizes the healing and forgiveness potential within the client.

Certain motivations to forgive the unrepentant abuser can be unhealthy for the client. Having extreme compassion for the abuser's life may lead a victim to pardon his actions toward her, thus continuing in her role as the object of his unresolved past. The client may feel that if she does not forgive, she will be rejected by the family, the church, the community, or the therapist. She feels she will be an outcast because she has not done the noble thing, so she convinces herself all is forgiven. She feels pressured to forgive and forget without understanding that she is being urged to do so only to make others more comfortable. It would not be true forgiveness. It would be a collusion of denial. The client may also believe that if she does not forgive then she is forever destined to a life of bitterness and anger. She does not see how she might be able to resolve her anger yet still withhold her forgiveness. Were the client to absolve her abuser for any of these reasons she leaves herself dangerously vulnerable to being revictimized in her future.

There is a misconception that not forgiving will lead to hatred, obsession, poor emotional health, or perpetual rage on the client's part. The implication is that forgiveness is the fullest release from the pain of having been so violated. This simply is not true. First of all, even the most severely abused children do not sustain hatred toward their abusive parents. The desire to feel loved by the parent is far stronger than any other feeling a child may experience. If there is any obsession, it is an obsession with love rather than hate or rage. Secondly, the release from the pain of betrayal comes through introspection, expression, perspective, and integration. Forgiveness is but one potential outcome of the process rather than the process itself.

If a client does not forgive her abuser, she retains a self-protective warning system. That system guards her from further harm from her abuser or other dangerous people. She will have developed the idea that some acts are unforgivable, especially those that involve powerful people mistreating the helpless. She remains forever aware that betrayal and violation are possible even from those she loves. This may cause her always to leave a piece of herself tucked away so that if she is ever hurt again she can survive again. In short, she will maintain a survivor's stance rather than a victim's stance. A victim believes that "No matter what pain someone causes me I will eventually offer my compassion and forgiveness," thus leaving herself open to any unkind act. A survivor says "Never again will anyone have the power to annihilate me."

THE THERAPIST'S ROLE

What can or should the therapist's role be as the client grapples with the question of forgiveness? Certainly the therapist must allow the client every opportunity to talk about her ambivalences and concerns. Certainly the therapist must help the client to resolve her rage before addressing matters of forgiveness; only then can the therapist support the client's spiritual or moral beliefs that help her make peace with this issue. But what about the therapist's assessment or moral judgment of the perpetrator? Should this be brought into the therapy?

Traditionally, therapists are trained to be quintessentially nonjudgmental. Anything short of this would hinder a good therapeutic relationship, which is clearly a very sound position. But in the course of treating incest survivors, clinicians hear stories that defy human understanding and compassion. Adults who sexually abuse children, in spite of their own abusive childhoods, are somehow *monstrous* or less than human. In a recent interview, Dr. Judith Herman said she believes there is no medical model, no diagnostic category, that can explain away the perpetrators of such crimes.

> They are just evil. . . . They do it because they want to and it gives them satisfaction. Research currently being done with sex offenders, where they are promised confidentiality in return for participation, indicates, essentially, that they have no empathy for their victims. They may look good on the outside, both socially and in terms of traditional mental health categories, but then so did S.S. officers. They had no psychosis; they had pets and wives and people they were kind to. [Hawkins 1991, p. 50]

The concept of evil is a new one to the mental health field and few psychotherapists feel comfortable defining human behavior in such terms. This idea is slowly being taken out of the closet by such respected clinicians as Judith Herman and Scott Peck. They are carefully introducing the idea that evil exists within many parents who sexually, physically, and emotionally abuse their children. They strongly urge vigorous discussion and research about the nature of evil, but they also suggest that clinicians can aid the healing process for their clients by identifying the perpetrators as evil individuals who have chosen dishonesty and destruction of others over truth and goodness.

Peck (1983) defines evil this way:

> Evil is in opposition to life. It is that which opposes the life force. It has, in short, to do with killing. . . . When I say that evil has to do with killing, I do not mean to restrict myself to corporeal murder. Evil is also that which kills the spirit. There are various essential attributes of life—particularly human life—such as sentience, mobility, awareness, growth, autonomy, will. It is possible to kill or attempt to kill one of these attributes without actually killing the body. [p. 42]

Seeing forgiveness of the abuser in the context of evil may clarify the dilemma for the client. When is it ever appropriate to forgive someone who has consciously tried to kill another human being?

The concept of perpetrators as evil is raised here to challenge therapists to think further about what Herman and Peck are observing. All clinicians treating incest survivors have wondered about the capacity for evil within human beings. The atrocities committed against small children certainly go beyond most psychiatric classifications. Whether or not an individual therapist will feel comfortable using such strong terminology with clients must come from that therapist's own examination of the concepts of evil and forgiveness.

8

The Therapist

THE THERAPIST'S LEVEL OF CLINICAL EXPERTISE

Incest treatment can easily overwhelm an inexperienced clinician. The therapy is complicated and the emotionality is intense. This is not an episodic crisis or a developmental stage. Incest leaves deep scarring that requires extensive longer-term psychotherapy with a confident therapist.

The skilled and seasoned therapist has accumulated enough years of experience to have a well-established therapeutic style. She or he has experimented with being too distant, not separate enough, overinvolved, too "touchy-feely," or too sterile to have arrived at a comfortable balance that is both very professional and very human. A demonstration or videotape of any of the truly great family therapists illustrates this point (for instance, O. Silverstein, J. Haley, S. Minuchin, P. Papp, H. Aponte). Because incest treatment relies so heavily on the confidence, comfort, and good boundaries of the therapist, it is hard to imagine a new clinician feeling adequately prepared to do this work.

Tolerating and working with extreme and intense emotions is not for every therapist. If this is an area of concern for a therapist, incest treatment will present many challenges. Even some experienced clinicians urge their clients to contain their strongest feelings. It would be advisable for the uneasy therapist to receive additional professional consultation and training in the realm of rage, grief, and release work.

Most therapists would agree that diagnostic skills improve steadily over time. The more clients one sees, the more honed assessment skills become. It is a matter of sheer volume and variety. What may have looked like a classic borderline disorder early in one's career may not appear so later on. Attention to subtleties and nuances provides for sharper diagnoses. This is a critical element for incest therapy. To the less-trained eye, survivors may appear quite patho-logical, which would set in motion an inappropriate treatment plan that may include, for instance, premature evaluations for medications, analysis, four appointments a week, or even hospitalization. A keen diagnostician would be able to separate pathology from survival coping mechanisms characteristic of Post-Traumatic Stress Disorder.

As has been illustrated earlier, incest treatment progresses well with an eclectic mixture of intervention strategies. Most graduate schools train students to do two or three things very well with a bit of working knowledge about other forms of treatment. It is usually during post-graduate training or clinical exper-imentation that a therapist expands her or his repertoire of innovative methods. The bigger the bag of tricks, the more creative the treatment can become. A therapist is prompted to learn some new tricks when the old stand-bys aren't enough, the presenting problem is unfamiliar, or there have been innovations in the field. The beginning practitioner is more taken up with establishing good basic skills within a specific treatment orientation. This is an appropriate goal but will not be enough for incest treatment.

If it should happen that a less-experienced or less-comfortable therapist must deal with incest issues with a client, supervision is recommended. There is unquestionably a great deal for the therapist to learn but it should not be at the client's expense. Because this is a new field of study and treatment, supervision by therapists who have specialized in incest treatment is prudent even for more experienced clinicians. There are many moments during the course of this therapy when the therapist may doubt her or his perspective or intervention strategies. Consultation can clarify these strategies and thus provide another avenue of protection for the client. If treatment becomes excessively stalled or difficult, it is important to reassess the client–therapist match. It may turn out that a particular client may never achieve the kind of confidence or trust in the therapist she will need in order to progress. Inviting a third-party consultant for one to three sessions can clarify the situation. As the therapist models getting help from other resources when relationships are stuck, the client receives affirmation for her choice to be in therapy. Bringing in a consultant minimizes the possibility for the client to feel rejected if the decision shows a need for a different therapist. Conversely, it can maximize the potential for a clearer therapeutic connection. Good supervision is simply good practice.

THE GENDER OF THE THERAPIST

Does it matter? Since the overwhelming majority of incest survivors are women and approximately 93 percent of the perpetrators are men (summary of research in Courtois 1988), most clients will select women therapists. Male survivors also have a tendency to select women therapists. An in-depth discussion about whether male therapists can be effective in incest treatment becomes largely an academic exercise since clients have already made their preferences perfectly clear. Very few women who are seeking a therapist to help them recover from the pain of incest will actively search for a male therapist. American culture today seems to equate men with aggressive and threatening behaviors and women with comforting and understanding traits. Whether or not this is true or the client's own experience confirms this, most clients feel a woman therapist is a safer choice.

But the question still remains. Does the gender of the therapist matter in incest treatment? Will the client progress more if her therapist is the opposite or same gender of her abuser? What about the gender of the primary nonprotector? Can the client perceive a woman therapist as truly safe if her mother never protected her from her abusive father? Will a male therapist inevitably be cast as the perpetrator and hopelessly impede the treatment? The truth is that for the incest survivor neither men nor women were appropriate or adequate in caring for her. But in most cases a man was the most overtly frightening and harmful force while a woman was a more passive and inaccessible player. This implies a greater comfort zone with women, although trust will be difficult. What the client needs most of all is a safe, appropriate, caring, and wise *adult*. If a client chooses to work with a male therapist he certainly can fulfill these functions.

If a male therapist is treating incest survivors there are special considerations. There is a need to establish not just clear but rigid boundaries within the therapeutic relationship without becoming too distant. If the boundaries are permeable, the client will be anticipating inappropriate behavior (even if it never happens). If the male therapist is too distant he becomes a threat. This is a very tricky balance to strike. In this context, touching of any kind will be exceptionally loaded. The client will probably not give the therapist permission to offer any form of physical comfort, and this must be respected. Even a casual pat on the back as the client leaves the room would be inadvisable.

Early in treatment when it is important for the client to be as explicit as possible about the incest experiences, the male therapist needs to be mindful that his questioning and encouragement not be viewed as voyeurism. Even if it is not the therapist's intent to be titillated by the sexual details, many clients find the male therapist's questions to be askew. For instance, when a female therapist is pressing for details she usually asks, "What happened next?" Many women clients report that a male therapist poses his question more like, "What did you and your father do in bed?" There is an undertone of sexual collusion in the man's question. There is a possibility that an incest client will be more overtly seductive with a male therapist. This is learned behavior and one that must be discouraged by the therapist. Were the therapist to feel flattered by the client's advances, the therapy would be endangered. This could present a particularly charged situation for the heterosexual client and therapist.

Developing a trusting relationship with a man will be a very trying experience for an incest survivor. All the previously discussed issues around trust building early in the treatment will be accentuated many times over. If the male therapist is skilled and well-boundaried, trust will eventually occur. The client will decide if it is worth the time and effort to struggle with issues of trust with a male. Survivors usually opt for a less loaded relationship with a female therapist to begin their lessons in trust. Some will go on to a second therapy with a male therapist after the bulk of their work is completed in order to resolve their remaining issues with men.

Women treating incest survivors have different concerns. It is easy for the client to perceive the female therapist as the mother or protector she never had. If the therapist remains only in that role she will not be effective enough in the treatment. She must be much more than just protective of the client. Conversely, the female therapist may experience maternal feelings toward the client. (This is not to imply that a male therapist could not also have nurturant feelings.) This would cause the therapist to infantalize the client, making the definition of the therapeutic relationship more like that of a parent and child; there would not be enough distance or appropriate boundaries.

In these days of feminism, women are enraged when they hear stories about violence toward women and children. The female therapist treating incest survivors will get quite an earful. As a woman, the therapist will identify with the client's anger and fears toward men who harm women and children. If both the therapist and the client are consumed with their rage the treatment will deteriorate. The female therapist will need to find private ways to resolve her own feelings. She cannot bring her anger at the abuser or men into the therapy. Likewise, male therapists need to confront their abhorrence of and identification with the abuser. These are vulnerable issues for therapists that need clarity or else the treatment becomes contaminated.

If a female therapist is treating a male survivor she will be faced with the same dilemmas as the female client–male therapist pairing. For male survivors who were abused by their mothers, trusting a female therapist will be especially problematic.

In general, incest clients will have already resolved the gender issues before searching for a therapist. The greatest majority of survivors will select a female therapist. The implication is that only a handful of male therapists will be approached to do this work; however, with adequate skill and training they can conduct effective treatment. Sensitivity to these concerns is important and client preference should prevail.

THE THERAPIST'S MOTIVES FOR TREATING INCEST SURVIVORS

Many therapists find themselves specializing in incest treatment simply because of the number of clients revealing sexually abusive childhoods. The work is challenging and interesting and the therapist studies to conduct the best possible therapy. For others, though, the motivation may not be just happenstance. There may be a personal ax to grind or an old score to settle or a campaign to launch. Many therapists treating survivors are incest or abuse survivors themselves. Others purport radical feminist politics and are ready to bring down the patriarchy. Still others harbor deep resentments and anger toward men without specific political rhetoric, as well as professional rescuers out to save the victims of oppression. These are some of the more dangerous motives a therapist can bring to incest treatment.

If a therapist approaches incest therapy with a personal agenda, she provides an underlying bias or feeling that will influence the client's direction. This brings the client under the therapist's spell and thus disempowers her, for she will have traded one influential figure for another and will still be subject to someone else's outlook and value system. She must uncover her *own* thinking, her *own* feelings, and her *own* resolutions. A therapist who, overtly or covertly, holds strong beliefs (other than that the sexual abuse of children is always wrong) or who sees these clients as needing a benevolent savior undermines the treatment and the client's potential growth.

Most therapists continue to do incest work because they have come to have the highest respect for these survivors. They are triumphant individuals who need to experience their power and efficacy. Many therapists are moved by their stories, their survival, and their growth; outrage over sexual and physical abuse of children is a common feeling among these therapists. These are appropriate feelings and motives to bring to this work.

IF THE THERAPIST IS AN INCEST SURVIVOR

The odds that the therapist is a survivor are high, so the question becomes how should she or he handle that fact while treating other survivors. First, the therapist should have completed extensive psychotherapy and feel sufficiently healed from the past. In the process, the therapist should have learned a great deal about setting and maintaining clear boundaries in relationships. This is an essential concern as the survivor-therapist needs to define nearly rigid boundaries in the therapeutic relationship. This is especially difficult when the client is working through emotionally volatile material. It is easy for the therapist's own issues to be triggered by the client. To maintain clarity about what feelings belong to whom can be truly difficult for the survivor-therapist. There is also a tendency to distance from the relationship when the therapy intensely evokes the therapist's own childhood feelings. This can get very bumpy but good supervision can smooth it out.

It is imperative that the survivor-therapist *not* reveal her identification with the client until the very end of treatment—if she feels she must. Disclosing her or his incestuous past with the client will have an adverse effect on the treatment. The client will tone down her own story, try to draw out the therapist's story, worry about upsetting the therapist, perceive the therapist as the ultimate role model of recovery, or generally contain herself. This completely hampers the client's treatment. She will attempt to be nurturing to the therapist and not receive the treatment she needs. If the therapist wants to tell the client that she or he is a survivor, too, this should only occur at the very end of treatment, but this is a choice, not a necessity. However, one advantage the survivor-therapist brings to incest treatment is his or her keen insights into the client's experience and psyche. The therapist's own personal struggles with incest and recovery lend rich perspective to this work.

ETHICAL GUIDELINES

Every psychological discipline has a standard of ethics that practitioners are expected to follow. Broadly speaking it includes keeping to professional guidelines, treating the client rather than the caregiver, abstaining from any sexual liaisons with clients, obtaining supervision, and referring clients to other clinicians when necessary. These are behaviors all clients, including incest clients, should expect from their therapists. However, for therapists who treat incest survivors there are other issues.

Many analytically trained psychotherapists still ascribe to Freud's postulation that incest reports are merely the sexualized Oedipus or Electra fantasies of the client. Although this notion has been greatly challenged, some therapists are still skeptical about the validity of their clients' memories. Even the slightest doubt from the therapist can be damaging for the client. It is unethical and immoral for therapists to approach incest as a figment of someone's imagination. Were a client to present these concerns to such an analytical purist, it would be proper for her or him to refer that client for a different kind of treatment. First and foremost, these clients deserve to be treated by therapists who believe them. (For an in-depth discussion of this issue see Miller 1990.)

Although therapists are trained to be rigorously nonjudgmental, it is impossible to always achieve this state. After all, therapists are human too. Where this might present a problem is with the therapist's own value system especially around spiritual or religious ideals, the sanctity of the family, sexuality, and retribution. As has been mentioned earlier in several contexts, the client must discover her own belief system and resolutions. If a therapist believes so fervently in the idea of forgiveness, especially as related to salvation, there is danger she or he will impose this on the client. If a therapist believes that all people should "honor thy father and thy mother" regardless of the sins of the parents, this will become a treatment goal. If a therapist feels that homosexuality is unnatural or wrong or sinful, the homosexual client will continue to feel shameful about her sexuality. And if a therapist believes all child molesters and abusers should be brought out into the light of day through public or private confrontation or through legal action, then the client will be goaded to pursue some form of retribution. None of these attitudes may be in the client's best interests. The therapist must be careful to tuck away her or his own beliefs about what would be the "correct" resolution to childhood trauma. The only correct solution is the one the client selects.

TAKING CARE OF THE CARETAKER

Incest treatment can get under a therapist's skin as can few others. The work is so intense, compelling, and potentially consuming, it becomes essential for the therapist to take good care of her- or himself in order to continue to provide help to these clients.

Because the therapeutic relationship becomes so intense, the therapist must be certain that her or his personal life already includes several important relationships. Otherwise there is the danger that the client–therapist relationship will be the source of personal gratification for the therapist. If the therapist's personal needs are not being met, there will be great temptation to fill that void with the richness of the therapy relationship, which would infuse the treatment with inappropriate expectations.

Conversely, there is a possibility of the therapeutic relationship spilling over into the therapist's personal life. There must be clear guidelines within the treatment to minimize the potential for constant intrusions. It is also important for the therapist to find as many ways as possible to shut off what occurs at the office, for there needs to be a clean break between what happens at work and what happens at home. Fulfillment and relaxation in the therapist's personal life make it possible to have the energy to work with incest survivors. Being able to keep work and play separate demonstrates the therapist's ability to maintain clear boundaries.

Consulting with other therapists treating incest survivors is a good way to manage the intensity of this work. Therapists need to tell their stories too. Given the confines of confidentiality, therapists don't generally go home and talk about their day at the office. Support from colleagues, input, and supervision revitalize the therapist who deals with incest. Limiting the number of incest clients is also useful. A therapist won't survive emotionally and psychically if she or he treats incest clients only.

Since psychotherapy is not an exact science, it does not provide precise answers for the issues already discussed. The point, however, is for the therapist who works with incest survivors to examine her or his own attitudes and beliefs and to be careful not to contaminate the treatment with certain biases or preconceived notions. Each client's history will be unique and each client's resolution must be her own.

Epilogue

Treating incest survivors is some of the most dramatic work a therapist can facilitate. The potential for growth, change, and repair within the client's inner and outer life is unequal to most other therapies. Although the childhood damage is so devastating, the prognosis for complete recovery is excellent. Long-term individual psychotherapy can bring about a magnificent metamorphosis for the incest survivor.

I have come to believe that if the therapist can enter the client's world from the abused child's perspective then the treatment can be unusually dynamic and expansive. To accomplish this, however, the therapist needs to make the treatment setting and therapeutic relationship comfortable for the child who still exists within the adult client. This is tricky to do and even more difficult to explain. I hope that the reader has been able to glean the intuitive quality to this work. So many of the richest treatment moments have been completely spontaneous and unique to that particular therapeutic connection, and duplication does not occur too often.

The intricacy of this therapy and the need to balance several perspectives at one time makes this incredibly creative work. For me, this has been very gratifying. At one moment I am doing straightforward talk therapy, and at the next moment I'm doing a guided visualization that leads to play therapy. I have the opportunity to move back and forth between working with an adult and working with a child. I can use ordinary adult therapeutic language and then elaborate visual imagery. In short, in this work I am able to draw on all my inner resources in order to create a healing experience for the client. The process of creative discovery keeps me very engaged in this form of treatment.

In the larger scheme of things—beyond the individual healing—there is tremendous value in doing effective treatment with incest survivors. The only way to stop the cycle of child sexual and physical abuse that is so prevalent in our culture is to heal formerly abused adults. Each survivor who seeks help in recovering from childhood abuse is painfully aware of his or her own potential to become abusive. Most will say, "I don't ever want to do to any child what was done to me." As clinicians, it is our responsibility to engage in the most extensive treatment possible to rid these individuals of their longstanding pain and sorrow so that the next generation does not have to suffer the same pain.

As a therapist who has been doing this work for many years, I continue to be in awe of the human will to survive. That this powerful force within us all develops so early in life is a wonderment to me. I have struggled without success to find just the right word to describe that inner strength. My clients use words like *soul* or *spirit* or *inner self* or *inner voice*. They all talk about a part of themselves that is untouchable, powerful, intelligent, and private that has guided them through the most difficult of times. I cannot describe how privileged I feel to have been allowed into so many of these souls. Each time I have felt that I was invited into an inner sanctum where the essence of humanness resides. I cannot describe in words the panoramas I have witnessed; I can only say that these survivors have my most profound respect. They are triumphant individuals who were once shattered but who have emerged from their chaos to become whole and integrated spirits.

I will end with Mariah's words. As you will recall from Chapter 1, Mariah's father "acknowledged" her 10th birthday by raping her. Over the course of five years of therapy we worked hard to create new rituals for Mariah—especially around her birthday. Each year her healing increased and those days became more and more joyful. Mariah celebrated her 33rd birthday shortly before we terminated her therapy. She asked me to meet her at a park by the river rather than in the office on the morning of her birthday. I gladly agreed. When I arrived, my eyes nearly popped out of my head! Spread on the grass by the edge of the river was a huge blanket filled with wrapped birthday presents, a bouquet of wildflowers, a bunch of helium balloons, and a birthday cake with candles. Mariah was excited to share all her "surprises" with me. She gleefully unwrapped several presents she had picked out for herself. Some were toys for "the little girl" and some were fancy gifts for the healed adult. She read each card aloud to me, blew out the candles on the cake, and served each of us a piece. Before we left she took the bunch of balloons in one hand and my hand in the other and led us to the shore. As she released the balloons into the sky and watched them drift high above us, she turned to me and said, "Now I can soar just like those balloons. Thank you so much for sticking by me." We both cried as we embraced in the fullness of our joy.

One of Mariah's birthday cards overwhelmed me. I knew I had just heard the last words of this book. With Mariah's permission, I share the card and her words with you. The printed inscription on the card reads:

For someone who means a lot to me.
Special—just one of the many words I could use to say how much you mean to me. . . .
Special—just one of the wonderful things I'm hoping your birthday will be.
Happy Birthday!

Mariah's handwritten words followed:

For the little girl. . . .
It's taken us a while to get where we are now. Times were tough but I'm so glad we've stuck together no matter what. Facing the challenges has helped us to grow. How wonderful it is to be able to enjoy the honesty, trust, and *love* we've built. There's such a warm, close feeling deep down inside and a quiet happiness that can only come from finally accepting and really caring for each other. Happy Birthday to us—I'm so happy you're a part of me and I of you. Let's take our love and hold it close!

References

Note: References marked with an asterisk (*) are appropriate for clients as well as for therapists.

American Psychiatric Association (1987). *Diagnostic and Statistical Manual of Mental Disorders-III-R.* Washington DC: American Psychiatric Association.

Bandler, R., and Grinder, J. (1982). *Reframing.* Moab, UT: Real People Press.

*Bass, E., and Davis, L. (1988). *The Courage to Heal.* New York: Harper & Row.

*Bass, E., and Thorton, L., eds. (1983). *I Never Told Anyone.* New York: Harper & Row.

Bettelheim, B. (1980). *Surviving and Other Essays.* New York: Vintage Books.

*Boston Women's Health Book Collective (1979). *Our Bodies, Ourselves.* Rev. ed. New York: Simon & Schuster.

Bowen, M. (1978). *Family Therapy in Clinical Practice.* New York: Jason Aronson.

Bowlby, J. (1988). *A Secure Base.* New York: Basic Books.

*Bradshaw, J. (1988). *The Family.* Deerfield Beach, FL: Health Communications.

* _____ (1990). *Homecoming.* New York: Bantam Books.

Braun, B. G. (1990). Dissociative disorders as sequelae to incest. In *Incest-Related Syndromes of Adult Psychopathology,* ed. R. Kluft, pp. 227–245. Washington, DC: American Psychiatric Press.

*Butler, S. (1985). *Conspiracy of Silence: The Trauma of Incest.* San Francisco: Volcano Press.

Calof, D. (1987). *Treating Adult Survivors of Incest and Child Abuse.* Workshop presented at Family Networker Symposium, Washington DC, March.

*Capacchione, L. (1988). *The Power of Your Other Hand.* North Hollywood, CA: New Castle Publishing.

Carter, E., and Orfanidis, M. (1976). Family therapy with one person and the family therapist's own family. In *Family Therapy*, ed. P. Guerin, pp. 193–219. New York: Gardner Press.

Courtois, C. (1988). *Healing the Incest Wound.* New York: Norton.

*Daugherty, L. (1984). *Why Me?* Racine, WI: Mother Courage Press.

*Davis, L. (1990). *The Courage to Heal Workbook.* New York: Harper & Row.

Dolan, Y. (1991). *Resolving Sexual Abuse: Solution-Focused Therapy and Ericksonian Hypnosis for Adult Survivors.* New York: Norton.

Erikson, E. (1950). *Childhood and Society.* New York: Norton.

——— (1968). *Identity: Youth and Crisis.* New York: Norton.

Fine, C. G. (1990). The cognitive sequelae of incest. In *Incest-Related Syndromes of Adult Psychopathology*, ed. R. Kluft, pp. 161–182. Washington, DC: American Psychiatric Press.

Finkelhor, D. (1979). *Sexually Victimized Children.* New York: Free Press.

Forward, S., and Buck, C. (1978). *Betrayal of Innocence: Incest and Its Devastation.* New York: Penguin Books.

Fraiberg, S. (1959). *The Magic Years.* New York: Scribner and Son.

*Frankel, V. (1959). *Man's Search for Meaning.* New York: Washington Square Press.

*Fraser, S. (1987). *My Father's House.* New York: Harper & Row.

Freud, S. (1940). An outline of psychoanalysis. *Standard Edition* 23:141–208.

*Gawain, S. (1978). *Creative Visualization.* New York: Bantam Books.

Gelinas, D. J. (1988). Family therapy: characteristic family constellation and basic therapeutic stance. In *Vulnerable Populations: Evaluation and Treatment of Sexually Abused Children and Adult Survivors*, vol. 1, ed. S. Sgroi, pp. 25–49, 51–76. Lexington, MA: Lexington Books.

*Gil, E. (1983). *Outgrowing the Pain.* New York: Bantam Doubleday Dell Publishing Group.

——— (1988). *Treatment of Adult Survivors of Childhood Abuse.* Walnut Creek, CA: Launch Press.

Goodwin, J. M. (1990). Applying to adult incest victims what we have learned from victimized children. In *Incest-Related Syndromes of Adult Psychopathology*, ed. R. Kluft, pp. 55–74. Washington, DC: American Psychiatric Press.

*Graber, K. (1991). *Ghosts in the Bedroom: A Guide for Partners of Incest Survivors.* Deerfield Beach, FL: Health Communications.

Groth, A. N. (1982). The incest offender. In *Handbook of Clinical Intervention in Child Sexual Abuse*, ed. S. Sgroi, pp. 215–218. Lexington, MA: Lexington Books.

Groves, D. (1987). *Resolving Traumatic Memories: Competency Based Training for Mental Health Professionals.* Munster, IN: David Groves Seminars.

Haley, J. (1973). *Uncommon Therapy.* New York: Norton.

Hawkins, J. (1991). Rowers on the River Styx: an interview with Dr. Judith Herman. *Harvard Magazine*, vol. *91*, pp. 43–52, March–April.

*Herman, J. (1981). *Father–Daughter Incest.* Cambridge: Harvard University Press.

——— (1990). Discussion. In *Incest-Related Syndromes of Adult Psychopathology*, ed. R. Kluft, pp. 289–293. Washington, DC: American Psychiatric Press.

Imber-Black, E., Roberts, J., and Whiting, R., eds. (1988). *Rituals in Families and Family Therapy.* New York: Norton.

Justice, B., and Justice, R. (1979). *The Broken Taboo.* New York: Human Sciences Press.

Kaplan, H. S. (1974). *The New Sex Therapy.* New York: Brunner/Mazel.

Kerr, M., and Bowen, M. (1988). *Family Evaluation*. New York: Norton.

Kinsey, A., Pomeroy, W. B., Martin, C. E., and Gebhard, P. H. (1953). *Sexual Behavior in the Human Female*. Philadelphia: Saunders.

Kirschner, D., and Kirschner, S. (1986). *Comprehensive Family Therapy*. New York: Brunner/Mazel.

Kluft, R., ed. (1990). *Incest-Related Syndromes of Adult Psychopathology*. Washington, DC: American Psychiatric Press.

Kramer, J. (1985). *Family Interfaces: Transgenerational Patterns*. New York: Brunner/Mazel.

*Lerner, H. G. (1985). *The Dance of Anger*. New York: Harper & Row.

*_____ (1989). *The Dance of Intimacy*. New York: Harper & Row.

*Loulann, J. (1984). *Lesbian Sex*. San Francisco: Spinsters.

*Maltz, W. (1991). *The Sexual Healing Journey: A Guide for Survivors of Sexual Abuse*. New York: HarperCollins.

*Maltz, W., and Holman, B. (1987). *Incest and Sexuality: A Guide to Understanding and Healing*. Lexington, MA: Lexington Books.

Masterson, J. (1976). *Psychotherapy of the Borderline Adult*. New York: Brunner/Mazel.

_____ (1981). *The Narcissistic and Borderline Disorders*. New York: Brunner/Mazel.

McGoldrick, M., and Carter, E. (1980). *The Family Life Cycle: A Framework for Family Therapy*. New York: Gardner Press.

McGoldrick, M., and Gerson, R. (1983). *Genograms in Family Assessment*. New York: Norton.

Meiselman, K. (1978). *Incest*. San Francisco: Jossey-Bass.

*Middelton-Moz, J., and Dwinell, L. (1986). *After the Tears*. Deerfield Beach, FL: Health Communications.

Miller, A. (1981). *Prisoners of Childhood*. New York: Basic Books.

_____ (1986). *Thou Shalt Not Be Aware*. New York: New American Library.

*_____ (1990a). *The Untouched Key*. New York: Doubleday.

*_____ (1990b). *Banished Knowledge*. New York: Doubleday.

Minuchin, S. (1974). *Families and Family Therapy*. Cambridge, MA: Harvard University Press.

*Morrison, T. (1987). *Beloved*. New York: New American Library.

Peck, M. S. (1983). *People of the Lie: The Hope for Healing Human Evil*. New York: Simon & Schuster.

Piaget, J. (1955). *The Language and Thought of the Child*. Cleveland: World Publishers.

_____ (1963). *The Origins of Intelligence in Children*. New York: Norton.

_____ (1965). *The Moral Judgment of the Child*. New York: Free Press.

Russell, D. E. H. (1986). *The Secret Trauma: Incest in the Lives of Girls and Women*. New York: Basic Books.

Schetky, D. H. (1990). A review of the literature on the long-term effects of childhood sexual abuse. In *Incest-Related Syndromes of Adult Psychopathology*, ed. R. Kluft, pp. 35–54. Washington, DC: American Psychiatric Press.

Sgroi, S., ed. (1988). *Vulnerable Populations: Evaluation and Treatment of Sexually Abused Children and Adult Survivors*. Vol. 1. Lexington, MA: Lexington Books.

Sgroi, S., and Bunk, B. S. (1988). A clinical approach to adult survivors of child sexual abuse. In *Vulnerable Populations: Evaluation and Treatment of Sexually Abused*

Children and Adult Survivors, vol. 1, ed. S. Sgroi, pp. 137–186. Lexington, MA: Lexington Books.

*Sharansky, N. (1988). *Fear No Evil.* New York: Vintage Books.

Sheehy, G. (1987). *The Spirit of Survival.* New York: Bantam Books.

Shengold, L. (1989). *Soul Murder: The Effects of Childhood Abuse and Deprivation.* New York: Ballantine Books.

*Sisk, S., and Hoffman, C. (1987). *Inside Scars.* Gainsville, FL: Pandora Press.

Spiegel, D. (1990). Trauma, dissociation and hypnosis. In *Incest-Related Syndromes of Adult Psychopathology,* ed. R. Kluft, pp. 247–261. Washington, DC: American Psychiatric Press.

Stone, M. H. (1990). Incest in the borderline patient. In *Incest-Related Syndromes of Adult Psychopathology,* ed. R. Kluft, pp. 183–204. Washington, DC: American Psychiatric Press.

*Tower, C. C. (1988). *Secret Scars.* New York: Penguin Books.

*Utain, M., and Oliver, B. (1989). *Scream Louder.* Deerfield Beach, FL: Health Communications.

Wachtel, E., and Wachtel, P. (1986). *Family Dynamics in Individual Psychotherapy.* New York: Guilford Press.

Wallas, L. (1985). *Stories for the Third Ear.* New York: Norton.

Walters, M., Carter, E., Papp, P., and Silverstein, O. (1988). *The Invisible Web: Gender Patterns in Family Relationships.* New York: Guilford Press.

*Whitfield, C. (1987). *Healing the Child Within.* Deerfield Beach, FL: Health Communications.

*Wisechild, L. (1988). *The Obsidian Mirror.* Seattle, WA: Seal Press.

*Woititz, J. G. (1985). *Struggle for Intimacy.* Deerfield Beach, FL: Health Communications.

*_____ (1989). *Healing Your Sexual Self.* Deerfield Beach, FL: Health Communications.

Index

171